Fifty Years of the Movies

Fifty Years of the Movies

Jeremy Pascall

Exeter Books

NEW YORK

To Adrian Scott, but for whom . . .

Front endpaper:
(Left to right) Donald O'Connor, Ethel Merman, Dan
Dailey, Mitzi Gaynor and Johnnie Ray in *There's No
Business Like Show Business*, director Walter Lang
(20th Century-Fox, 54)

Half-title page:
W.C. Fields in *The Bank Dick*, director Eddie Cline
(Universal, 40)

Title page:
2001: A Space Odyssey, director Stanley Kubrick
(MGM, 68)

Back endpaper:
Peter O'Toole in *Lawrence of Arabia*, director David Lean
(Columbia, 64)

Publisher's note:
Every attempt has been made to capture the original
technical quality of the photographs reproduced
in this book

Copyright © 1981 by The Hamlyn Publishing Group Limited
Second impression 1982

First published in USA 1981
by Exeter Books
Distributed by Bookthrift
Exeter is a trademark of Simon & Schuster
Bookthrift is a registered trademark of Simon & Schuster
New York, New York

ISBN 0-89673-086-7

Printed in Spain

Contents

Introduction

On 6 October, 1927, the audience at Warner Theatre caught the first, most famous words in movie history. There had been experiments with sound for years but the results were disappointing at best, and laughable at worst. The general opinion in the industry was that nobody – not the public, not the studios – wanted or needed sound; the silent film still cast its spell. However, one studio *did* need sound; or at least something that would restore its ailing fortunes.

Warner Brothers were desperately hard-pressed and Sam Warner had become convinced that the system being developed at Bell Telephones had real potential. Warners pushed ahead and by 1927 synchronized music and speech had become a reality. On screen in *The Jazz Singer* an exuberant Al Jolson declared, 'You ain't heard nothin' yet!'

Prophetic. It started a trend which became a craze which, by the turn of the decade, was a revolution. Within a few years, the silents – for all their art and beauty, their pace and excitement – had become redundant. Cans of nitrate stock were allowed to rot away on dusty shelves. Glittering careers were broken. Now the microphone became the great arbiter of stardom, greater even than the studio moguls or the audience. Some, like Emil Jannings, who won an Oscar in 1928, were declared too gutteral for Hollywood pictures. (He returned to Germany.) Corinne Griffith was adjudged too nasal, and May McAvoy was discovered to have a thtrong lithp.

For the first time in the history of the movies, there was a language barrier. And it was not only to affect actors. Hollywood films could no longer be exported worldwide to be understood by any audience, thanks to the cheap method of translating a few captions.

Actually, sound set cinema techniques back by a decade or more. The microphone was king. It was static, cumbersome and cranky. It imposed a tyranny on movie-makers. Audiences used to the flowing, incident-packed action of the great silent pictures soon became bored with the novelty of hearing their favourite stars speak huddled around a vase of flowers (or whatever device was used to disguise the mike) and spewing forth page after page of stilted dialogue. Nearly three years after the revolution, Hollywood could still think of few better ways of using its new toy than to photograph Broadway hits just as performed on stage.

Sound was to impose yet other restrictions. In the early Twenties there had been a backlash against the permissiveness of movie content, and the Hollywood moguls, alarmed that they might have restrictive censorship forced on them, pre-empted such a move by appearing to put their own house in order and inviting a man of unquestioned moral rectitude to oversee their product. Will H. Hays became the 'Czar' of Hollywood, wielding his blue pencil as President of the Motion Picture Producers and Distributors of America (which became generally known as the Hays Office).

Initially he was no more than a figurehead; he simply advised and warned – after all, it was difficult to censor the way a handsome actor looked at a beautiful actress. But with the coming of sound, he became a force in Hollywood. He was all too aware that the audience had not heard anything yet. A suggestive look was one thing, a *double entendre* quite another. In 1929 he and others (notably representatives of the influential Catholic community in America) drew up a code of practice that would govern the representation of human behaviour – particularly human sexual behaviour – on the screen. In 1930 it was adopted, becoming known as the Hays Code. It covered just about everything from the depiction of nudity to the length of a screen kiss, from the uttering of the mildest expletive to forcing married characters to sleep in uncompanionable single beds. For, by 1930, the talkies were dominant and Hays was not going to allow them to pollute the eyes and ears of his huge flock.

As the decade prepared to turn the loudest sound heard was the crash which resonated from Wall Street as the US Stock Exchange collapsed. Its echoes bounced around the world as the States and then Europe plunged into the worst recession in history. The Depression subsequently blighted the Thirties and offered Hollywood massive audiences hungry for romance, thrills, laughter, music – anything to lift them out of the misery of their daily lives. This, then, was the scene which heralded the greatest decade in the history of movies, the Golden Age of Hollywood.

Jeremy Pascall.

the Thirties

At first the Depression hit Hollywood severely. Desperate to keep up with its competitors, every studio was pouring money into the crippling investment needed to re-equip with the hardware of sound recording just at the time that funds were drying up. Nonetheless, the decade that started in uncertainty ended with Hollywood in a position of unchallengeable supremacy. All the great studios, all the great stars, all the great directors were in Hollywood, and by 1939 most of the great movies were being made there too.

It was the stars that made Hollywood pre-eminent, and the studios made the stars. Metro-Goldwyn-Mayer (MGM) were to boast they had more stars than there are in heaven; a typical piece of Hollywood hype but undoubtedly the seven major studios collected a greater galaxy of star names than have ever been assembled in one town. The studios dominated film-making: they were dream factories and great estates. In its golden years MGM covered over 100 acres and its 22 sound stages annually turned out more than 40 movies.

These vast complexes were often run as their personal fiefs by the moguls who controlled them. They could (and did) make and break stars, commission million-dollar movies at their personal whim, and dictate every aspect of movie-making from finance to artistic interpretation.

The Big Five were: MGM (run by Louis B. Mayer, it had the longest roster of stars, producing the glossiest product); Paramount, headed by Adolph Zukor; 20th Century-Fox which, unlike the others which were well-established by the Thirties, was not formed until 1935 when the Fox Film Corporation and Twentieth Century Pictures merged; RKO (it got its initials from its founding companies – Radio Corporation of America and the Keith-Orpheum cinema chain), which as well as producing its own films also released the often outstanding movies of independents like Sam Goldwyn (he had ducked out of MGM soon after the merger) and David O. Selznick; and, of course, Warner Brothers, which before *The Jazz Singer* (27) were an ailing last in the league but as a result of their gamble on talkies went, briefly, to the top.

There were several other studios in Hollywood, most specializing in low-budget 'B' features, but between them and the Big Five came the Little Two – Universal (run by Carl Laemmle), which achieved good results on small budgets, especially with its horror movies, and Columbia, which was lorded over by the foul-mouthed, boorish and occasionally monstrous Harry Cohn (known with good reason as King Cohn).

These were the people who dictated what the Hollywood studios would produce; these were the men who, knowing stars were their most valuable asset (even though they often treated them like cattle), rushed to find actors and actresses 'who could talk', when sound turned their town upside down. By 1930 the weeding-out process was coming to an end. Established stars had been vetted, and the hunt was on for new stars who could not only talk agreeably but could deliver dialogue convincingly.

Only two of the very greatest silent stars still resisted the microphone – Charlie Chaplin and Greta Garbo. The pressure on Chaplin was not as intense as it had been on others. His talent and popularity rested on his incomparable genius as a mime, and, although he incorporated a music score into his films, he was not to prove he could talk until *The Great Dictator* (40).

Garbo's position was not so secure. Divine she may have seemed, but were the ethereal face and form coupled to an impenetrably Svedish aksent? The industry and the audience held their breath for two years during which, one by one, the rest of the Hollywood pantheon exercized their vocal cords on film for better or worse. In 1930, the goddess was finally ready. GARBO TALKS! screamed the hoardings for *Anna Christie*. She appeared in a dockside bar and spoke her first words: 'Gif me a visky, ginger ale on the side, and don't be stingy, baby.' An accent there surely was, but that and the timbre in which it was delivered were so perfectly married to her image that she succeeded triumphantly. Garbo proved that an accent need not be a bar to talkie stardom.

Indeed her career flourished through movies like *Grand Hotel* (32), *Queen Christina* (33), *Anna Karenina* (35) and *Camille* (36). She was the most popular dramatic actress of her time. Many miles of prose have been devoted to the attempt to define her talent and words like 'mystery' and 'enigma' tend to crop up a lot. Those the camera loves, it reveals. All, that is, but Garbo, claim her admirers. In 1939 she was ready to broaden from tragedy into comedy: GARBO LAUGHS! was the new headline and the audience laughed with her in *Ninotchka*,

Enigmatic Garbo, queen of MGM: (*top left*) *Anna Christie*, director Clarence Brown (30); (*top right*) *Susan Lenox, Her Fall and Rise* with Clark Gable, director Robert Z. Leonard (31); (*above*) *Camille* with Robert Taylor, director George Cukor (36); (*left*) *Ninotchka* with (left) Melvyn Douglas, director Ernst Lubitsch (39)

Marlene Dietrich in *Morocco* (*above*), director Josef von Sternberg (Paramount, 30) and (*above right*) *The Scarlet Empress* with John Lodge, director Josef von Sternberg (Paramount, 34)

proving she had the staying power to rise to even greater heights. But she was becoming increasingly reclusive; *Two-Faced Woman* (41) was not a success and she took the excuse of a failure to retire from the screen at 36.

Marlene Dietrich reversed the journey of many of her compatriots by travelling from Germany to Hollywood and stardom. *The Blue Angel* (30) was made in Germany by Josef von Sternberg and shot in both German and English. Her part as Lola-Lola, a cabaret singer whose sexual domination over an aged professor (Emil Jannings) leads to his ruin, caused a sensation. Occasionally a role makes a star but it is usually because the director lavishes extreme care and attention on the actor or actress. John Ford was to do this for John Wayne in *Stagecoach* at the end of the decade; in 1930 von Sternberg allowed his loving camera to linger lustfully over Dietrich. The image of her seated on a barrel, a top hat on her head and her amazing legs sheathed in silk stockings drawn taut across her thighs by black suspenders is the stuff of masturbatory dreams. Couple this near-fetishism to Dietrich's mystery and to that crooning, seductive voice husking out 'Falling In Love Again' and it is not difficult to see why she was a sensation.

She was summoned to Hollywood and rushed into *Morocco* (30) to play opposite another rising star, Gary Cooper. In this and subsequent films – *Dishonoured* (31), *Shanghai Express* (32), *Blonde Venus* (32), *The Scarlet Empress* (34) and *The Devil Is A Woman* (35) – von Sternberg seems to have devoted himself to enhancing Dietrich's innate mystery and eroticism, and, although the Hays Code rigorously, and often ridiculously, clamped down on overt sexuality in films, von Sternberg suffused his with an erotic aura that seems to shimmer from the screen. Dietrich usually played a whore or, at least, a woman of very elastic virtue – 'It took more than one man to change my name to Shanghai Lily,' she whispers with a sultry bawdiness in *Shanghai Express*.

For a while, she seemed to rival Garbo as the new queen of the talkies. Both were European and both had broken the sound barrier because of, not despite, their accents. And, of course, because they were luminescent women and magnificent actresses.

Hollywood needed its new stars, stars who could act dialogue, stars who could sing and dance, because the rage was for '100% Talking, 100% Singing, 100% Dancing' pictures. (No one worried about statistical impossibilities!)

RUDY VALLEE JIMMY DURANTE ALICE FAYE ADRIENNE AMES
GREGORY RATOFF CLIFF EDWARDS GEORGE WHITE

The first musicals were brought straight from Broadway and mounted as filmed stage shows. The technical limitations of early sound recording had a disastrously disjointed effect on dialogue and made simultaneous singing and movement virtually impossible. A song had to be delivered directly to the microphone and the results were of necessity stilted. These were *filmed* musicals rather than the true, fluent musicals that Hollywood was quickly to make its own.

The turning point was *Broadway Melody* in 1929, and the twist was that the story was set *behind* rather than *on* the stage. The backstage musical, which was to be such a feature of the Thirties, was born. The idea was simple: follow the fortunes of a set of hoofers or singers, and interject into this wafer of a plot spectacular singing/dancing set pieces.

As the decade progressed the plots got thinner and the set pieces became more spectacular, thanks to Busby Berkeley. He used his chorus girls as animated tiles in vast, ever-shifting mosaics. He dressed them up preposterously as coins and musical instruments, he dressed them down in wisps of gauze, he undressed them entirely behind screens, ensuring of course that they were backlit so that the audience could see all they had to offer in silhouette!

He started the trend in 1933 with *42nd Street*, to which he contributed the musical numbers. For the

opposite and left
Lobby cards, publicity
material for display in or
outside cinemas: *Blonde
Venus* with Dietrich and
Cary Grant (Paramount, 32);
George White's Scandals
(Fox, 34); *Ready, Willing and
Able* with Ruby Keeler and
Lee Dixon (Warners, 37);
Gold Diggers of 1935 (First
National)

Dietrich in two more von
Sternberg movies: (*above
left*) *Shanghai Express* with
Warner Oland (seated) and
Clive Brook (Paramount, 32)
and (*above*) with Cesar
Romero in *The Devil Is A
Woman* (Paramount, 35)

left
The King of Jazz, director
John Murray Anderson
(Universal, 30)

left
The King of Jazz, director
John Murray Anderson
(Universal, 30)

below left
Dick Powell and Ruby Keeler
in the 'Pettin' In The Park'
number from *Gold Diggers of
1933*, director Mervyn
LeRoy, choreographed by
Busby Berkeley (Warners,
33)

time, they were astonishing. In the title song Ruby
Keeler and Dick Powell, who were to become one
of the most popular teams of the period, cavorted
amidst a set representing the Manhattan skyline.
In successive films, Keeler and Powell acted as the
innocent foils to the extravagant sexuality that
whirled around them.

Busby Berkeley made his casts give their all. The
success of *42nd Street* spawned a string of rather
similar movies which he either choreographed or
directed: *Gold Diggers of 1933* (there were also
Gold Diggers of 1935, of 1937 and *In Paris*), *Roman
Scandals* (33), *Fashions of 1934*, *Dames* (34) and so
on, each outdoing the previous extravaganza in
exotic, erotic flamboyance. He was generally faithful to his trusted performers; just as Powell and
Keeler frequently played the young lovers, glamour
was often supplied by Joan Blondell and Ginger
Rogers.

Most of the Busby Berkeley movies were pure
froth to raise depressed spirits. They were bright
and brash and packed with classic numbers (mostly
written by Harry Warren and Al Dubin) which
remain fresh to this day: 'We're In The Money'
(from *Gold Diggers of 1933*), 'I Only Have Eyes For
You' (from *Dames*), ('By A Waterfall') (from *Footlight
Parade* in 1933) and 'Lullaby Of Broadway' (from
Gold Diggers of 1935).

However, Berkeley did not ignore the harsh
realities that existed outside the cinemas. In *Gold
Diggers of 1933* he included a bitter plea for social
justice entitled 'Remember My Forgotten Man'.
Joan Blondell sings it with anger while around her
we see lines of wounded servicemen limping back
from the First World War to find the promise of
'homes fit for heroes' betrayed as the shuffling
parade becomes a dole queue. Not everyone

12

Busby Berkeley extravaganzas: (*right*) *Gold Diggers of 1933*, director Mervyn LeRoy; (*below*) Ruby Keeler in *42nd Street*, director Lloyd Bacon (33); (*below right*) *Footlight Parade*, director Lloyd Bacon (33, all Warners)

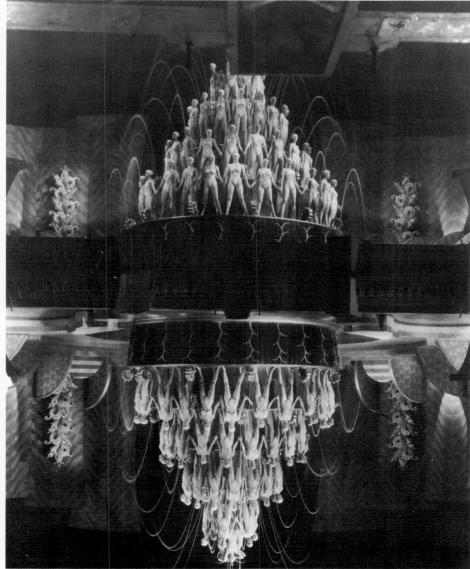

approved: The New York Times considered the song and staging 'a shabby theme of bogus sentimentality'.

Berkeley for all his excesses and occasional lapses of taste had shown that cameras and performers could be liberated from the tyrannical immobility imposed by cumbersome microphones. Soon technology had to keep pace with directors, and Hollywood quickly learned how to come up with new ideas which gave films pace and verve and excitement. Ernst Lubitsch, whose legendary 'touch' was so light, elegant and witty it became a byword for transforming frothy schmaltz into something artful, slyly sexy and glowingly beautiful, set his stamp on the musical in *Monte Carlo* (30). He liberated the form by having Jeanette MacDonald sing 'Beyond The Blue Horizon' as she sped in a train across country, the song's rhythm being taken up by the clattering express and its chorus joyfully chanted back at her by workers in the fields.

This and others – *One Hour With You* (32) and *The Merry Widow* (34) – helped to establish MacDonald as a star name in musicals. Her first partnership (in both these movies) was with Maurice Chevalier, another foreigner whose voice was more than acceptable to the microphone. But in 1935 she was teamed with the man with whom her name became inextricably linked – Nelson Eddy – in *Naughty Marietta*. Next came *Rose Marie* (36) and the team was established, Eddy's rather wooden personality throwing MacDonald's liveliness and vivacity into sharp relief.

Perhaps Jeanette MacDonald is seen at her best in *Love Me Tonight* (32), another film which advanced the musical, directed by another master, Rouben Mamoulian. The superb song 'Isn't It Romantic?' is made more memorable by Mamoulian's treatment of it. Starting in the streets of Paris, it is carried by passers-by, train passengers and parading soldiers until it finally reaches MacDonald, who trills the catchy tune from her castle window. (In contrast to this soufflé of a film, Mamoulian also brought his genius to bear in *Doctor Jekyll and Mister Hyde* in 1932, which is notable – among many other things – for the brilliance of Fredric March's transformation from respectable citizen to ghoul.)

As the musical gained force and popularity Hollywood continued to plunder the New York stage for talent. One man who trekked across country to find film fame gave what an RKO producer described as a 'wretched test', noting in a memo that he was 'uncertain' about the man, not least because of his 'enormous ears and bad chin line'. But what that perspicacious producer (David O. Selznick) *had* spotted was the man's 'tremendous' charm, and so he signed the little guy, intending him for *Flying Down to Rio*, a spectacular musical which was running into a few problems.

While the difficulties were being ironed out, Selznick left for MGM and another musical, *Dancing Lady*. The little guy was called in from RKO, where he was still kicking his prancing heels, for a celebrity spot in Selznick's new musical. And

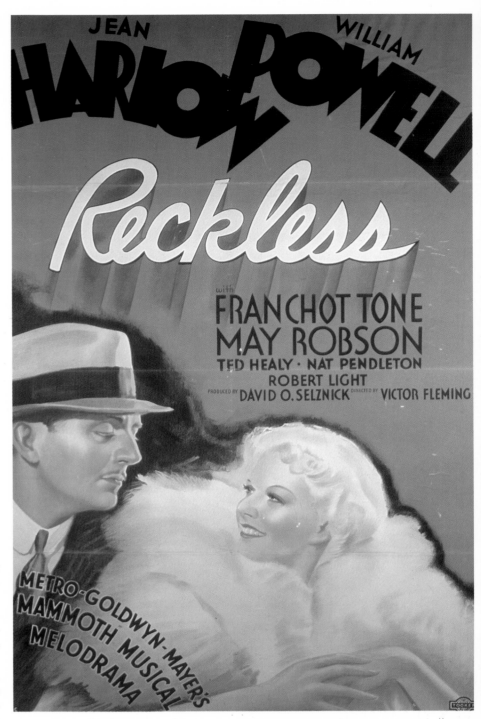

opposite top, above and above right
Thirties posters: *Reckless* (MGM, 35); *Public Enemy* (Warners, 31); *Curly Top* (Fox, 35)

right
Jeanette MacDonald and Nelson Eddy in *Rose Marie*, director W.S. van Dyke (MGM, 36)

opposite bottom
Vivien Leigh and Clark Gable in *Gone with the Wind*, director Victor Fleming (MGM, 39)

so, in his introduction to the movies Fred Astaire played himself. Something he was to do, to a greater or lesser degree, throughout his brilliant screen career. *Dancing Lady* (33) was a huge hit and brought Astaire, who was already famous on the Broadway and London stages, to a world audience. His contribution was noted but he didn't yet click. Something was missing.

Somebody was missing. He found her in *Flying Down to Rio*. No genius planned the sublime partnership of Fred Astaire and Ginger Rogers; it

15

just sort of happened. In fact, their dance in the movie, 'The Carioca', had little, if anything, to do with the plot and seems to have been filleted in to display Fred's dancing genius. The movie is none the .worse (indeed it is much the better) for that. When it was released, in December 1933, Ginger Rogers was far more familiar to movie audiences. She was already a veteran of 19 films, including small but flashy roles in Berkeley's *Gold Diggers of 1933* and *42nd Street*, so Fred was billed below her – the last time that was to happen.

It seemed to be a match made in heaven. Together they floated through the Thirties, singing and dancing marvellous songs in marvellous movies – *The Gay Divorcee* (*The Gay Divorce* in GB) followed in 1934, the first, and in many ways the stereotype, Astaire/Rogers vehicle. Next came something of an oddity, *Roberta* (35), which was not truly their film in that the lovely Irene Dunne headed the billing, had the best song, 'Smoke Gets In Your Eyes', and provided the main romantic interest with Randolph Scott. But Fred and Ginger scored heavily with 'I Won't Dance' and confirmed their compatibility.

The team really hit their stride with *Top Hat* (35). This is vintage stuff: particularly a memorable Irving Berlin score – 'No Strings', 'Isn't This A Lovely Day?', 'Cheek To Cheek' and, of course, 'Top Hat, White Tie And Tails', which became a signature tune for Astaire. The plot is the usual on-off-on-again-off-again-happy-ending that taxed no one, but the dancing is divine, especially the silken smoothness of 'Cheek To Cheek'.

The next year saw them in *Follow the Fleet* and *Swing Time* (the latter complete with 'The Way You Look Tonight', 'Pick Yourself Up', and 'A Fine Romance'). *Shall We Dance* followed in 1937, *Carefree* in 1938, and they ended the decade untypically with a biography of a dance partnership, *The Story of Irene and Vernon Castle* (39). By now the sparkle was going out of the team – Fred was getting bored and itched for greater challenges. He had only made one picture without Ginger since *Rio* (*A Damsel in Distress* in 1937 with Burns and Allen); Ginger had 'freelanced' more but felt, probably correctly, that she was being regarded merely as Fred's partner, and a junior one at that. When they split, after *The Castles*, Astaire continued to be the finest song-and-dance man in the business and Ginger proved what she had always known – she could act as well, if not better, than she could dance. In 1940 she won an Oscar for her role as *Kitty Foyle*. Ten years after the break, they came together for *The Barkleys of Broadway* (49); Judy Garland should have played opposite Fred but she was ill. It was not an unhappy reunion, though perhaps both Fred and Ginger realized there is no going back.

The nine films they made during the Thirties had raised the Hollywood musical to new heights of sophistication and glamour, and together they achieved a light-hearted (and heart-lightening) elegance that has never been matched.

Throughout the decade the tap-tap-tap of patent-shod feet was almost drowned by the rat-a-tat-tat of machine guns. For example, James Cagney sang and danced in *Footlight Parade* (33) but he was more readily identified in the public mind as he swore and swaggered in *The Public Enemy* (31). Cocky, feisty, twitching and fretting with ill-suppressed rage, exploding into psychotic violence, spitting at cops, slapping down broads, beating up hoods, blasting speakeasies apart – that was the Cagney the public flocked to see.

Crime was the growth industry of the Thirties. Prohibition ended in 1933 but the crime wave did not end with it. People like Bonnie Parker and Clyde Barrow, 'Ma' Barker, 'Baby Face' Nelson and John Dillinger filled the nation's headlines and were elevated to near-heroic stature. Al Capone's evil rule over Chicago was fresh in the memory and a bum could achieve a fame almost equal to that of a Hollywood star by being proclaimed Public Enemy No. 1.

This was a rich vein for movies. *But*, the studios protested, they were aware of their social responsibilities: 'Crime does not pay,' they warned before the reels showed gang bosses in flashy fedoras making out with busty blondes in sumptuous apartments. Warners' attitude was ambivalent but, if people in the cinema noticed, they probably didn't care. They were swept away by the sheer excitement of screeching tyres, yattering Thompsons, and the force and power of stars like James Cagney and Edward G. Robinson. These movies, Warners declared, were 'torn from today's headlines' and their stars punched their personalities into the public consciousness.

Robinson led the way in 1930 with *Little Caesar* as Caesar Enrico Bandello – Little Rico – a character based closely on Al Capone. The movie, directed by Mervyn LeRoy, virtually set the style for the genre. Robinson snarled and bullied, threatened and menaced his way to gangland supremacy. The pace of action and dialogue was furious, the latter almost entirely in underworld slang. These were dramas from the streets, streets familiar to many in the cinemas. The gangsters had found a way to rise out of them . . . for a while.

It was obligatory that retribution followed the violent deeds of the screen hoodlums. But retribution did not always come from the cops: Tom Powers got his at the hands of rivals – almost cut apart by bullets, they dumped him on his mother's doorstep. Powers was a nasty piece of work. He had astonished and shocked audiences by smashing a breakfast grapefruit into Mae Clarke's pretty face! That action more than any other established James Cagney as the meanest, ballsiest gangster of them all. *Public Enemy* (31), directed by William Wellman, made him a star, and one of the most imitated actors of all time.

Who does not instantly recognize the twitch of the shoulders, the hitch of the elbows, the stiff-legged straddle and the growled 'You dirty rat, you'? Cagney never said it and, what's more, although he is forever remembered as the best (meaning worst) gangster in screen history, he

didn't make that many gangster movies. The majority of his parts in the Thirties were non-criminal – everything from a motor-racing driver in Howard Hawks's *The Crowd Roars* (32) to airline pilot in *Ceiling Zero* (36), from a prison governor in *Mayor of Hell* (33) to Bottom in Max Reinhardt's brave but flawed *A Midsummer Night's Dream* (35).

He made two more gangster films that endure as classics: *Angels with Dirty Faces* (38) and *The Roaring Twenties* (39). In both the tone has softened slightly. In Michael Curtiz's *Angels with Dirty Faces*, he is prevailed upon by a boyhood friend (who becomes a priest) to 'act yeller' as he takes the walk to the electric chair so that the local street

Cagney and the Dead End Kids in *Angels with Dirty Faces*, director Michael Curtiz (Warners, 38)

And with Humphrey Bogart in *The Roaring Twenties*, director Raoul Walsh (Warners, 39)

an Oedipal thug in *White Heat* in 1949, again for Walsh), winning an Oscar for his portrayal of patriotic composer George M. Cohan in *Yankee Doodle Dandy* (42). Despite the mayhem and murder he caused on screen, years later he confessed, 'I was always a hoofer at heart.'

Odd how dancers seemed to make convincing villains: George Raft was another. An excellent dancer, he is probably still best remembered for the insouciance with which he spun a coin in *Scarface* (32). Although the title was Al Capone's nickname, there were few other parallels with the role Paul Muni played on screen. Along with *Little Caesar* and *Public Enemy*, this was one of the classic gangster pix of the period.

Muni was an effective psychopath, but not really an archetypal gangster. He attempted to be The Great Actor, perhaps moulding himself on George Arliss, who was much regarded for his rather theatrical performances in a range of stately characters, particularly in the name part of *Disraeli* (29). In the later Thirties Muni also specialized in biopics of the eminent which carried humanist messages, like *The Story of Louis Pasteur* (35), *The Life of Emile Zola* (37) and *Juarez* (39) – but in 1932 he essayed a part that set another trend for the times.

Mervyn LeRoy's *I Am a Fugitive from a Chain Gang* might be described as a crime movie with a conscience. Based on fact, it tells of Jim Allen, who returns from the First World War and becomes

gang will see him as a coward. And Raoul Walsh's *The Roaring Twenties* had him as a veteran of the First World War who drifts into crime and finally gives up his own life so that the husband of the woman he has loved, and lost, may live. Despite the mawkish ending, the film lives up to its title, with a pace set by Cagney. It was probably the last great gangster movie to come out of Warners. 'He used to be a big shot,' says a moll of Cagney. It is an epitaph for the genre but not for Cagney, who went on expanding his range (although he did return as

unwittingly implicated in a crime. He is sentenced to a chain gang, where he is treated with callous savagery. It was a searing, damning indictment of the penal system which caused an uproar of protest, and it pioneered a new trend of socially aware dramas on issues that affected the everyday lives of the audience.

These were another speciality of Warners. Following *I Am a Fugitive from a Chain Gang*, they again featured Muni in a powerful and outspoken film, *Bordertown* (34), in which he played a Mexican lawyer who is the victim of racial prejudice. And in the following year Michael Curtiz starred Muni in *Black Fury*, another movie based on fact, this time about a miner's strike in which a leader was beaten to death. Warners' *Black Legion* (37) starred Bogart in the true story of a basically decent man whose patriotism is perverted by a secret society strongly resembling the Ku Klux Klan. Mob violence was also depicted in Mervyn LeRoy's *They Won't Forget* (37), which, together with Fritz Lang's *Fury* (36 for MGM), condemned lynching.

Not every director, or star, made his, or her, point with unremitting drama. Instead of tears and tragedy, some looked to laughter and comedy. Frank Capra was a director who believed that, despite the dark forces pressing on individuals, a man or a woman could fight back and triumph. He knew people felt helpless to alter the way politics and economics were shattering their lives and he made films – fairy tales, really – to prove that an

individual could do something to alter the system for the better. Capra films showed courage and love and integrity but most of all they were witty.

Two bear strong similarities – *Mr Deeds Goes to Town* (36) and *Mr Smith Goes to Washington* (39). They tell the stories of simple honest men who take on the system and, by courage and folksy good humour, beat it. Gary Cooper (Mr Deeds) and James

Cagney with Anita Louise in *A Midsummer Night's Dream*, directors Max Reinhardt and William Dieterle (Warners, 35)

Paul Muni (centre) with Vladimir Sokoloff in *The Life of Emile Zola*, director William Dieterle (Warners, 37)

Social comment handled dramatically: Paul Muni in (*top left*) *I Am a Fugitive from a Chain Gang* with David Landau (*right*), director Mervyn LeRoy (Warners, 32) and (*top right*) *Black Fury*, director Michael Curtiz (Warners, 35); and (*above*) *Fury*, director Fritz Lang (MGM, 36). The humorous approach: Jean Arthur and Gary Cooper (seated) in *Mr Deeds Goes to Town* (*above right*), director Frank Capra (Columbia, 36)

Stewart (Mr Smith) were actors who seemed to epitomize Capra's concept of the ideal American, the inheritor of Abraham Lincoln's mantle. They both had a sure touch for comedy that made them hilariously bumbling as well as laudably unswerving in walking their righteous paths. Longfellow Deeds is a tuba-playing, small-town boy who inherits $20 million. His efforts to do good land him in a law court where his sanity is disputed, but with humorous shrewdness he routs his enemies. Jefferson Smith is a starry-eyed idealist who becomes a senator. He sets out to expose a fraud and has to filibuster for 23 hours before a Senate Committee to defeat the actions of a group of corrupt politicians.

Capra also made one of the great classic 'crazy' comedies of the Thirties, *It Happened One Night* (34). Somehow the film distilled magic. Gable was

already the dream man of female fantasies, one other men strove to emulate – big, handsome, macho. To these qualities he brought, for the first time, a marvellous sense of humour. He proved that men could be tough *and* funny. His playing of a worldly-wise, out-of-work journalist strikes exactly the right note as he acts as nanny to a self-willed, poor-little-rich girl who is dashing across country away from a demanding father who's annulled her marriage. The pace of the film and the comedy is fast, interjected with scenes which stick in the memory – like the two sharing a motel room and partitioning it with a blanket ('the walls of Jericho'). It won an Academy award as Best Picture of 1934, Gable and Colbert got Oscars as Best Actor and Actress, Capra was Best Director, and the script won a fifth statuette. It was the first time one movie swept the board.

Capra again : (*above*) James
Stewart and Jean Arthur in
Mr Smith Goes to Washington
(Columbia, 39); (*left*)
Claudette Colbert and Clark
Gable in the 'Walls of
Jericho' scene from *It
Happened One Night*
(Columbia, 34)

right
Cary Grant and May Robson (centre) in *Bringing Up Baby*, director Howard Hawks (RKO, 38)

below
Irene Dunne and Grant in *The Awful Truth*, director Leo McCarey (Columbia, 37)

Crazy or 'screwball' comedies became a rage. Capra made another in 1938 with *You Can't Take It With You* (Oscar for Best Film), the story of the loony Vanderhof family, who turn their back on money to pursue their own obsessions, which include making fireworks in the basement, a novelist who is never published, and a ballet dancer with the grace of a rhino. The essence of screwball comedies was their improbability. In *Topper* (37) we willingly accept that a young couple (Cary Grant and Constance Bennett) could be killed in a car crash and then come back as fun-loving ghosts (high spirits, one supposes) to convert their staid banker friend Cosmo Topper to their pleasure-seeking ways.

British-born Cary Grant dominated this genre. He was the consummate light comedian of his time. Suave, almost unbelievably good-looking, he initially seemed better suited to the dashing heroic style of another British import, Ronald Colman. Perhaps Grant could have emulated Colman's roles in films like *Bulldog Drummond* (29), *Raffles* (30), *A Tale of Two Cities* (35), *Lost Horizon*, or *The Prisoner of Zenda* (both 37). Certainly the studio tried him in such parts and even as a caddish sexual predator, the sound equivalent of Valentino, but somehow a smile rather than a snarl seemed most at home on his lips. His comic talent shone through in *Topper*, was honed in Leo McCarey's *The Awful Truth* (37) opposite Irene Dunne as a divorcing couple who really *do* want to part but . . . and came into full bloom with the magnificently wacky *Bringing Up Baby* (38).

The plot is absurd: Grant is a dry-as-dust palaeontologist who is reconstructing a dinosaur skeleton when Katharine Hepburn's dog steals a vital bone. To compound this, Hepburn – who has a manic genius for causing chaos – also owns a pet leopard named Baby, which escapes (at the same time as a wild and vicious one, naturally), *and* she is determined to hook Grant. Throw into this confusion the inspired comic acting of Grant and a previously undiscovered talent for comedy in Hepburn, plus an asylum of supporting actors AND Howard Hawks's mastery of the form, and you have a film that is still guaranteed to provoke gales of laughter decades after it was made.

This film demonstrates the incredible versatility demanded by Hollywood in its great days. Katharine Hepburn, for example, was already known as a fine, if rather heavy, actress. Before *Baby* she had been in a long series of costume films starting with *Little Women* (33) through *Mary of Scotland* (36) and *A Woman Rebels* (36) to *Quality Street* (37), and powerful dramas which commenced with her first movie *A Bill of Divorcement* (32) and continued with *Morning Glory* (33), *Alice Adams* (35) and *Stage Door* (37). From the start her relationship with Hollywood had been uneasy. Spotted by David O. Selznick (the man had a genius for finding talent) in a New York play, he took her west for a screen test. Years later he recalled the impact she made: '"Ye gods, that horse face!" they cried, and, when the first rushes [of *A Bill of Divorcement*] were shown, the gloom around the studio was so

above
Douglas Fairbanks Jr (left) and Ronald Colman in *The Prisoner of Zenda*, director John Cromwell (United Artists, 37)

left
Katharine Hepburn (far right) in *Little Women* with (left to right) Frances Dee, Spring Byington, Joan Bennett and Jean Parker, director George Cukor (RKO, 33)

bottom
Adolphe Menjou and Katharine Hepburn in *Morning Glory*, director Lowell Sherman (RKO, 33)

Although they admired her talent, the audience did not automatically flock to each new Hepburn film. Shortly before *Baby* she had been dubbed 'box-office poison' and her career was in the balance. The movie resurrected her career, a career that brought her three Oscars – for *Morning Glory*, *Guess Who's Coming to Dinner* (67) and *The Lion in Winter* (68) – and *eight* other Academy nominations! An unprecedented feat that deserves to be marked by listing the films for which she came so close to winning an Oscar: *Alice Adams*, *Philadelphia Story* (40, another delicious comedy which also starred Cary Grant plus James Stewart), *Woman of the Year* (42, and notable as the first of nine films made opposite Spencer Tracy, a partnership that was as close off screen as on), *African Queen* (51), *Summertime* (55, *Summer Madness* in GB), *The Rainmaker* (56), *Suddenly Last Summer* (59) and *Long Day's Journey into Night* (62). A most remarkable woman.

The director of *Bringing Up Baby* was Howard Hawks and people who have only seen that movie or one of his other great comedies – *His Girl Friday* (40), *Ball of Fire* (41) or *I Was a Male War Bride* (49) – might be excused for thinking he stayed with the genre exclusively. They might also be very surprised to learn that he directed *Dawn Patrol* (30), *Scarface* (32), *Barbary Coast* (35) and *Only Angels Have Wings* (39), every one packed with action. And then he ventured successfully into the world of the private eye with *The Big Sleep* (46), the musical with *Gentlemen Prefer Blondes* (53), and even more successfully into Westerns – *Red River* (48), *Rio Bravo* (58), *El Dorado* (67) and *Rio Lobo* (70), all starring John Wayne.

Hepburn was primarily an actress who made occasional, welcome excursions into comedy. Sound displayed another type – the comedy actor or actress who would, occasionally, make excursions (not always successful) into heavier parts. Two of the most sparkling performers of the day were Myrna Loy and William Powell. Individually they were delightful, together they were uproarious, one of the great movie teams. Both had started in silents and put in a great deal of work before they moved into the star category, but in 1934 they

Hepburn's versatility: (*top*) in *Alice Adams*, director George Stevens (RKO, 35) and (*above*) with Roland Varno in *Quality Street*, director George Stevens (RKO, 37)

heavy you could cut it with a knife.' But when the film was completed, the audience recognized within the first minutes that a new and startling personality had come to movies. 'You could almost feel, and you could definitely hear, the excitement in the audience. . . . In those few simple feet of film a new star was born.'

opposite bottom
Richard Barthelmess (far left) and Douglas Fairbanks Jr (fourth from left) in *The Dawn Patrol*, director Howard Hawks (First National, 30)

Bette Davis and Leslie Howard in contrasting movies: (*above*) *Of Human Bondage*, director John Cromwell (RKO, 34) and (*left*) with Charley Grapewin (far left), Dick Foran and Humphrey Bogart in *The Petrified Forest*, director Archie Mayo (Warners, 36)

found themselves in *Manhattan Melodrama*, sharing the bill with Clark Gable.

Powell had already distinguished himself as a suave villain and then, playing Philo Vance, as an urbane private detective. His second talkie in 1929 was *The Canary Murder Case*, which started a run of four Vance thrillers, the last in 1933. He became increasingly debonair, rivalling Cary Grant for sophisticated good looks (and light comedy talent) and Fred Astaire in dapperness, particularly when wearing top hat, white tie and tails.

Director W.S. van Dyke noted Powell's elegance, Loy's charm and the pair's evident compatibility in *Manhattan Melodrama* and decided to try them as a team in a modest movie based on Dashiell Hammett's private-eye novel, *The Thin Man* (34). The chemistry was impeccable; as Nick and Nora Charles, the rich socialites who stumble over mysteries, Powell and Loy were perfect. They brought to life the witty, bright, loving, sexy but flip, gay and giddy married couple who, when they are not helping baffle the police, drink to the point of alcoholism. Comedy thrillers seldom work well, but in *The Thin Man* a delicate balance is struck, thanks, in no small part, to the stars, who knew exactly how to underplay a gag.

So successful was the formula (even the dog Asta made a hit) that sequels were ordered. In all the series ran to six features – the original being followed by *After the Thin Man* (36, which, remarkably, was very nearly as good as the first), *Another Thin Man* (39), *Shadow of the Thin Man* (41),

above
Cary Grant and Rita Hayworth in *Only Angels Have Wings*, director Howard Hawks (Columbia, 39)

right
Myrna Loy and William Powell in *The Thin Man*, director W.S. van Dyke (MGM, 34)

The Thin Man Goes Home (44) and *Song of the Thin Man* (47) – the last two, as Loy admitted, being pretty awful.

Powell and Loy so enjoyed acting together that they made six other movies between being Nick and Nora – *Evelyn Prentice* (34), *The Great Ziegfeld* (36, in which Powell played the celebrated impresario and Loy his second wife, Billie Burke), *Libeled Lady* (36, which also starred Spencer Tracy and Jean Harlow), *Double Wedding* (37), *I Love You Again* (40) and *Love Crazy* (41) – to most of which they brought their warm, gentle comedy touch with great success. It was the Second World War which finally interrupted the movies' most delightful comedy partnership, and after it both reduced their work rates.

Chaplin keeps silent for
(*above*) *City Lights* with
(seated) Harry Myers (United
Artists, 31) and (*left*)
Modern Times (United
Artists, 36)

opposite top
Stan Laurel (left) and Oliver
Hardy in *Our Relations*,
director Harry Lachman
(MGM, 36)

right
Voluptuous Mae West in
typically provocative pose

The Thirties were splendidly full of comedic talents. Sound had destroyed the careers of many who relied on pantomimic comedy – Buster Keaton never adapted and was a tragic loss. Others, like Harold Lloyd, continued to flourish. Chaplin, of course, maintained his individuality and contributed only two movies in the decade, both silents: *City Lights* (31) and *Modern Times* (36).

Few comedians made a more successful transition to talkies than Laurel and Hardy. Already stars in the silent era, they added verbal idiosyncrasies to their pantomime which actually broadened their characterizations rather than detracting from their comedy, as with some of their contemporaries. With sound Ollie became more pompous – 'Another fine mess you've gotten me into' – and Stan more whimperingly, simperingly daft. Sound even gave another dimension to their slapstick – how much more effective was the resounding clang that rang from Stan's empty head when struck by an infuriated Ollie! They went from strength to strength with comedy classics like *You're Darn Tootin'* (28), *Big Business* (29), *Hog Wild* (30), *Towed in the Hole* (33), *Sons of the Desert* (33), *Babes in Toyland* (34), and dozens of others which have convulsed subsequent generations.

To a new wave of comedians, sound also offered a golden opportunity. How could Mae West display her unique style to its best advantage without it? Now she sashayed across the screen and drooled out lines like, 'Is that a gun in your pocket or are you just pleased to see me?' 'It's not what I do,' she declared, 'but how I do it. It's not what I say, but how I say it. And how I look when I do it and say it.' She looked incredible, an overblown parody of sexuality, and when she deserted the stage for the screen she made the ears and eyes of millions pop.

It's ironic that she's best known for a line she never said – 'Come up and see me sometime' – but what she *did* say caused consternation among the puritans who oversaw the morals of Hollywood movies. *I'm No Angel* (33) was described by one of these gentlemen as: '. . . a vehicle for a notorious characterization of a scarlet woman whose amatory instincts are confined exclusively to the physical. There is no more pretence here than on a stud farm.'

What the pompous fool could not see was that Mae West was sending up sex and men and herself rotten. Over the next few years her films were subjected to a barrage of attacks, her scripts were torn apart, and her grossly overdrawn, vampish character stripped of its earthiness, warmth and, most destructive of all, its humour. As each successive film was shorn of its essential qualities her popularity waned and by the end of the decade she had virtually retired. However, her best, least censored, movies remain to delight us – *I'm No Angel* and *She Done Him Wrong* (33).

Mae West, said W.C. Fields, was 'the finest woman ever to walk the streets'. They appeared together in what was virtually her last film before retirement (she was tempted back in 1943 for *The Heat's On*). *My Little Chickadee* (39) should have been a memorable meeting but the parts never made a satisfactory whole. Probably because they each insisted on writing their own material! Vintage Fields is to be found in *It's a Gift* (34) and *The Bank Dick* (40). In both the miserly, misanthropic, cheating, lying, cowardly, braggadocio is seen in all his shabby, disreputable glory.

The great thing about Fields is that he hated *everyone*. What made this so convincing was that the screen Fields seems to have been but an extension of the real Fields. He laced a child actor's orange juice with gin, and, when the unfortunate infant was too sozzled to perform, went around complaining, 'The kid's no trouper.'

He was notoriously snug with his money: years of scratching a hand-to-mouth living in vaudeville had taught him financial caution. Eventually, he put some of his wealth into a splendid house with a beautiful lawn; one day a friend heard shots coming from the back yard and, upon investigating, found Fields shooting – and missing – birds perched in the trees above his prized lawn. When asked why he was doing it, he replied, 'I'll shoot 'em till they learn to shit green!'

All of his foibles and petty meannesses spilled over into his screen persona, as did his richly florid use of the English language. A leering lecher (and voyeur) he boarded, accosted and wooed ladies with such pretty compliments as: 'My ravishing little pineapple . . . my little Mexican jumping bean . . . my little titmouse.' His humour was sometimes cruel, years before such comedy was fashionable. In *It's a Gift* there's a scene in which a blind man gropes his way towards Fields's store. Shouting, 'The blind man! The blind man!' he rushes to open the glass door. Too late: the blind man walks straight through it! After the tears have dried, one

Mae West with Cary Grant (*above*) in *She Done Him Wrong*, director Lowell Sherman (Paramount, 33), and W.C. Fields (*left*) in *My Little Chickadee*, director Edward Cline (Universal, 39)

W.C. Fields with child-actor Freddie Bartholomew in *David Copperfield* (*right*), director George Cukor (MGM, 35) and in *It's A Gift* (*below*), director Norman Z. McLeod (Paramount, 34)

feels ashamed of laughing at so heartless a gag.

Although a true original who ploughed his own comic furrow, W.C. Fields was asked to try one part outside his forte. He was a perfect Micawber in the 1935 version of *David Copperfield*.

Groucho Marx described Fields as 'A great comedian . . . I liked the way he said, ''To hell with the whole world'' and *he meant it*!' Groucho Marx and his brothers exhibited much the same attitude. Perhaps the one word to describe their comedy is anarchic. They seemed dedicated to reducing any situation to a shambles – Groucho with his double talk, Chico with his fractured English, and Harpo with his manic physical assaults. Theirs was an entirely new screen humour. It involved a certain amount of slapstick but essentially relied on the verbal dexterity of Groucho.

The Marx Brothers had also toured the United States as vaudevillians, working up an act of stunning attack, a manic free-for-all that left audiences breathless. Eventually they reached Broadway and

became huge stage stars. In 1929, while appearing in 'Animal Crackers', Paramount signed them to film a previous stage hit, *The Cocoanuts*. It was a poor thing: static filming techniques could not capture the break-neck pace of the Marxes. The next year they filmed *Animal Crackers* with more success and crossed the country in 1931 to take up residence in California and work out the rest of their five-film contract for Paramount.

Originally there were six Marx Brothers: Manfred, who died at the age of three in 1888; Chico (born Leonard, 1886), Harpo (Adolph, 1888), Groucho (Julius, 1890), Gummo (Milton, 1897) and Zeppo (Herbert, 1901). Five of them appeared in vaudeville and four in pictures. Gummo quit after serving in the First World War and Zeppo, who was relegated to rather stiff and self-conscious romantic roles, after the Paramount deal ended. But in the early years they were, in the words of a song from *Animal Crackers*, 'four of the three musketeers'. ('It's all for one and two for five!')

Today four of the five Paramount movies are regarded as classics and command huge and devoted followings but at the time *The Cocoanuts, Animal Crackers, Monkey Business* (31), *Horse Feathers* (32) and *Duck Soup* (33) were no more than moderate successes at the box office. Perhaps the humour was too frantic, too surreal and extraordinary, too unstructured and indisciplined to appeal.

An important ingredient of many of the movies was a lady who became an honorary Marx, a Marx Sister – Margaret Dumont. This tall, stately, statu-

esque, immensely dignified matron was the butt of Groucho's verbal gymnastics and the dupe of the group's shady dealings. She is a monument of patience, standing rock solid while mayhem runs rampant around her, seeming quite unable to understand what is funny about her massive calm in the face of chaos. Poor Margaret Dumont, she surely never deserved the barrage of abuse Groucho poured on her. In *Duck Soup* she tells him, 'I've sponsored your appointment because I feel you are the most able statesman in all Freedonia.' This provokes a torrent of invective:

'Well, that covers a lot of ground. Say, you cover a lot of ground yourself. You'd better beat it. I hear they're going to tear you down and put up an office building where you are standing. You can leave in a taxi. If you can't leave in a taxi you can leave in a huff. If that's too soon, you can leave in a minute-and-a-huff. You know you haven't stopped talking since I came here? You must have been vaccinated with a phonograph needle.'

This is quintessential Groucho – the stream-of-consciousness, double-talking nonsense that builds absurdity upon absurdity.

Duck Soup, for all its comic pyrotechnics, was a comparative flop and Paramount refused to renew the Marxes' contract. Their movie career might have ended there but for the intervention of 'The Boy Genius', Irving Thalberg. Thalberg is an almost legendary figure in the Hollywood of the Thirties. Groucho considered him to be 'the greatest producer', an opinion shared by many but one it is difficult to assess because he died at the tragically

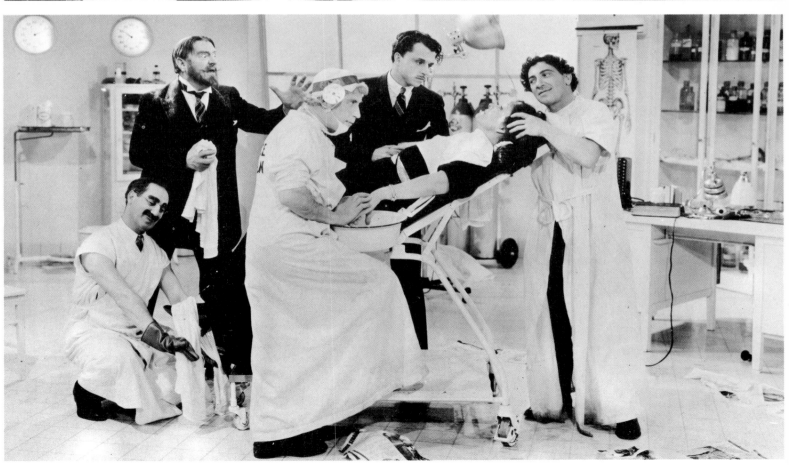

Shirley Temple with James Dunn in *Bright Eyes* (*top*), director David Butler (20th Century-Fox, 34), and (*above*) with Bill 'Bojangles' Robinson in *The Littlest Rebel*, director David Butler (20th Century-Fox, 35)

Laughton and Clark Gable) and the Leslie Howard/Norma Shearer version of *Romeo and Juliet* (36).

Groucho later recalled that Thalberg told him: 'The first five pictures weren't real pictures because they weren't about anything. Sure, they were funny, but you don't need that many laughs in a movie. I'll make a picture with you fellows with half as many laughs, but I'll put a legitimate story in it, and I'll bet it will gross twice as much as *Duck Soup*.'

Thalberg was as good as his word. *A Night at the Opera* (35) did pull in twice the revenue of *Duck Soup* and it had less laughs. But those it did have were memorable, not least the cabin scene in which a succession of people cram into a tiny space. But the zaniness of the earlier films was sacrificed to a story line which included a romantic sub-plot featuring Allan Jones, who took over the straight role from Zeppo, and it is notable that this and *A Day at the Races* (37, the second of the two great MGM movies) flag badly when the Marxes are elbowed aside so that the plot may progress.

After Thalberg's death (he died during *A Day at the Races*) there was nobody who could bring the same touch to the Marx Brothers, and their later films – *Room Service* (38), *At the Circus* (39) and *Go West* (40) – were patchy, the true Marxist madness being allowed to splutter only occasionally into life. They made three more – *The Big Store* (41), *A Night in Casablanca* (46) and the best forgotten *Love Happy* (49) – but their Thirties work remains a testament to lunatic humour at its best.

It is a problem assessing which stories about the Marxes are true and which are invented. Groucho claims that while making *Horse Feathers* Harpo was much taken by a small child and offered her parents $50,000 to adopt her. The parents refused, which is hardly surprising, but cynics might say they already knew their daughter was worth much more. She became Hollywood's biggest smallest star – Shirley Temple!

There were virulent rumours circulating that this moppet was, in fact, an adult dwarf, so assured was her acting, singing and dancing on screen. This was a calumny but it *is* supposed to be true that the ringlets which were her cherubic trademark were not her own. Shirley's hair refused to curl so false pieces were woven in to produce the tresses.

Shirley Temple was a star at five years old and by 1938, after a string of amazing successes like *Little Miss Marker* (34), *Bright Eyes* (34, in which she warbled 'On The Good Ship Lollipop'), *The Littlest Rebel* (35), *Wee Willie Winkie* (37), *Heidi* (37) and *Rebecca of Sunnybrook Farm* (38), she was earning a phenomenal $100,000 per film (it would rise to $300,000 in 1939) and reputed to be the second highest wage-earner in Hollywood. Only Louis B. Mayer took home more!

Shirley Temple was the ideal child of the Thirties, the sweetest-natured, best-behaved paragon which parents held up to their own brats as an example. But, of course, she had to grow up eventually and by the decade's end, at the decrepit age of 11, she was finding the transition from talented tot to acclaimed adolescent difficult. Her career was fitful

early age of 37. However, his contribution is still impressive. In his twenties he was made executive producer at MGM and given charge of production. His aim – which he achieved – was to present the public with the very best talents available, and the results of their work were sumptuous, starry prestige pictures like *The Barretts of Wimpole Street* (34), *Mutiny on the Bounty* (35, with Charles

during the Forties and virtually non-existent by 1950, when she retired. In 1939 she had switched from 20th Century-Fox to MGM, who announced that one of her forthcoming films would be *Babes on Broadway*, sharing star billing with two of Metro's brightest young talents – Judy Garland and Mickey Rooney. It never happened but it would have been fascinating to see Temple and Rooney trying to charm each other off the screen.

In many respects Rooney was the male equivalent of Shirley Temple. He too started young in films – he made his first, a silent, at the age of six in 1926, but his rise to stardom was not as meteoric. Until 1933 he was known as Mickey McGuire, the name of a character in a series of shorts in which he featured. When the McGuire series ended, he had to find a new handle. Rejecting his own – Joe Yule – he settled on Rooney and into a steady career as juvenile support in numerous movies, although his interpretation of Puck in *A Midsummer Night's Dream* (35) was well received.

In 1937 he played opposite another child star, Freddie Bartholomew, in *Little Lord Fauntleroy*, and the teaming was so successful that they were put together again that year in *Captains Courageous*, for which the star, Spencer Tracy, won a deserved Oscar. (It seems Rooney brought Tracy luck: in

37

1938 they appeared together again, in *Boys' Town*, for which Tracy got his second Academy award.) In the meantime, Rooney had appeared in a gentle small-town story, *A Family Affair* (37), as the son of Judge Hardy. This was a prototype 'family' film that idealized the virtues of Mom, Pop and apple pie. It was not a huge success but Louis Mayer decided that it was the sort of film MGM ought to make and the sort the great American public *ought*

to flock to see. (Eventually Hollywood agreed and presented the Hardy Family series with a special Oscar for 'furthering the American way of life'.) *You're Only Young Once* appeared in 1938 with Lewis Stone taking over the part of lovable, understanding Judge Hardy from Lionel Barrymore. The series was established and continued with *Judge Hardy's Children, Love Finds Andy Hardy* (both 38, the love interest being Judy Garland) and then on and on. Altogether 15 were made and the Hardys became the best-loved family in the States.

The series only showed one side of Rooney. He could sing, he could dance, he could play musical

Rooney as Andy Hardy: in *You're Only Young Once* (*above*) with Lewis Stone and Cecilia Parker, director George B. Seitz (MGM, 38), and with Judy Garland (the romantic interest) in *Love Finds Andy Hardy* (*above right*), director George B. Seitz (MGM, 38)

right
The team with June Preisser in *Babes in Arms*, director Busby Berkeley (MGM, 39)

Garland in *The Wizard of Oz*, with Margaret Hamilton and Ray Bolger, director Victor Fleming (MGM, 39)

instruments, and he could do impressions. He did all with a bouncing, rather aggressive, self-confidence which probably found its best expression in *Babes in Arms* (39), in which he and Judy Garland played a couple of kids who decide to put on a show. It was rather a hackneyed theme but they put it across with such verve and dazzle that they knocked the cobwebs clean off it. You don't break up a winning formula and MGM poured all its expertise into three more vehicles to showcase their youngsters – *Strike Up the Band* (40), *Babes on Broadway* (41) and *Girl Crazy* (43). By the mid-Forties there were few more popular or highly paid stars than this pair, both of whom were old pros and barely into their twenties!

(And both were faced with the problem encountered by other child stars – growing into adult actors. Rooney's lack of stature and cherubic features made this doubly difficult. There were few parts that could match both his talents and his seemingly endless adolescence. In later years he also developed a weight problem which made casting even more difficult. Apart from good roles in *The Bold and the Brave* (56) and *Baby Face Nelson* (57), he was mostly relegated to guest shots and character cameos in other people's films.)

Following the policy that movies should appeal to a family audience, at the end of the decade Mayer's studio, MGM, produced *The Wizard of Oz* (39), one of the finest examples of family entertainment ever. There is no more charming, captivating

and enchanting fairy tale in movies outside the animated films of Disney. The story of Dorothy, who is whisked over the rainbow and meets up with the Wicked Witch, the Cowardly Lion, the Tin Man and the Scarecrow (the last three being played by Bert Lahr, Ray Bolger and Jack Haley respectively) as she follows the Yellow Brick Road with Toto her dog to find 'the wonderful wizard of Oz', has retained its spellbinding quality over the years and continues to draw huge audiences.

Originally Mayer intended to cast Shirley Temple (then 11) as Dorothy. He was so keen to get her he offered to swap Gable and Jean Harlow, his most popular team, in a one-film trade with 20th Century-Fox. Sadly, Harlow died before the deal was concluded and Mayer turned to his own galaxy of stars and selected Garland. She was 16 – too old for the part – and her burgeoning puberty had to be disguised behind a tight bandeau. But, except for her age, she was perfect. In addition to the casting (every part is beautifully played), the warmth of the fantasy, and the excellent score, much of *The Wizard of Oz*'s success lies in its brilliant use of Technicolor. When seen on a good print, this is ravishing and it is even more effective because the early scenes set in Kansas and leading up to the whirlwind that carries Dorothy off are in black and white.

It was one of the best examples of the use of colour in a feature (as opposed to cartoon) film in the Thirties, but it was by no means the first.

Disney's first full-length
cartoon: *Snow White and the
Seven Dwarfs* (37)

Hollywood had been using a crude colour system – which gave a limited range of tones – since the Twenties. *The King of Jazz* – a lavish revue based around Paul Whiteman and his Orchestra – had used it effectively in 1930, but it was an expensive and unreliable technique which often gave very poor results. Technicolor continued experimenting and eventually produced a better, more reliable system which recorded the whole colour range faithfully.

The first use of the improved process was in a Walt Disney short, *Flowers and Trees* (32), which won an Oscar and, significantly, Disney also won a special award that year for creating Mickey Mouse. Mickey appeared first in a sound film, *Steamboat Willie*, in 1928 and grew into a legend – probably the most popular, certainly the most internationally famous, cartoon creation ever (although Donald Duck might dispute this, even though he did not appear until 1934). Disney's first great technical achievement was in perfectly synchronizing animated movement to dialogue and music, the latter being an important ingredient in Disney products. Many of the songs used in his movies became big hits.

Walt Disney was not content to confine himself to making cartoon shorts, profitable though they were. His purpose was to prove that animation could do everything that the best of Hollywood feature films had to offer, and more. He determined to produce a full-length sound movie, using full colour. The universal opinion was that he'd gone crazy and would quickly bankrupt himself. Ignoring such pessimism, he set to work on *Snow White and the Seven Dwarfs* (37). No one had ever attempted anything like it before and Disney virtually had to invent the many systems and processes required as he went along. The project also extended his financial resources to the limit and he was close to proving his detractors right by the time *Snow White* got into the cinemas. However, it proved to be a monster hit and a vast money-maker.

Triumphantly vindicated, Disney pressed on. *Pinocchio* followed in 1940 and then, in the same year, the even more ambitious *Fantasia*, in which he choreographed his animated creations to classical music (Mickey Mouse appeared in 'The Sorceror's Apprentice'). Next came *Dumbo* (41) and *Bambi* (42), which is widely regarded as the pinnacle of animation art, so beautiful and perfect are the effects he achieved. The studio went from strength to commercial strength, branching out into live-action films (the first being *Treasure Island* in 1950), documentaries (*The Living Desert* in 1953) and musicals which combined live action with animation such as the immensely successful *Mary Poppins* (64). He did not abandon full-length animated features, but they were becoming prohibitively expensive to produce to his own standards and by the Fifties and Sixties they retained their charm but not their technical brilliance.

Disney dispensed sweetness and light but most of his movies did not neglect the darker side of life. He realized that children enjoy being thrilled and most of his films had an element of horror. Adults share this masochistic delight and their tastes were well catered for during the decade.

The first great star of horror movies was Lon Chaney, 'The Man of a Thousand Faces', who had transfixed audiences with his gallery of grotesques in the silent era. In 1930 he took the plunge with *The Unholy Three* (a sound remake of his 1925 picture), playing a cast of characters each of which needed a different voice. Chaney supplied them all and even swore an affidavit to that effect. His performance was hailed by the critics and he was all set to become the first horror star of talkies, when tragically, not long after the release of *The Unholy Three*, he died of cancer.

His mantle or, to be more precise, his cloak fell to Bela Lugosi, a Hungarian with a lisping, strongly accented voice that seemed to carry infinite menace. There have been uncounted actors since who have attempted the role of the vampire count, but none has put his stamp on the role as firmly as Lugosi in *Dracula* (31). So seductively threatening was he, so atmospheric was the film, that together

they seemed to set a style for sound horror at the very first attempt.

Universal made *Dracula* and the studio became virtually synonymous with the horror genre in the Thirties. After Lugosi's success, Universal wanted him to star in another horror epic, *Frankenstein* (31). Perhaps his greatest asset as a horror actor was his voice; however, unaccountably he was screen tested as the monstrous creation, who has no dialogue at all beyond gutteral grunts and gruesome groans.

Eventually a new actor was brought in to play Frankenstein's creature. Boris Karloff was not, as his name implied, Russian, nor was he in real life anything like the ghouls he played on screen. He was a modest, well-bred, cricket-loving Englishman, born William Pratt in 1877. Beneath the 48 pounds of make-up he wore to portray Frankenstein's monster can be seen a pair of sad, gentle eyes that reflect the misery of the creature, giving him humanity, and it was this quality which helped him become the pre-eminent star of horror movies in a career which lasted for nearly 40 years.

Lon Chaney in *The Unholy Three*, director Tod Browning (MGM, 30)

Bela Lugosi in *Dracula*, director Tod Browning (Universal, 31)

Boris Karloff with Elsa Lanchester in *The Bride of Frankenstein*, director James Whale (Universal, 35)

He followed *Frankenstein* with *The Mummy* (32) and *The Old Dark House* (32), in which he played a murderous deaf and dumb butler, and came together with Bela Lugosi in *The Black Cat* (34) and one of the inevitable sequels to *Frankenstein – The Son of . . .* (39). Before these, though, there had been *The Bride of Frankenstein* (35). Most sequels are shoddy things but *Bride* with Karloff and Elsa Lanchester very nearly matched its predecessor for style, atmosphere and quality.

Universal seemed to have gained a copyright in horror but other studios were keen to reap the rewards, not least MGM and, in the rush to cash in, Irving Thalberg made one of his few major miscalculations. He admired the work of director Tod Browning (who had made *Dracula*) and was keen

to give him his head. They settled on a story set in a circus in which a trapeze artiste murders her rich midget husband. Entitled *Freaks* it tells how the midget's misshapen colleagues transform the lovely Cleopatra into (don't snigger) a human chicken. It was, of course, absurd but it had enormous power, mainly because Browning cast the roles of the circus freaks with unfortunates who had been deformed since birth.

Freaks (32) is considered a classic today but when it was first shown reports claimed people rushed screaming from the cinema. MGM were appalled, the censors slashed the movie, and it was not shown in Britain until 1963. The film almost ruined Browning's career.

It was generally safer to rely on movie magic to

create monsters and by the Thirties the state of the movie art was such that amazing illusions could be conjured. In 1933 two movies relying on 'switchcraft' appeared – *The Invisible Man* from Universal and *King Kong* from RKO.

Claude Rains, as the evil scientist in *The Invisible Man*, is only brought to retribution when his footsteps in snow betray his progress. (Rains went on to a distinguished and varied acting career which encompassed *The Adventures of Robin Hood* (38), *Mr Smith Goes to Washington* (39), *Casablanca* (42) and many others but returned to horror in 1943 as

the mutilated composer who haunts Paris in *The Phantom of the Opera*.)

King Kong was, and remains, a much more remarkable technological achievement. For a start

Horror stalks the screen: Fredric March with Miriam Hopkins in *Dr Jekyll and Mr Hyde* (*above left*), director Rouben Mamoulian (Paramount, 32); eponymous *Freaks* (*above*), director Tod Browning (MGM, 32); and (*left*) *King Kong* with Fay Wray, directors Merian C. Cooper and Ernest Schoedsack, special effects by Willis O'Brien (RKO, 33)

Kong was supposed to be 50 feet tall, large enough to climb the Empire State Building and still not be dwarfed by it. A little-known genius named Willis O'Brien who had worked for years on a method of frame-by-frame photography came up with the answer. An intricately detailed, 18-inch model was constructed on which tiny adjustments could be made to the limbs and facial features between each frame exposure. At its simplest, this means that to raise an arm the model was photographed with the limb fractionally adjusted several times. The precise amount of adjustment was worked out with incredible care so that when the film was run at normal speed the arm appeared to move smoothly. It sounds simple but to achieve 1 minute of animation on screen 960 separate movements and 20 hours of filming were required.

There were also scenes in which the brute had to be seen in correct scale against human actors – for example, when it plucks Fay Wray from a tree. To achieve this, two enormous models were built: a huge paw and an immense bust of the beast's head and shoulders. So large was the head that three men could climb inside to work the controls which operated its eyes (each as big as melons), nostrils, mouth (6 feet across with 10-inch teeth) and other features. *King Kong* took two painstaking years to film and cost $650,000 – a derisory sum today and not a particularly high budget even then.

As these movies showed, Hollywood's expertise had grown very fast. For all its sophistication, though, it still had elements of the Western town it had once been, and there were enough people around who had ridden into Hollywood on a horse, punched cows for a living, and thought that acting, or at worst, stunting in the movies would be an easier way of making a pay packet.

Gary Cooper had started like that. As a string-bean kid who'd worked as a cowboy on his father's ranch, he talked his way onto a location shoot for Henry King's *The Winning of Barbara Worth* in 1926. Then won a small but flashy part when an actor failed to turn up. He was to become the finest film actor in Hollywood, a man who acted so naturally that during a take he didn't seem to be doing anything. But he knew exactly what the camera could catch and he had only to flicker an eyelid to convey a wealth of meaning.

Cooper started in silents as a supporting actor and worked his way up the ladder. When sound arrived, the Western – always a popular silent genre – had a problem; the cumbersome recording equipment couldn't move to the wide open locations that gave them their glamour. There were a couple of years during which the cowboy film languished until the technology could catch up but by 1929 it was ready and so was Cooper. The irony is that Cooper's first all-talking picture, *The Virginian*, is also the one in which his dialogue is almost monosyllabic. This is the movie where he gained the reputation for a conversational ability that was limited to 'yep', 'nope' and 'smile when you say that'!

Although now often best remembered for his work in Westerns – particularly his Oscar-winning role as Marshall Will Kane in *High Noon* (52) – he made very few in the Thirties, the most notable being *The Plainsman* (36), in which he played Wild Bill Hickok to Jean Arthur's Calamity Jane. His range during the decade was astonishingly wide: from Hemingway's *A Farewell to Arms* (32) to the White Knight in *Alice in Wonderland* (33), taking in British Empire heroics in *Lives of the Bengal Lancers* (35) and *Beau Geste* (39) and playing opposite Marlene Dietrich in *Morocco* (30) and *Desire* (36).

His finest performances – even amidst the incomparable work he did elsewhere – were as the decent, quiet American who knows what is right and that it must be done whatever the odds. *Mr*

Gary Cooper goes to war: with Adolphe Menjou in *A Farewell to Arms* (*below*), director Frank Borzage (Paramount, 32), and Ray Milland in *Beau Geste* (*bottom*), director William Wellman (Paramount, 39)

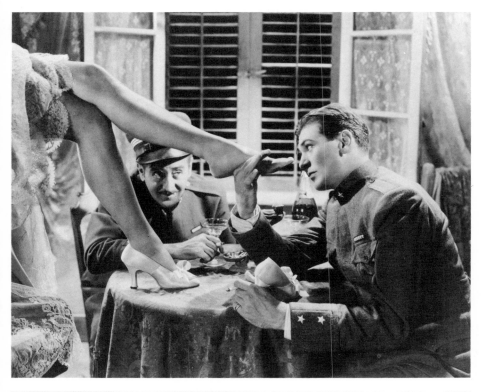

Deeds Goes to Town (36) gave him a perfect opportunity to play this paragon and show a skill for comedy. *Sergeant York* (41) had him playing a real-life pacifist who became one of the most-decorated heroes of the First World War. He won a deserved Oscar for his sensitive portrayal, and his second award-winning role, in *High Noon*, confirmed him as the gentle man with an iron will.

It is, perhaps, surprising that until the Fifties and films like *Distant Drums* (51), *Springfield Rifle* (52), *Vera Cruz* (54), *Man of the West* (58) and *The Hanging Tree* (59) he was offered little opportunity to prove that few could ride higher in the saddle than he. As Clyde Jeavons has commented, 'Out of doors no other actor cut a finer figure. He was the Westerner's Westerner.'

Now, this claim can be disputed and most ardent John Wayne fans probably will. But in the context of the Thirties there's no doubt that Wayne was very firmly in the second rank. His friend and mentor, John Ford, had suggested Wayne to director Raoul Walsh for the lead in *The Big Trail* (30), one of the first epic sound Westerns. It should

have been The Duke's big break but he fluffed it. Perhaps he was too young and inexperienced, but something was missing and that, as far as most of Hollywood was concerned, was that. He was relegated to the 'oaters', the production-line 'B' Westerns that were churned out as programme fillers. He might have languished there with popular, but second-rate, stars like William Boyd (Hopalong Cassidy) and the singing cowboys including Gene Autry, Tex Ritter and Roy Rogers, who were to dominate the Western in the Thirties and early Forties and set back its development. However, John Ford had not given up on him.

Ford once introduced himself to an audience: 'My name's John Ford. I make Westerns.' It was one of the great understatements of Hollywood. In fact, he virtually invented the Western as we know it and had an uncanny feel for the West and its men. As he told a student audience: 'I *have* been a cowboy and I punched cows awhile. The boss's daughter fell in love with me. She was six feet two and weighed about 210 pounds so I stole a horse and rode away and came to California. But I have been a cowboy and I know the West pretty well.'

He started making movies in 1914 when he moved out to Hollywood to join his brother Francis, who was a director. In 1917 he directed, wrote, acted and stunted in his first solo venture, *The Tornado*, a Western, of course. Before the arrival of sound he made over 60 films, the vast majority Westerns. It was with sound that his reputation really grew but he did not make a Western between 1926 (*Three Bad Men*) and 1939. And his reputation as the greatest director of Westerns actually rests on a rather small body of work – of the 59 sound features he made between 1926 and 1966, only 13 were Westerns.

But what Westerns! They include some of the all-time classics – *My Darling Clementine* (46, based on the stories of the gunfight at the OK Corral told to him by Wyatt Earp), the cavalry trilogy of *Fort Apache* (48), *She Wore a Yellow Ribbon* (49) and *Rio Grande* (50), *The Searchers* (56) and *The Man Who Shot Liberty Valance* (62).

The rest of his movies were as diverse as they were usually brilliant. He seemed to move effortlessly from comedy to drama, from historical to modern subject. For example, in 1935 successive Ford movies were *The Informer*, a powerful drama about a Sinn Feiner who betrays a friend to the police for the reward which will take him to the States (it won Oscars for the director and Victor McLaglen, who starred as Gypo Bolan), and then *Steamboat Round the Bend*, in which Will Rogers (in his last film) plays a medicine drummer who converts an old steamboat and races it down the Mississippi to save his nephew, who has been falsely convicted of murder. Although the latter could have been a sombre subject, it is handled with a lightness and humour that is delightful.

Versatility was second nature to Ford: in 1936 he directed Katharine Hepburn in *Mary of Scotland*; in 1937 he directed Shirley Temple in *Wee Willie Winkie*. Later he tackled, and triumphed, with *Young Mr Lincoln* (39), *The Grapes of Wrath* (40, for which Henry Fonda and Jane Darwell won Oscars), *Tobacco Road* (41), *How Green Was My Valley* (41, Oscar for Best Director), and *The Fugitive* (47) – all serious subjects for which he demanded, and received, magnificent performances from his actors, especially Henry Fonda, who starred in three of them. Ford made history in 1952 when his sparkling Irish comedy *The Quiet Man* (starring Wayne, in unusually humorous form, and Maureen O'Hara) won him his fourth Oscar as Best Director; no one else had achieved this honour.

Perhaps the best-remembered Ford film, certainly the best-remembered Western, was *Stagecoach*, his only Western of the Thirties. It rehabilitated the genre, which apart from a few exceptions – *Billy the Kid* (30), *Cimarron* (31) and the jokey *Destry Rides Again* (39, starring the unlikely but effective combination of James Stewart and Marlene Dietrich) – had fallen into the 'B' picture limbo. It also made John Wayne a star. Ford gives him one of the best introductions into a picture that any actor could ask. When we first see him he is waving down the stage, twirling his rifle,

Contrasting styles and subjects from John Ford: (*left*) Victor McLaglen and Una O'Connor in *The Informer* (RKO, 35) and (*below*) Will Rogers and Anne Shirley in *Steamboat Round the Bend* (20th Century-Fox, 35)

bottom
Some of the passengers in Ford's *Stagecoach*: (left to right) Andy Devine, George Bancroft, John Carradine, Donald Meek, Louise Platt, Claire Trevor and John Wayne (United Artists, 39)

and the camera zooms straight into his face, giving that big, handsome mug the tightest, largest, most flattering close-up.

Once seen, who can forget *Stagecoach*? Apart from Wayne as The Ringo Kid, there is a truly excellent cast, including Claire Trevor as the prostitute Dallas, John Carradine as the gentlemanly gambler Hatfield, Thomas Mitchell as the drunk Dr Boone (he won an Oscar for it) and so on. And then there is the magnificent backdrop of Monument Valley with its towering rock columns and the outstanding stunt work. Yakima Canutt, the doyen of Hollywood stunting and the man who would years later stage the chariot race in *Ben Hur* (59), supervised and undertook the death-defying walk along the stampeding team of horses.

The technical genius of people like Canutt, people who were bringing entertainment movies to an unprecedented standard in every area from stunts to make-up, from set building to camera trickery, from colour processing to costume design, established Hollywood as the centre of the film world, and talented actors, technicians and directors from other countries were attracted to the town. Two men from very different backgrounds made that long journey. Director Michael Curtiz set out from Hungary and arrived in 1926; actor Errol Flynn started from Tasmania and after a long, adventurous, roistering, philandering peregrination fetched up in California in 1935. Together they made some dashing, daring, freebooting dramas.

Few men swashed a finer buckle than Errol Flynn. Before the booze and debauchery ravaged his face and body, he was almost unbearably handsome. As Jack Warner (of Warner Brothers) commented, 'He was all the heroes in one magnificent, sexy, animal package.' And to crown it, he had a merrily mischievous twinkle in his eyes. He was a man born to swing from the deck of a buccaneer's brigantine, to dive from a crenellated rampart, to bound through Sherwood Forest. A man equally at home with a cutlass in his fist or a woman in his arms. Curtiz was one of Hollywood's characters: he stomped around the set in riding boots and breeches, brandishing a fly whisk. Despite these eccentricities he was a fine commercial film-maker who knew just how to get the best out of Flynn.

Together they made some marvellous filibustering adventures – *Captain Blood* (35, in which Flynn first sailed the bounding main), *The Charge of the Light Brigade* (36), *The Adventures of Robin Hood* (38) and *The Sea Hawk* (40) among others. Of them, *Robin Hood* is the most accomplished. Flynn is perfect for the role – a springing, leaping, laughing outlaw who captivates Olivia de Havilland (as Maid Marion). Flynn and de Havilland made a comely team in several pictures; perhaps the dynamism of their playing was partly due to the fact that Flynn, the great lover and libertine, met his match in the lovely Olivia. Bette Davis believed that she was one of the few women he deeply and genuinely loved. The film itself is a beautiful, romantic evocation. Made in colour, it matches *The Wizard of Oz* (39) for sheer eye-pleasing loveliness, particularly in the gentle muted greens of the

above
Richard Dix (kneeling) and William Collier Jr in *Cimarron*, director Wesley Ruggles (RKO, 31)

left
Johnny Weissmuller and Maureen O'Sullivan in *Tarzan and His Mate*, director Cedric Gibbons (MGM, 34)

Swashbuckling Errol Flynn: with Olivia de Havilland in *Captain Blood* (*opposite, top left*), director Michael Curtiz (Warners, 35); in *The Charge of the Light Brigade* (*opposite, top right*), director Michael Curtiz (Warners, 36); and (*opposite centre*) with Bette Davis in *The Private Lives of Elizabeth and Essex*, director Michael Curtiz (Warners, 39)

opposite bottom
Buster Crabbe as superhero *Flash Gordon* with Priscilla Lawson, director Frederick Stephani (Universal, 36)

forest. All in all, it was probably Flynn's finest hour and one of Curtiz's major achievements, one to be set beside *Yankee Doodle Dandy* and *Casablanca* (both 42). He was another of the craftsman directors who were able to bring equal deftness to almost every style of film.

Curtiz flourished as an emigré in Hollywood and others flocked to the town to emulate his success.

In 1938 Alfred Hitchcock made the trip across the Atlantic; he had worked in the British film industry since 1921, but he recognized that it was in a different, lower league and he had always looked to Hollywood as his inspiration. By the time he was summoned by David O. Selznick to make *Rebecca* (40), he was among the forefront of British filmmakers.

The British film industry had never really found the confidence to get on equal terms with its American cousin. It had reacted slowly to sound, mostly because it was virtually bankrupt when the revolution came, and it produced only one mogul who could make even the smallest claim to rivalling the giants of Beverly Hills. Alexander Korda was a Hungarian who had worked in Hollywood but he made a huge impact in Britain in 1933 when he

Charles Laughton in two of his best-remembered roles: with Clark Gable in *Mutiny on the Bounty* (opposite, top left), director Frank Lloyd (MGM, 35), and (opposite, top right) with Binnie Barnes, in *The Private Life of Henry VIII*, director Alexander Korda (London Films, 33)

Robert Donat with Godfrey Tearle in (opposite bottom) *The Thirty-Nine Steps*, director Alfred Hitchcock (Gaumont British, 35), and *The Citadel* (right), director King Vidor (MGM, 38)

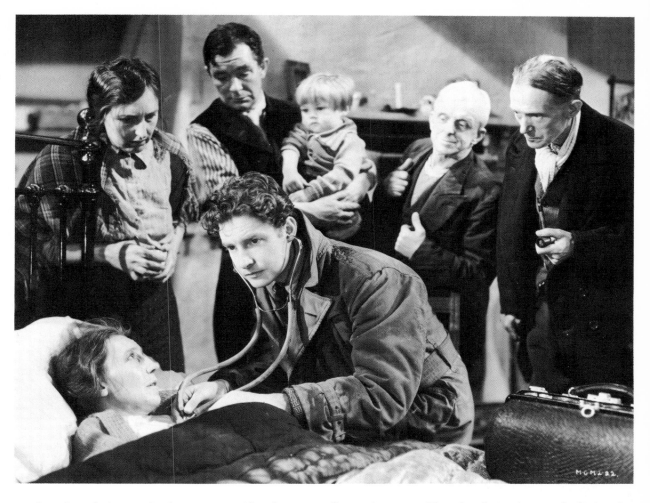

below
Jessie Matthews in the 'Dancing On The Ceiling' number from *Evergreen*, director Victor Saville (Gaumont, 34)

produced and directed *The Private Life of Henry VIII* starring Charles Laughton. For a brief, glorious period this single film looked as if it was heralding a golden age of British cinema to rival Hollywood: *Henry VIII* was one of the very few British films that was exported to the States and scored a hit there.

On the crest of this wave Korda overstretched his ambitions. He set up London Films and established a vast studio at Denham. Sadly, the Americans never reacted in the same way to another of Korda's films, and although he produced a string of fine pictures – *The Scarlet Pimpernel* (34), the chillingly prophetic *Things to Come* (35), the acclaimed *Rembrandt* (37, with another magnificent performance from Laughton), and *The Four Feathers* (39) – his ambition always outstripped his assets. However, Korda and the rest of the British industry did contribute one important asset to film-making – a stable of actors who, because their native country had so little to offer, swiftly became exports to Hollywood. Besides Laughton there was Robert Donat, who had come to prominence in *Henry VIII*, *The Thirty-Nine Steps* (35), *The Citadel* (38) and *Goodbye Mr Chips* (39); he was followed in the Forties by Rex Harrison, James Mason and others like Margaret Lockwood and Trevor Howard, who did not settle so easily.

Gracie Fields also made the journey across the Atlantic, having scored successes in Britain with warm-hearted movies like *Sally in Our Alley* (31) and *Sing As We Go* (34), but other great ladies of the British cinema either never got or refused to answer Hollywood's call. Both Jessie Matthews and Anna Neagle were doing very nicely at home, Matthews with her featherlight musicals, of which *Evergreen* (34) is best remembered, and Neagle with musicals like *Bitter Sweet* (33) and biopics like *Nell Gwynn* (34), *Victoria the Great* (37), and *Nurse Edith Cavell* (39). Neagle did make three movies in the States but then returned for a series of flowery romances, of which *Spring in Park Lane* (48) was probably most successful.

Alfred Hitchcock had been following his own course. *Blackmail* (29) was his first talkie, a thriller,

51

above
Laurence Olivier and Merle
Oberon in *Wuthering
Heights*, director William
Wyler (Samuel Goldwyn, 39)

below and opposite
The incandescent Jean
Harlow: in *Dinner at Eight*,
director George Cukor
(MGM, 33), and with Gable
in *Red Dust*, director Victor
Fleming (MGM, 32)

and Robert Powell in the Seventies. In addition he made *The Man Who Knew Too Much* (34, which he remade in 1955 with James Stewart and Doris Day), *The Lady Vanishes* (38, another enduring classic) and *Jamaica Inn* (39) from the Daphne du Maurier novel; this author also provided Hitchcock with *The Birds* (63) and that first Hollywood movie, *Rebecca* (40).

Its star, playing the mysterious Max de Winter, the master of Manderley, was Laurence Olivier, another of those who had been lured to Hollywood. He had gone in 1938 to play Heathcliff in *Wuthering Heights* (39), leaving behind the woman with whom he was passionately in love. She was missing him desperately and, on a whim, decided to spend five reckless days with him. On the third day of her stay Olivier dined with Myron Selznick, one of Hollywood's leading agents. Vivien Leigh joined them and afterwards Myron took the couple to a backlot where his brother was about to start shooting his new picture.

David O. Selznick's new film was running into trouble. For a start the producer was having problems with Clark Gable. Gable had many strengths but among them could not be listed an impeccable taste in choosing films. He'd bucked at doing *It Happened One Night* (34) and two years before that he had grouched about being cast in *Red Dust* because he was unhappy with his co-star, Jean Harlow. He disapproved of her screen image.

the type of film with which his name will forever be associated. His British work in the early Thirties rivals Hollywood for style, craft and inventiveness. *The Thirty-Nine Steps*, in which Robert Donat as John Buchan's hero Richard Hannay is chased across the Highlands (handcuffed for some of the way to the delicious Madeleine Carroll, which provokes a very saucy scene when she is forced to take off her stockings!), is a classic and far superior to the remakes starring Kenneth More in the Sixties

Jean Harlow looked like a tart with her radiant platinum blonde hair, her hard little body, her flinty face dominated by hooded, come-to-bed eyes and her bottom-drawer accent. She dressed like a tart in clinging, low-cut backless dresses beneath which she wore no underwear. She became the first sex symbol of the sound era simply by saying

to Ben Lyon, 'Do you mind if I put on something more comfortable?' in *Hell's Angels* (30). Like Mae West, it wasn't so much *what* she said as the way she said it, and the simmering look which accompanied a line. And, again like West, she knew that sex and laughs could go together. She had a deft comic touch, especially for the wisecrack when it was delivered with a swing of the hips, as she showed in Capra's *Platinum Blonde* (31).

When she was paired with Gable in *Red Dust* (32) the shower of sexual sparks thrilled audiences. The two seemed complementary: both knew who they were and what they were about. She was a tramp but honest and forthright. He was a decent man whose past was less than immaculate. They just needed to look at each other with frank lust for the chemistry to work.

Despite Gable's misgivings it was a big hit, one which MGM could not ignore. In 1933 they were re-teamed, less successfully, in *Hold Your Man*, but they hit form again in *China Seas* (35). The plot was little different from *Red Dust* – Gable is torn between his attraction for a classy society dame (Rosalind Russell; it had been Mary Astor in *Dust*) and a woman of loose morals. Although capable of mixing in the lady's rarefied world, he meets his true mate in the dame.

So self-assured on screen, Harlow seemed unable to match it in real life. Allegedly promiscuous, she made three disastrous marriages, the first when only 16 and the others after she achieved stardom. Eventually she seemed to find the man to

Harlow in *Libeled Lady* (*above*) with William Powell (left) and Spencer Tracy, director Jack Conway (MGM, 36), and in *China Seas* (*right*) with Gable, Rosalind Russell and C. Aubrey Smith, director Tay Garnett (MGM, 35)

make her happy – William Powell. It was, from all accounts, a grand passion and they were to be married but in 1937 she fell ill. She suffered from a kidney complaint which she should have soon got over but her mother, a fanatical Christian Scientist, refused to allow doctors to attend her and, by the time she was given medical treatment, it was too late. Her's was an untimely death which robbed the movies of an incandescence that would not be seen again until Monroe two decades later.

Harlow's last film, *Saratoga* (37), was unfinished on her death. Instead of shelving it, MGM shot some of the later scenes using a double, a clumsy and inadequate substitution which should have been laughed out of the cinemas. Astonishingly, *Saratoga* took $2 million at the box office, the most profitable movie of the year. Its success undoubtedly owes a lot to public curiosity and a good deal to the popularity of its two stars, for by now Clark Gable was the acknowledged 'King of Hollywood', voted such by the fans.

His friend Spencer Tracy, a far superior actor, presented him with a joke crown. Arguably Tracy was Hollywood's best actor – a record nine Oscar nominations and awards for *Captains Courageous* (37) and *Boys' Town* (38). He was equally commanding in drama (*20,000 Years in Sing Sing*, his first hit in 1933) or comedy (*Father of the Bride*, 50), in biopics (*Edison the Man*, 40) or Westerns (*Broken Lance*, 54). He carried *Bad Day at Black Rock* (55) single-handed and worked in successful teams: three pictures opposite Gable and a long partner-ship (discreetly continued off-screen) with Kath-arine Hepburn in nine pictures from *Woman of the Year* (41) to his last film, *Guess Who's Coming to Dinner* (67). Throughout his 37-year career his strength, conviction and personality won the love of the public and the unalloyed respect of his peers.

Great though Tracy was, he couldn't topple Gable. There will probably never again be a star as popular or as enduring as Clark Gable – he was the biggest, the handsomest, the best. He had more presence, more appeal, more charm than anyone else. When he consciously tried to act, in *Parnell* (37), for example, in which he played the Irish statesman, he could be a disaster. His secret was that he knew how to project himself. 'What people see on the screen is me,' he once admitted. 'The only reason they come to see me is that I know life is great and they know that I know it.'

When he started, though, he wasn't the magni-ficently handsome specimen of manhood that the world later loved and respected. His ears looked like 'a pair of open cab doors', his teeth were crooked and his hands enormous. Nothing could be done about the hands but the ears were surgically pinned back and the teeth were first capped (rather inadequately) and then entirely replaced by plates. These were not as tight-fitting as might be and more than one actress complained of his halitosis!

Nothing diminished the fact that he was a big, proud, very masculine man. From his early film appearances in 1930–31, audiences recognized that here was a new type of man, a great lover who was

also rugged and virile. John Barrymore described him as 'Valentino in the body of Jack Dempsey'. He loved women but treated them rough, preferring them (both on and off the screen) to be all-woman in bed but one of the boys elsewhere.

He made 14 pictures before *Red Dust* (32), starting as a cowboy in *The Painted Desert* (30) – he was to return to Westerns later in his career with *Across the Wide Missouri* (51), *Lone Star* (52), *The Tall Men* (55) and *The Misfits* (61) in a modern setting – and played a variety of parts including romantic lead opposite Garbo in *Susan Lenox – Her Fall and Rise* (31) before finding the characterization that was to be his trademark, the independent, strong-willed, devil-may-care, gentlemanly roughneck that was an extension of his own personality. His subsequent rise to pre-eminence was meteoric, helped by *It Happened One Night* (34, he won the Best Actor Oscar), *Mutiny on the Bounty* (35) and *San Francisco* (36).

In 1936 his personal life matched the happy success of his career when he fell crazily in love with Carole Lombard, and she with him. They had met four years earlier when they played opposite each other in *No Man of Her Own* (32) and had argued. They continued to argue, but he divorced his second wife and settled down with an actress who shared many things in common with Jean Harlow.

Lombard was a great beauty who looked rather fragile but beneath the porcelain exterior was a tough, raunchy, dirty-talking broad who was easily a match for her man. She talked just like a man, and she was as at home in the outdoors, fishing and shooting and drinking beer, as any of Gable's boon buddies. It was a hugely successful marriage and its end in 1941 when her plane crashed in Nevada very nearly destroyed him. It was the lowest point of his life and a stark contrast to the peaks he had achieved only two years before, peaks Lombard urged him to scale.

Everyone had known that Gable was the only man who could play the lead in David O. Selznick's new film, *Gone with the Wind* (39). Everybody except Gable: he was genuinely afraid that he could not match the public's expectation. But persuading Gable turned out to be the least of Selznick's problems. Leslie Howard, his first choice as Ashley Wilkes, shunned the role; 'I haven't the slightest intention of playing another weak, watery character,' he announced. Eventually, though, he succumbed. Selznick's biggest problem, however, was in casting the heroine: 'Seventy-five million people would want my scalp if I chose the wrong Scarlett.'

Whereas the male stars were reticent, the grande dames of Hollywood were elbowing each other out of the way to land O'Hara. But Selznick soon realized that his Scarlett would have to be an unknown. He initiated the biggest talent hunt in Hollywood history – 14,000 hopefuls were interviewed, 90 given tests, $50,000 spent. Nobody suitable was discovered.

By November 1938 Selznick was desperate: he had to get the movie started and he also had to clear a ramshackle city of old sets off his lot before he

could build Tara. His answer was to put the existing sets to the torch, start his Technicolor cameras rolling, load doubles for Gable and the future Scarlett into a buggy and capture the destruction of Atlanta, a key scene.

The night he started his conflagration was the night brother Myron dined with Olivier and Vivien Leigh. The date was not accidental. Myron had taken one look at Miss Leigh and confirmed what she already knew. She was Scarlett. Together they connived the most dramatic, unorthodox audition yet recorded. David would first meet Vivien in the light thrown from Atlanta's glowing ruins. It was carefully timed – the small party arrived after the excitement but while David was still buoyed up by getting his first feet of film in the can. Myron guided Vivien through the crowds and greeted David with 'Meet your Scarlett O'Hara!'

The problems didn't end there. Tears and tantrums marked the shooting. Vivien Leigh didn't get on with the second and third directors. Gable didn't get on with Selznick. And Vivien Leigh and Clark Gable didn't get on!

GWTW opened on 15 December, 1939, in, appropriately, Atlanta, Georgia. It had taken three years to make – from the buying of the rights to the premiere – and cost $4,250,000. No one had ever spent that much on a movie before (today you would probably have to multiply it by six to get an equivalent figure). It was, as everybody knows, a fabulous success, possibly financially the most successful film ever made. Others have subsequently out-grossed it – *The Sound of Music* (65) eventually knocked it off its No. 1 spot in Variety's list of All-Time Film Rental Champs – but *GWTW*'s figures have never been adjusted for inflation. It is almost certainly true to say that more people have paid money to see it than any other movie ever made.

Everything about it worked. Decades after it was first shown it still has the power to enthrall, to put a lump into the most cynical throat. One proof being that CBS Television paid $35 million in 1978 to show it 20 times over 20 years! If such a thing is possible, it became an instant classic, a feat recognized by the Academy of Motion Picture Arts and Sciences which awarded it eight Oscars (including one to Vivien Leigh as Best Actress, Best Picture, to Victor Fleming as Best Director and to Hattie McDaniel for her part as Mammy, the first ever given to a black performer) as well as two special prizes – one honorary award to William Cameron Menzies for 'outstanding achievement in the use of colour' and the Irving G. Thalberg Memorial Award – given only for exceptional merit – to David O. Selznick.

Gone with the Wind is the pinnacle of commercial movie-making, one of Hollywood's greatest and most enduring triumphs. It confirmed that the industry which had started the Thirties in such uncertainty had unequivocally earned the position of the foremost producer of movies in the world.

'30s Oscars

YEAR	BEST FILM	BEST ACTOR	BEST ACTRESS
1929/30	*All Quiet on the Western Front/* Universal	George Arliss/ *Disraeli*	Norma Shearer/ *The Divorcee*
1930/31	*Cimarron/* RKO Radio	Lionel Barrymore/ *A Free Soul*	Marie Dressler/ *Min and Bill*
1931/32	*Grand Hotel/* MGM	Fredric March/ *Dr Jekyll and Mr Hyde*	Helen Hayes/ *The Sin of Madelon Claudet*
1932/33	*Cavalcade/* Fox	Charles Laughton/ *The Private Life of Henry VIII*	Katharine Hepburn/ *Morning Glory*
1934	*It Happened One Night/* Columbia	Clark Gable/ *It Happened One Night*	Claudette Colbert/ *It Happened One Night*
1935	*Mutiny on the Bounty/* MGM	Victor McLaglen/ *The Informer*	Bette Davis/ *Dangerous*
1936	*The Great Ziegfeld/* MGM	Paul Muni/ *The Story of Louis Pasteur*	Luise Rainer/ *The Great Ziegfeld*
1937	*The Life of Emile Zola/* Warner Brothers	Spencer Tracy/ *Captains Courageous*	Luise Rainer/ *The Good Earth*
1938	*You Can't Take It with You/* Columbia	Spencer Tracy/ *Boys' Town*	Bette Davis/ *Jezebel*
1939	*Gone with the Wind* MGM	Robert Donat/ *Goodbye Mr Chips*	Vivien Leigh *Gone with the Wind*

Best Actor award for Paul Muni in *The Story of Louis Pasteur*, with Josephine Hutchinson, director William Dieterle (Warners, 35)

'30s Oscars

BEST DIRECTOR	BEST SUPPORTING ACTOR	BEST SUPPORTING ACTRESS	YEAR
Lewis Milestone/ *All Quiet on the Western Front*			1929/30
Norman Taurog/ *Skippy*			1930/31
Frank Borzage/ *Bad Girl*			1931/32
Frank Lloyd/ *Cavalcade*			1932/33
Frank Capra/ *It Happened One Night*			1934
John Ford/ *The Informer*			1935
Frank Capra/ *Mr Deeds Goes to Town*	Walter Brennan/ *Come and Get it*	Gale Sondergaard/ *Anthony Adverse*	1936
Leo McCarey/ *The Awful Truth*	Joseph Schildkraut/ *The Life of Emile Zola*	Alice Brady/ *In Old Chicago*	1937
Frank Capra/ *You Can't Take It with You*	Walter Brennan/ *Kentucky*	Fay Bainter/ *Jezebel*	1938
Victor Fleming/ *Gone with the Wind*	Thomas Mitchell/ *Stagecoach*	Hattie McDaniel *Gone with the Wind*	1939

The annual Academy awards, or Oscars, are presented by the Academy of Motion Picture Arts and Sciences, an organization founded by the industry in 1927 to raise the 'cultural, educational, and scientific standards' of film. Since 1954 any film shown in a commercial theatre in the Los Angeles area for a minimum of one week during the preceding year has been eligible for an award. But for the first six years, the period ran from 1 August to 31 July of the following year. Voting policy has altered several times; since 1957 voting has been restricted to the Academy, whose numbers also select the nominations. Over the years, the list of categories for which awards are made has lengthened. Today it includes acting, directing, writing, cinematography, art direction, sound, music, editing, costume design, best picture, best foreign-language film, best short and best documentary.

Robert Donat gets Best Actor for *Goodbye Mr Chips*, director Sam Wood (MGM, 39)

the Forties

Britain declared war on Nazi Germany on 3 September, 1939, and briefly the emphasis shifted from Hollywood, where American neutrality was reflected in the continuing production of entertainment movies and some broadly anti-Nazi pictures.

The ailing British film industry thrived with its back to the wall. It had a sense of purpose: it was part of the war effort and, despite great difficulties, including the requisition of skilled men and studios, rose manfully to the task, providing comfort, cheer, propaganda and a much-needed morale boost. Production declined steeply but what the industry lacked in sheer numbers it more than made up for in quality.

Although the majority of British films contained an element of propaganda, the British temperament has never been given to stridency and consequently much of the propaganda in feature films was not overt. Unable to resist leavening even the most serious films, there was often some degree of humour, usually rather underplayed.

The image of the bumbling, pompous, stiff-upper-lipped Englishman prevailed. In Carol Reed's *Night Train to Munich* (40) it is exemplified by Naunton Wayne and Basil Radford, who had first surfaced in 1938 as Caldicott and Charters in Hitchcock's *The Lady Vanishes*. Although in the heart of Nazi Germany, they continue to talk incessantly about cricket and grumble that *Punch* magazine is not available on the bookstall of Munich station! Professor Horatio Smith was cast in much the same mould: another archetypal Englishman,

Anton Walbrook (left), Deborah Kerr and Roger Livesey in *The Life and Death of Colonel Blimp*, directors Michael Powell and Emeric Pressburger (General Film Distributors, 43)

this time of intellectual bent, a professor of archaeology whose vague mind seemed full of dust. But beneath Smith's gentle exterior lies an iron core; he is smuggling Jewish refugees out of Nazi Germany. If this has a familiar ring about it, no wonder. Howard's character is based on Baroness Orczy's 'Scarlet Pimpernel', which the star (who also produced and directed) refashioned as *Pimpernel Smith* (41).

The abiding faults of a certain type and class of Englishman are blinkered conservatism and a general blustering rigidity. These were satirized by newspaper cartoonist David Low in a character called Colonel Blimp. In 1943 Michael Powell and Emeric Pressburger (a prodigious team who, under the name 'The Archers', wrote, directed and produced some of the most intriguing, off-beat and thought-provoking movies of the period) took a Blimpish character and traced his service life from the Boer War to the Second World War. *The Life and Death of Colonel Blimp* is an extraordinary film, believed by some to be one of the most outstanding ever to emerge from Britain.

It owes a great deal to Hollywood (particularly in use of set pieces and colour) and in feel and mood it has borrowed from the European film-makers (due, in no small part, surely to Pressburger's Hungarian background) but in sentiment it is entirely British. This latter notwithstanding, Churchill and his Minister of Information, Brendan Bracken, did much to frustrate its making. They prevented Laurence Olivier playing the role of the Blimpish hero, Clive Candy, and then ordered sizeable cuts in the finished version because they considered its message defeatist. It is difficult to see why. The point that comes across most clearly is that Candy cannot blind himself to reality any more; he must see that modern warfare is a dirty, vicious fight for survival and not a ritual played by the laws of cricket by officers who are first and foremost gentlemen.

Roger Livesey, who brilliantly filled the role intended for Olivier, is impressive and moving as he ages from fiery young soldier to crusty, blinkered old warhorse (although Powell retrospectively considered that 'Olivier would have done a much more vicious job'). But the strength of the allegory is that Candy is not disparaged. For all his faults, there is much to admire in the man and he remains, to the end, a heroic figure.

The Archers started their war fairly convention- ally. *Contraband* (40, *Blackout* in US) was, in Powell's words, 'quite a well-made thriller, if rather contrived'. They followed this with their first attempt to depict the Germans as ordinary human beings with strengths and weaknesses, faults and follies: *The 49th Parallel* (41, *The Invaders* in US). A U-boat is sunk off Canada and the survivors try to escape into the then neutral United States. In various episodes it is revealed that these men, though Nazis, are not all brutes: a remarkable attempt, considering it was partly financed by the British government. Pressburger won an Oscar for the script.

One of Our Aircraft Is Missing (42) was rather more orthodox. Set in 1941, it follows the desperate escape through Holland, assisted by the Dutch people, of the survivors of a stricken bomber. But it has another of The Archers' original touches – no music track is used; they believed that music would introduce an element of 'false emotion'.

By 1946 victory had been won by the Allies and the Ministry of Information was concerned with improving and cementing Anglo-American post- war relations. The Archers responded with an extraordinary fantasy entitled *A Matter of Life and Death* (46, *Stairway to Heaven* in US), in which Squadron Leader Peter Carter (David Niven) cheats death in a burning bomber and is put on trial in a heavenly court where his case for life is argued by the doctor (newly deceased) who tried to cure him against a prosecutor (played by Raymond Massey) who is rabidly anti-British as he was the first American killed in the War of Independence.

The doctor (Roger Livesey, who, on his showing in Powell–Pressburger movies, never received the acclaim he deserved) has a seemingly hopeless task. The jury consists entirely of representatives of peoples who have been historically oppressed by or at war with the blood-thirsty British – Irish, French, Chinese, Indian, Russian etc. When he objects, they are turned into GIs, each one a

Kim Hunter and David Niven (middle distance) in *A Matter of Life and Death* (US: *Stairway to Heaven*), directors Powell and Pressburger (GFD, 46)

naturalized American citizen of Irish, French, Chinese, Russian, etc. descent. Livesey ultimately fights, and wins, his case on the power of love between the British pilot and an American girl.

In many respects this is a charming fable, delightfully acted and full of inventiveness, including the splendid device of showing all the earthly scenes in warm colour and the heavenly scenes in rather chilling black and white. But the trial scene is so full of lumpish rhetoric in the cause of propaganda that it destroys the light airiness of the rest of the film.

Nevertheless, the majority of this movie, together with most of the rest of their work (in 1948 they scored a huge hit with *The Red Shoes*), mark Michael Powell and Emeric Pressburger as men who radically altered the British film industry's view of itself.

It is interesting to compare their handling of Anglo-American relations with that of Anthony Asquith, another fine British director who rose to deserved prominence at the time. He tackled the subject rather more satisfactorily in *The Way to the Stars* (45). In a series of flashbacks the story revolves around two RAF bomber pilots (John Mills and Michael Redgrave) and their American counterparts (Douglass Montgomery and Bonar Colleano), showing the tensions and then friendships that develop as their lives and loves and deaths are inextricably interconnected.

His first three contributions to the war effort – *Freedom Radio* (40), *Cottage to Let* (41) and *Uncensored* (42) – are not today remembered as outstanding, but *We Dive at Dawn* (43) – the story of a submarine's pursuit of a German battleship – and *The Demi-Paradise* (43) indicate his potential as one of Britain's finest directors. (This promise was later confirmed with the chilling *Fanny by Gaslight* (44), *The Winslow Boy* (48), *The Browning Version* (50) and *The Importance of Being Earnest* (52) among many others.) *The Demi-Paradise* shows Asquith's flair with comedy and attempts, as does *The Way to the Stars*, to build bridges between nations – this time the British and their relatively new allies, the Russians. Laurence Olivier is a Soviet engineer, the inventor of a propeller, who journeys twice to Britain to oversee its production, in this satire designed to encourage the British to abandon their prejudices and fight together against a common enemy.

Although the starch had to be taken out of some upper lips, the gritty British qualities remained and were seldom better exhibited than in Noel Coward's affectionate, yet unromanticized tribute to the Royal Navy, *In Which We Serve* (42), based on a true incident – the sinking of HMS *Kelly* during the Battle of Crete. Coward begged its commander, Lord Louis Mountbatten, a close friend, to be allowed to write a film around the *Kelly*. The latter agreed as long as the character of the captain was disguised and he made some further conditions which, ultimately, gave the film its great strength, adding, '. . . above all, remember that the heroine of the story is the ship, certainly not the Captain or even the other men.'

Coward was faithful to all but one of the provisos: the character of the captain remains recognizably Mountbatten. *Kelly* became HMS *Torrin* and Coward created a ship's company who, together with their families, serve to give the film credibility and the quiet dignity of truth that marks it as one of the best ever made about fighting men. Richard Attenborough, incidentally, made his film debut as the coward of the lower decks – a role in which

Moira Shearer in *The Red Shoes*, directors Powell and Pressburger (GFD, 48)

The Way to the Stars (US: *Johnny in the Clouds*), with (left to right) Anthony Dawson, David Tomlinson (centre) and Trevor Howard, director Anthony Asquith (Two Cities, 45)

right
Eric Portman (left) and John
Mills in *We Dive at Dawn*,
director Anthony Asquith
(Gainsborough, 43)

below
Edith Evans (left), Joan
Greenwood and Michael
Denison in *The Importance of
Being Earnest*, director
Anthony Asquith (Rank/
Two Cities/Javelin, 52)

he was briefly typecast before going on to a distinguished acting career and rather less success as a director of movies such as *Oh! What a Lovely War* (69), *Young Winston* (71) and *Magic* (78).

In Which We Serve was a great success and remains moving without being mawkish. For Coward it was a personal triumph – the first film script he'd ever written and, in addition, he acted outstandingly as the captain, provided the music score, and produced and co-directed with a young David Lean in this, Lean's first directorial chance. (Coward won a special Academy award for an 'outstanding production achievement'.)

Coward had celebrated the British spirit and character in a 1939 play, *This Happy Breed*, which David Lean brought to the screen in 1944. It wasn't the happiest translation but two other Lean/Coward collaborations were unusually felicitous – *Blithe Spirit* (45), a sparkling comedy, and *Brief Encounter* (45), the tender story of a middle-class housewife (beautifully portrayed by Celia Johnson) who falls in love with a doctor (Trevor Howard in the part that made him a star).

David Lean, who was a film editor before Coward gave him his directorial break, is one of Britain's most distinguished film directors and yet his reputation rests on a remarkably small body of work – less than 20 movies in 30 years. *Brief Encounter* is a 'small' film: it centres around two people torn between their love and their duty and is mostly enclosed in the dusty railway station where they make their assignations. It offers no clue to the direction Lean would take. He followed it with two excellent realizations of Dickens novels – *Great Expectations* (46) and *Oliver Twist* (48) – probably the finest of all the many attempts to bring the great man's work to the screen (and both packed with exemplary casts, including stand-out performances from Alec Guinness as, respectively, Herbert Pocket and Fagin).

He then made only seven films – notably *The Sound Barrier* (51) and *Hobson's Choice* (53) – before expanding his canvas to the epic with *The Bridge on the River Kwai* (57), *Lawrence of Arabia* (62), *Dr Zhivago* (66) and *Ryan's Daughter* (70). These were epics not just in size and length and cost but in the prodigious labours lavished on them by their

right
In Which We Serve, directors
Noel Coward and David
Lean (Rank/Two Cities, 42),
with Coward (front right)
and John Mills (behind him)

far right
Celia Johnson and Trevor
Howard in Lean's *Brief
Encounter* (Cineguild, 45)

John Howard Davies (as
Oliver) and Francis L.
Sullivan in *Oliver Twist*,
director David Lean (GFD/
Cineguild, 48)

opposite, top left
Patricia Roc and Gordon
Jackson (foreground) in
Millions Like Us, directors
Frank Launder and Sidney
Gilliatt (Gainsborough, 43)

Carol Reed movies:
(*opposite, top right*) Orson
Welles in *The Third Man*
(London Films, 49), and
(*opposite bottom*) Bobby
Henrey and Ralph Richardson
(right) in *The Fallen Idol*
(London Films, 48)

director. What sets Lean apart from other directors
of epic subjects is that, although he can handle
spectacle brilliantly, he is foremost a cinematic
artist: the films are, when necessary, bold and

thrilling and full of stunning effects, but they are
beautiful as well. And perhaps his greatest gift is
in not allowing people to be lost in the huge sweep
of the story; people – often extraordinary and

tormented – are at the heart of these massive films. Both *Kwai* and *Lawrence of Arabia* won Best Picture and Best Director awards, and in *Ryan's Daughter* John Mills won an Oscar for his supporting role as the village idiot, while Freddie Young, one of the world's finest cameramen, completed a hat-trick – his work on Lean's latter three films had gained him three Oscars for cinematography.

The war offered British directors like Lean the chance to prove they were world class. Carol Reed also moved into the front rank. He had started the decade, and the war, strongly with the comedy-thriller *Night Train to Munich* (40) and then made a cherishable version of H.G. Wells's story of a modest draper who comes into money and tries to enter Society, *Kipps* (41, *The Remarkable Mr Kipps* in US). It had an excellent script by Frank Launder and Sidney Gilliatt, who themselves later wrote and directed two notable movies – *Millions Like Us* (43), an anthem to the citizenry who contributed to the war effort, in this case women in aircraft factories, and a superior love story, highlighting the pressure on service marriages, *Waterloo Road* (44).

Reed's only other war-related movie was *The Way Ahead* (44), showing how the army forged a disparate group of reluctant recruits (including David Niven, William Hartnell and Stanley Holloway) into a cohesive, comradely fighting unit. It is another example of how, in the hands of a good director, an unpromising subject could be turned into an entertaining and often amusing film, which managed to get across its moral (and morale) in a subtle, intelligent way.

In the Forties and Fifties Reed was at the height of his powers, particularly in strong subject matter which he could emphasize with his characteristically stark cinematography and a tremendous feel for mood. *Odd Man Out*, about an IRA gunman on the run (played by James Mason), was made in 1946 and then followed two adaptations of Graham Greene stories – *The Fallen Idol* (48) and his masterpiece, *The Third Man* (49), a brilliant evocation of the sinister and evil set in Vienna and pulling

Ealing comedy: (top) *Whisky Galore* (US: *Tight Little Island*) with Gordon Jackson (left) and Morland Graham, director Alexander Mackendrick (48); (centre) Stanley Holloway and Barbara Murray in *Passport to Pimlico*, director Henry Cornelius (49); and (above) Dennis Price (left) and Alec Guinness in *Kind Hearts and Coronets*, director Robert Hamer (49)

excellent performances from Orson Welles as gangster/drug pusher Harry Lime and Joseph Cotten as his one-time friend, a novelist who tracks him down and engineers his death. The scene set in the giant wheel and the chase through the sewers remain as vivid today as they were then.

Although Reed's subsequent work was consistently interesting, he never really recaptured the form of *The Third Man*. He seemed most at home with confined, claustrophobic subjects which exercised his pinpoint vision, but in 1968 he burst

back with *Oliver!*, which had tremendous verve, and revealed an unsuspected talent for the musical. Indeed, he matched Hollywood, something it acknowledged by awarding both him and the film Oscars.

One of the pinnacles of British film-making in the Forties came in 1944 when Laurence Oliver made a spirited, muscular, hugely entertaining version of *Henry V*. The Bard does not always translate well to the screen but Olivier, as star, producer and director, succeeded in giving us a reading that is instantly comprehensible to audiences unfamiliar with Shakespeare, while remaining faithful to the dramatist's original work.

Olivier was already regarded as Britain's finest stage actor and had received the summons to Hollywood after some good work in not particularly distinguished British films. His initial experiences in the States were not happy. Contracted to RKO, he was dismally underused in 1931–32 in films that scarcely deserve mention and then taken up by MGM, who sought to cast him opposite Garbo in *Queen Christina* (33), but she insisted on John Gilbert for the role. He returned home, disillusioned, until the call came to star as Heathcliff opposite Merle Oberon's Cathy in *Wuthering Heights* (39). He scored another hit in *Rebecca* (40) and his star was in the ascendant. He delighted as Darcy in *Pride and Prejudice* (40) and helped the British cause in the US as Nelson in *That Hamilton Woman* (41, *Lady Hamilton* in GB). His extraordinary good looks as well as his talent had him marked for superstardom, but he wished to contribute more to the war effort and turned down staggering offers, preferring to return to Britain and join the Fleet Air Arm, from which he was given leave to make the occasional film like *49th Parallel* (41) and *The Demi-Paradise* (43).

After *Henry V* he alternated between stage and screen, usually doing his most acclaimed work for the former but contributing to the latter with some excellent performances, notably *Richard III* (56), *The Devil's Disciple* (59) and *The Entertainer* (60). Mostly he seemed content to offer cameos or meaty supporting roles in epics like *Spartacus* (60), *Khartoum* (66), *Oh! What a Lovely War* (69) and *The Battle of Britain* (69). His work as a movie leading-man was less happy – and very nearly disastrous when co-starred with Marilyn Monroe in *The Prince and the Showgirl* (58), which he also directed – although he was strong in *Sleuth* (72). In his seventies he made a sortie back into films, getting paid a great deal of money for work that stretched him not at all (except perhaps physically: he had overcome a succession of serious illnesses) but he was chilling as a Nazi dentist in *Marathon Man* (76).

Olivier became Britain's first actor-peer, but others received knighthoods and both Sir Ralph Richardson and Sir John Mills enjoyed distinguished film careers. Mills was suitably stiff-lipped in wartime dramas like *In Which We Serve* (42) and *The Way to the Stars* (45) and is probably best recalled for his film work; *Great Expectations* (46), *Scott of the Antarctic* (48), *Hobson's Choice* (53) and,

particularly, *Tunes of Glory* (60) were milestones on the way to his Oscar for *Ryan's Daughter* (70). Richardson, on the other hand, was primarily a man of the theatre who would frequently grace

films, latterly with scene-stealing cameos – *The Four Feathers* (39), *Anna Karenina* (48), *Richard III* (56) and *A Long Day's Journey into Night* (62) among many other memorable performances.

Alfred Hitchcock, another, more permanent British expatriate, also wanted to swing opinion behind Britain, even though the US was, until Pearl Harbor, strictly neutral (at least in theory). His second Hollywood movie was *Foreign Correspondent* (40), a reasonably straight thriller about an American newspaperman who gets involved in Nazi machinations in Holland and Britain which ends with a spectacular fight at the top of the tower of Westminster Cathedral, London. The message is not allowed to interfere with the pace of the plot, but Joel McCrea (as the reporter) represents the US's straddling stance as he tries to remain an objective observer but is finally committed to the Allies' part.

Hitchcock directed five more feature films during the war years, of which three were unrelated to the conflict: the extremely untypical, non-suspense comedy *Mr and Mrs Smith* and the excellent *Suspicion* with Cary Grant and Joan Fontaine (both 41), and the less remarkable *Shadow of a Doubt* (43). His next to have a war-related theme was *Saboteur* (42), which is almost an American equivalent of *Foreign Correspondent*. This time a young munitions worker is wrongfully accused of sabotage after being framed by a group of American fascists; the

climax is another vertiginous sequence in which the villain literally hangs by a thread from the top of the Statue of Liberty. Again the moral is present but not dominant.

In 1940–41, however, he made a picture that was overtly propagandist. *Lifeboat* (which was released in 1943 after the Americans had entered the war) is a remarkable film, not least because the action is entirely centred around a disparate group of survivors from a U-boat attack adrift in a lifeboat. In an atmosphere of increasing tension, they pick up an officer from the U-boat, largely because of his navigation skills, but he secretly resolves to steer towards a German supply vessel and kills one of the others when his plot is discovered, whereupon the others gang together and beat him to death. Here, then, was a clear instruction to 'the democracies to put their differences aside temporarily and gather their forces to concentrate on the common enemy, whose strength was precisely derived from a spirit of unity and determination'.

To make the point clear, the 'baddie' had to be portrayed as more capable than the 'goodies', a concept that was not always popular in the US. *Lifeboat* was given a rough ride, which worried Hitchcock not at all. He knew exactly where his

above and opposite, centre left
Hitchcock warns of the Nazi threat: *Foreign Correspondent*, (United Artists, 40), and John Hodiak and Tallulah Bankhead in *Lifeboat* (20th Century-Fox, 43)

sentiments lay and to prove it he left the States for his native country. Back in Britain, the Ministry of Information asked him to celebrate the bravery of the French Resistance, a task he undertook with typical energy, directing *Bon Voyage* and *Aventure Malgache* in 1944.

He returned to Hollywood in 1945 to a period which found him working up to the height of his powers with *Spellbound* (45) and *Notorious* (46, this dealing with the aftermath of war, with Ingrid Bergman as the innocent daughter of a Nazi spy who is persuaded to penetrate an espionage ring by American agent Cary Grant). He was yet to achieve the pre-eminence as master of suspense which marked his work in the Fifties and Sixties and was still liable to patchiness. Both *The Paradine Case* (47) and *Rope* (48) are excellent in parts but *Under Capricorn* (49), a costume drama set in Australia, is a disaster.

Hitchcock's need to throw his talents into the war effort was being increasingly shared by others in Hollywood. When the US was pitched irrevocably into the conflict on 7 December, 1941, after the Japanese attack on Pearl Harbor, the entire Hollywood community threw itself into the fray. Unlike the British, the Americans saw no need to reassess where they stood philosophically. To them the issues were quite clearcut, and the American war movie took its lead from the Western. The heroes

The Master in more typical mood: (*top*) with Joan Fontaine and Cary Grant in *Suspicion* (RKO, 41) and (*centre right*) Grant with Ingrid Bergman in *Notorious* (RKO, 46)

right
James Stewart and Margaret Sullavan in *The Mortal Storm*, director Frank Borzage (MGM, 40)

69

wore white tin helmets and the enemy wore black ones, emblazoned with a swastika. To some extent Hollywood had been gearing up in advance. *Foreign Correspondent* (40) had been an appeal to the US to abandon its isolationist policy, and a few other films urged that the world's greatest power could not sit on the fence for ever.

This is not to say that in the years leading up to Pearl Harbor the American film industry was not anti-Nazi; the community was run and staffed by too many European refugees (most of them Jews) for Hitler's threat to go unnoticed. Chaplin had lampooned Hitler (as Adenoid Hynkel) in *The Great Dictator* (40), warning of his evil but rather dissipating the message through a heartfelt but ultimately futile plea for world peace. In 1939 Anatole Litvak had cast Edward G. Robinson as an FBI agent who smashes a German espionage ring in *Confessions of a Nazi Spy*, and started a vogue for films (all of them inferior) in which the Nazi spy canker is purged from the body politic. And in 1940 *The Mortal Storm* (credited to Frank Borzage's direction, although Victor Saville later claimed the work was mostly his) unequivocally depicted the anti-Semitism of Nazi Germany.

However, once Hollywood got into full swing it churned out gung-ho!, patriotic, do-or-die, all-American heroic films as though they were Liberty ships. Inevitably, the vast majority were utter rubbish and have deservedly sunk into oblivion. Some were borderline cases. Errol Flynn swaggered through the war with typical aplomb, mopping up the opposition with a burst from his machine gun but he ran into trouble over *Objective, Burma!* (45). This one movie very nearly undid all the good work

Robert Mitchum in *The Story of GI Joe*, director William Wellman (United Artists, 45)

of improving Anglo-American relationships. The British were incensed and deeply insulted because the film seemed to be declaring that the Americans were winning the war unaided. Burma, where the British 12th and 14th Armies had fought an unusually nasty war against the Japanese, was a sensitive issue. Viewed today, *Objective, Burma!* is certainly no worse than most of the comic-book heroics of the period, and probably rather better (it was, after all, directed by Raoul Walsh) and it certainly exemplifies the blood-and-thunder, cavalier and rather mindless attitude of the majority of Hollywood's flag-waving, hell-for-leather output.

Hollywood's best work came from movies that treated the war in an oblique manner. But such movies were far thinner on the ground. *Sergeant York* (41), which won Gary Cooper an Oscar, was one, and a really odd-ball movie, *To Be Or Not To Be* (42), was another. The latter displays Ernst Lubitsch at his deftest as a director, and he has valuable help from his stars, Carole Lombard and, particularly, Jack Benny. Benny is marvellous as the leader of a troupe of actors who attempt to outwit the Nazis just after the fall of Poland. To escape from the oppressors they have to put all their thespian talents to the test, including a range of impersonations which includes Hitler himself. It is to Lubitsch's credit that the farce in no way minimizes the tragedy of the Polish agony; indeed the one throws the other into sharp relief. Although the film lampoons the Nazis, one never forgets the depth of evil they represent.

It is to be regretted that more conventional Hollywood war pictures seldom came close to achieving such distinction. It wasn't until the war was almost won that a couple emerged to set the account a bit straighter. William Wellman's *The Story of GI Joe* (45) was based on the despatches of correspondent Ernie Pyle and movingly follows the progress of 'the poor bloody infantry' as they wearily battle their way up through Italy. Lewis

Milestone's *A Walk in the Sun* (45) also approaches the lot of the common GI with a degree of truth that was usually lacking in contemporary films. Again it concentrates on a small group, a platoon of soldiers, again in Italy and again it shows bravery and courage (and despondency and boredom and despair and exhaustion) while eschewing mock-heroics.

John Ford's *They Were Expendable* (45) is also significant. A fictionalized account based around the man who pioneered the PT boats in the Pacific, it is unusual in that it deals with the Americans' worst military disaster of the war in the Philippines, and, although the movie pays magnificent tribute to the men involved, it does not try to conceal the basic truth of the debacle. Ford would not allow himself to fall into the trap of romanticizing history (in the way that Dunkirk was occasionally treated almost as a victory in British films when, in truth, it was a horrendous failure).

For a dourer, sourer, more realistic view of the war, we have to wait for those films which look back at it, their vision unclouded by the need to persuade audiences that we were winning or, at the very least, that the war was winnable.

In the meantime, movies concerning the war but not directly depicting the battlefield usually needed a soft centre and soft focus. After 1942 Hollywood's attitude became romantically pro-British – *Random Harvest* (42) and *The White Cliffs of Dover* (44) persuaded American audiences (and confirmed for British audiences) that there really always would be an England. But the most lyrical and sentimental paean of praise was *Mrs Miniver* (42), which still stands as a four-Kleenex weepie.

The story of a 'typically' British middle-class couple (Greer Garson and Walter Pidgeon), *Mrs Miniver* is a tribute to their sterling qualities and the abiding virtues of the British character. In fact, it's a load of absolutely wonderful hokum. An entirely American view, it is about as accurate as a movie about a Mid-Western family made and acted in Surrey would be!

Somehow it doesn't matter that the whole thing is spurious because it captures an image of Britain and the British that appealed to the Americans and flattered the British. The struggles of this cosy couple against the mounting horrors of the war did more to win the hearts and minds of the US than any amount of strident propaganda could ever have achieved. It scooped the pool at that year's Academy awards – Best Picture with further Oscars to director William Wyler, Greer Garson (Best Actress), Teresa Wright (Supporting Actress) and two others.

The following year the Oscar for Best Picture was won by *Casablanca*, which has since been described as 'the best bad movie ever made'! It could have been, perhaps *should* have been, an absolute stinker. For a start the story is fairly preposterous and it is constantly in danger of sinking under its own sentimentality. But the miracle is that the movie was ever made at all.

In her autobiography, Ingrid Bergman relates that 'There had to be all sorts of changes in the

script. So every day we were shooting off the cuff: every day they were handing out the dialogue and we were trying to make some sense of it. No one knew where the picture was going and no one knew how it was going to end, which didn't help any of us with our characterizations.' In short, it was chaos. And right up to the last day of shooting, there were two possible endings. It wasn't until Curtiz had actually filmed Bogie putting his arm around the shoulders of the previously ambivalent police captain and walking off with him into the fog ('Louis, I think this is the beginning of a beautiful friendship') that they realized they had the perfect ending.

For all its faults (Bergman really *did* say as she and Bogart kiss while the Germans enter Paris, 'Was that cannon fire, or is it my heart pounding?') the film is transcendent. Bergman is stunningly beautiful and the rest of the cast – Paul Henreid, Claude Rains, Sidney Greenstreet, Peter Lorre and Dooley Wilson as Sam (picking out the haunting strains of 'As Time Goes By') – flesh out a thin tale with finely-tuned performances. Central to it all is Bogart and his cynical, world-weary, heavy-hearted characterization of Rick, the man on the outside who finally comes down against tyranny. He, more than anybody or anything else, transforms *Casablanca* into a film that rides high in the list of almost everyone's ten *favourite* movies.

Humphrey Bogart is a quintessential Forties man. Dishevelled, battered, and ironical, he seemed to match the mood of the war-torn decade. He had made one attempt to break into movies in 1930–31, landing a goodish part supporting Spencer Tracy, who became a life-long friend, in *Up the River*, but after a promising start the studios didn't know what to do with him. He returned to New York and some difficult, jobless years through the Depression until he landed the part of Duke Mantee, a psychotic gunman in the Broadway production of 'The Petrified Forest'. The star, Leslie Howard, promised Bogie that if it was filmed he would play the same part on screen. Warner Brothers had other ideas and gave the role to Edward G. Robinson, but Howard interceded, faced Warners down, and got Bogart the job. He capitalized on his chance and made a hit in *The Petrified Forest* (36) but again the studio didn't know how to use him. Warners had

Robinson and Cagney; they didn't need another tough guy. Instead of stepping up to top spot, he spent the rest of the decade playing support; 'I was always the guy behind the guy with the gun,' he recalled.

He finally got his big break because Raft, Robinson and Cagney all turned down the part of an ageing killer on the run in *High Sierra* (41). Bogie moulded it into a very fine performance. Raft did him a favour again that year by refusing to star in the first movie of an untried young director, John

Bogart: with Dooley Wilson in *Casablanca* (*top left*), director Michael Curtiz (Warners, 43); with Ida Lupino in *High Sierra* (*top right*), director Raoul Walsh (Warners, 41); and with Peter Lorre (second from left), Mary Astor and Sidney Greenstreet in *The Maltese Falcon* (*above*), director John Huston (Warners, 41)

ably the seminal hard-boiled private-eye movie to which each later one would be compared. And, as Sam Spade, who was 'not as crooked as I'm supposed to be', Bogart shot to the top echelon, establishing the tough loner character that is now forever associated with him. Spade and Bogart are one: the laconic lines spill from his scarred lips; the self-possessed arrogance oozes from his cocky stance. He spits out Huston's gritty dialogue as the cigarette dangles or is gripped tensely on the inside of finger and thumb – Bogart could do more with a butt than most actors can do with a machine gun! He stalks through the movie, sparking off scene after memorable scene against Sidney Greenstreet, Peter Lorre, Elisha Cook Jr and, in particular, Mary Astor as the two-timing dame who tries to play him for a sap.

In private life he was a gentle man who weathered three stormy (and, in the last case, violent marriages) before he met Lauren Bacall on the set of *To Have and Have Not* in 1945. One of the most spectacular love affairs in Hollywood settled into one of the town's most idyllic marriages and lasted until his death from cancer in 1957.

After his rightful position as a star was confirmed with *The Maltese Falcon*, Bogart saw celluloid war service in *Across the Pacific* (42), *Action in the North Atlantic* (43), *Sahara* (43), *Passage to Marseille* (44) and *To Have and Have Not*. A fairly routine bunch except for the last, which was saved from silliness by the sexual clash between Bogart and Bacall, who dragged this travesty of the Hemingway story up to respectability. Who can forget the image of Bacall lolling seductively against a door and drawling, 'If you want me, just whistle. You know how to whistle, don't you? You just put your lips together . . . and blow!'?

This magic worked again in Howard Hawks's *The Big Sleep* (46), in which Bogart essayed another great fictional detective – Philip Marlowe. The success of *The Maltese Falcon* (41) initiated a trend for private-eye movies and producers looked inevitably to the novels of Raymond Chandler for plots. The first, and in many ways the most successful, adaptation was *Murder My Sweet* (44, *Farewell My Lovely* in GB, Chandler's original title), in which Dick Powell deserted his tap shoes and shrugged on a dirty trenchcoat to play Marlowe very convincingly. In the same year as Bogart played the man 'who must walk down mean streets', *The Lady in the Lake* also appeared. This used the subjective camera technique, in other words the main character is never seen but all the action is viewed through his eyes (i.e. the lens). Robert Montgomery put the voice to the part but the film remains, of necessity, static.

The Big Sleep is a marvellous movie, so good that the viewer is swept along by it and hardly bothers about the plot. This is just as well because it is incomprehensible. It doesn't matter: Bogart was very nearly perfect as Marlowe (although Powell was so good you can argue about it all night) and Bacall smouldered and traded sexual wisecracks with him. Their on-screen partnership ran to two further movies: *Dark Passage* (47) and the superior *Key*

Teamed off and on screen: Bogie and Lauren Bacall (*above*) with Hoagy Carmichael in *To Have and Have Not*, director Howard Hawks (Warners, 45), and (*right*) in *The Big Sleep*, director Hawks (Warners, 46)

Huston. Bogart couldn't afford to be choosy, even though the film didn't look too promising; it was, after all, the third remake of a Dashiell Hammett novel and the two previous ones hadn't made much impression.

In the event, *The Maltese Falcon* (41) was not only a directorial triumph for Huston; it was also prob-

Humphrey Bogart with Bobby Blake in *The Treasure of the Sierra Madre*, director John Huston (Warners, 48)

Largo (48), which is also noted for excellent performances by Edward G. Robinson (as a gangster who takes over an isolated hotel) and Claire Trevor, who won an Oscar for her part as an ageing moll.

This was a further alliance between Bogart and Huston, who in 1948 had also made the outstanding *Treasure of the Sierra Madre*. It elicited one of Bogie's best performances as Fred C. Dobbs, a down-and-out who with two partners – Walter Huston and Tim Holt – goes in search of gold. His slow, inexorable slide into paranoia as suspicion, greed and gold-fever possess him is brilliant. And yet this performance was matched by Holt's and excelled by wily old Walter Huston (John's father) who pinched the movie from them to win an Oscar. (John got two for this one – Best Director and Screenplay.)

Typically, Bogart refused to analyse his stardom and would never be drawn on his skills as an actor – 'I'm a professional,' he once stated flatly. 'I'm an actor. I just do what comes naturally.' It was natural to him not to give a bad performance and occasionally to turn one in that is as good as anyone else's best. *Sierra Madre* stretched him and so did another Huston picture, *The African Queen* (51).

This was a film of contrasts. No two co-stars were more unlikely than Bogart and Katharine Hepburn – he as elegant as a bag of spanners, she the epitome of class. No plot more unlikely than having the two of them tow an old rustbucket along a river to attack a German gunboat. No love affair less likely than Charlie Allnut, the greasy, uncouth, sweat-stained old soak, winning the affection of a determined, prim, chaste missionary lady. And it was these very incongruities that made *The African Queen* a classic and finally won Bogart his much-deserved Academy award. He was nominated again in 1954 for his portrayal of the psychotic Captain Queeg in *The Caine Mutiny* and showed an unexpected aptitude for comedy in *We're No Angels* (55) but by then the disease which would kill him was taking hold.

Nothing died with Bogart, his popularity has, if anything, increased as successive generations recognize those qualities that Lauren Bacall summed up: 'He is the only man I have ever known who truly and completely belonged to himself . . . . His convictions about life, work and people were so strong they were unshakable. . . . He had the greatest gifts a man could have: respect for himself, for his craft, integrity about life as well as work.'

Bogart's contribution to the war, like that of so many of the older stars of Hollywood, was in entertaining demoralized troops (and their folks at home) but it's doubtful whether they did as much to aid the rest and recuperation of tired fighting men as Betty Grable's legs. They were insured for $1 million (outpricing even Astaire's) and a particular photograph was pinned-up on every bulkhead, behind every locker, on the notice board of every mess in every theatre of war. It is arguably the most famous pin-up in history. She was, as one commentator has pointed out, the one accessible female movie star of the period. No great beauty, she had the attraction of the pretty girl behind the Woolworth's counter; she was 'strictly an enlisted man's girl', a good sort, a sport.

The films she made were trifles, skimpy comedies or lightweight musicals with forgettable scores like *Down Argentine Way* (40), *Moon Over Miami* (41), *Sweet Rosie O'Grady* (43), *Pin Up Girl* (44) or the immensely popular but negligible *The Dolly Sisters*

above left
Alan Ladd and Veronica
Lake in *This Gun for Hire*,
director Frank Tuttle
(Paramount, 42)

above
Dick Powell in *Murder My
Sweet* (UK: *Farewell My
Lovely*) with Claire Trevor,
director Edward Dmytryk
(RKO, 44)

left
James Cagney, Edmond
O'Brien (centre) and Wally
Cassell in *White Heat*,
director Raoul Walsh
(Warners, 49)

(45). Perhaps the best-recalled today is *How To Marry A Millionaire* (53), in which she was one of a trio of gold diggers, the other two being Marilyn Monroe and Lauren Bacall.

If Grable was strictly the girl to warm the . . . er . . . cockles of a dog soldier's heart, then Rita Hayworth was, as someone once said, 'the intellectual's glamour girl'. Or, as Hollywood would have it, The Love Goddess. She was breathtakingly beautiful, astonishingly erotic, and she seemed to possess every attribute that men fantasize about in redheaded women.

Rita Hayworth, born Margarita Cansino and cousin of Ginger Rogers, earned her early living as a dancer. She got to Hollywood in 1935 and appeared under her given name mostly in 'B' pictures until 1937, when she was re-christened. But it wasn't until *Only Angels Have Wings* (39) that she started making waves. She was still known as an actress rather than dancer when the big break came with *Strawberry Blonde* (41) and she sizzled opposite Tyrone Power in *Blood and Sand* in the same year.

Then it was decided to capitalize on her ability as a hoofer and she was paired with her cousin's ex-partner, Fred Astaire, in *You'll Never Get Rich* (41). She concentrated on musicals (or dramas in which she had a number) for most of the decade. The fact that she had no voice was overlooked (and it was overdubbed) because the sight of that gloriously sensual body moving, that mane of hair tossing wildly, and that delicious mouth thrown open in ecstasy were more than enough compensation. She re-matched with Astaire for *You Were Never Lovelier* (42) and then changed partners to dance with Gene Kelly in *Cover Girl* (44), probably

above
Rita Hayworth and Fred Astaire in *You Were Never Lovelier*, director William A. Seiter (Columbia, 42)

left
Gene Kelly (second from left), Rita Hayworth and Phil Silvers in *Cover Girl*, director Charles Vidor (Columbia, 44)

Rita Hayworth doing her 'glove strip' routine in the 'Put The Blame on Mame, Boys' number from *Gilda*, director Charles Vidor (Columbia, 46)

John Garfield and Lana Turner in *The Postman Always Rings Twice*, director Tay Garnett (MGM, 46)

her best-remembered film, not least for the wistful 'Long Ago And Far Away'.

Cover Girl was a high-point and, except for *Gilda* (46) – a thriller in which she and Glenn Ford kindled a sexual glow (remember the striptease in which she took off nothing but her gloves?) – her career seemed to slip away. This was partly because of her hectic private life, which, with its series of romances, marriages and divorces, pulled her away from the screen. Another reason was that she started repeating her performances – the glove strip from *Gilda* was also featured in *Miss Sadie Thompson* (53) and again in *Pal Joey* (57) – and it seemed that neither she nor the studio knew what to do next. The post-war years were mostly frittered away in sub-standard films – though she was excellent in *Separate Tables* (58) – and with them went her stunning beauty. She was still fascinating, the face full of life, but the sheer breathless excitement she generated in the Forties, in the better musicals and *Gilda*, was gone.

Acting ability was not a primary requisite of light entertainers in these days. Esther Williams looked great in a bathing suit. She started as an athlete and was selected to represent the US in the 1940 Olympics but the war put an end to that career and she became a star of the Aquacade. MGM spotted her and thought she might be their answer to 20th Century-Fox's Ice Maiden, Sonja Henie, who had skated her way to fame. Consequently they put her into movies (the names don't really matter as one is barely distinguishable from another) which were usually submarine equivalents of Busby Berkeley spectaculars and depended far more on her ability to smile while contorting herself beneath the waves than to emote on terra firma. As Fanny Brice said, 'Wet, she's a star. Dry, she ain't!' It didn't matter: she was easy on the eye and a marvellously mindless antidote to the horrors which daily confronted audiences.

What Esther Williams did for the swimming costume, Lana Turner did for the sweater. She was amply endowed and did nothing to hide the fact, pulling on a sweater that was at least two sizes too small. In fact, so erotic was she as she jiggled beneath this humdrum apparel that the censor soon clocked the fact and banned 'sweater shots'. Although she vied with Grable as a pin-up queen, the studio thought she had more than the average acting abilities of her sisters. After bunging her into the usual rubbish during the late Thirties, they built her up with a lead in *Ziegfeld Girl* (41) and then, amazingly, put her into *Dr Jekyll and Mr Hyde* (41), where she was easily and unsurprisingly outclassed by Spencer Tracy and Ingrid Bergman. She was better suited to rather racier roles opposite Clark Gable in *Honky Tonk* (41) and *Somewhere I'll Find You* (42). Then she did some routine wartime morale boosters before very nearly proving she was an actress of consequence in *The Postman Always Rings Twice* (46), in which she played a sluttish, ruttish wife who overwhelms John Garfield, using his lust for her to induce him to murder her husband. Torrid is the word to describe her and between them Garfield and Turner make this third version

of James M. Cain's thriller into one of the tensest of the decade.

Bad women were fashionable, especially bad women who used their bodies. Mary Astor had tried to subvert Bogie in *The Maltese Falcon* (41) and Lizabeth Scott (a Lauren Bacall look-alike, but not act-alike) invoked a similar ploy in *Dead Reckoning* (47) but the outstanding wicked woman was Barbara Stanwyck in Billy Wilder's brilliant *Double Indemnity* (44).

Written by Wilder and Raymond Chandler from another James M. Cain novel, it is the story of a conniving woman who lures an insurance agent (Fred MacMurray) into an adulterous relationship. Totally besotted by her, MacMurray is persuaded into killing her husband for the insurance money. He nearly gets away with it, and would have done had it not been for the dogged persistence of his boss (Edward G. Robinson), whose ulcer twinges when he suspects fraud.

Stanwyck is one of those who proved that, despite the need for glamour, not all Hollywood stars needed to be sex symbols. Bette Davis was so far from being a sex symbol that on first sight Carl Laemmle, head of Universal who signed her in 1930, commented cruelly, 'I can't imagine any guy giving her a tumble.' It wasn't relevant; Bette Davis became . . . well, perhaps not a great actress, but certainly one of the most instantly recognizable and formidable screen actresses of her generation. Whatever else she might be, Bette Davis was always, and transcendently, Bette Davis. She would not fit into any mould Hollywood tried to press her into. Indeed, for a while in 1936 she didn't even seem to fit into Hollywood.

Her career to that date had been checkered. At first Universal didn't know how to use her but gradually she had fought her way to respectable parts. She moved to Warners, where her stormy relationship with bosses continued; she bullied Jack Warner for six months to release her to Selznick to play Mildred Rogers in Somerset Maugham's *Of Human Bondage* (34) opposite Leslie Howard. The part of the whorish, slatternly Cockney waitress with whom the club-footed hero becomes besotted and by whom he is so badly treated had few redeeming features and every other star shied away from it. Finally Warner gave way.

In the event Davis was triumphant – 'Probably the best performance ever recorded by a US actress,' said *Life* – and she should have got an Oscar.

She didn't get many meaty parts to match her talents either, until *Dangerous* (35). *Dangerous* is typical Davis material. It is 'a weepie' and that curious creature 'a woman's picture'. Hollywood believed, possibly rightly, that women had a particular yearning for films in which the heroine

Barbara Stanwyck in *Double Indemnity*, director Billy Wilder (Paramount, 44)

is wrenched by conflicting passions, put-upon by brutal men or bitchy women, and suffers the torments of unrequited love, or a love that is doomed, or a love that cannot be enjoyed without guilt.

In *Dangerous* she plays a booze-sodden ex-star who is going down the drain until saved by the love of a noble man. Pure molasses from start to finish but she 'worked like ten men' (including some acting that went right over the top) to save it. It's no better, probably rather worse, than *Of Human Bondage* and yet she won an Oscar for it.

She looked set fair to enjoy the hyper-emotional parts in which she could be a blazing bitch or a neurotic ugly duckling, and followed *Dangerous* strongly with *The Petrified Forest* (36), being terrorized by Humphrey Bogart, but then the studio began pushing her into inferior productions. Never one to take such treatment passively, she staged a walk-out and quit Hollywood. It was virtually unheard of for any contract star to oppose the might of a studio. Even arguing with a mogul could have dire consequences; the usual punishment was relegation to supporting roles in 'B' pictures, exile to an inferior studio or suspension. The dispute eventually went to court. She lost and had costs awarded against her. Every sage in Hollywood predicted the end of Bette Davis. To everyone's surprise, when she returned, entirely

Katharine Hepburn and Spencer Tracy (centre) in *Woman of the Year*, director George Stevens (MGM, 42)

79

unrepentant, to Hollywood, she was welcomed back and eventually her parts improved.

In 1938 came *Jezebel*, in which she is a hoity-toity society girl who is used to getting what she wants. She wants Henry Fonda and outrages the New Orleans élite by wearing a red dress to a grand ball rather than the traditional white gown of the un-married virgin. This scandalous behaviour so humiliates Fonda that he leaves her and marries another! Absolute nonsense, of course, but then the plots of most of Bette Davis's most successful pictures don't stand close scrutiny. It is a tribute to her that she manages to make them seem im-portant and heart-rending as she strides through them. She so bowled along in *Jezebel* that she won her second Academy award in three years.

As she went into the Forties, she entered the richest, weepiest phase of her career. The tone was set in 1939 with *Dark Victory*, in which she is suffering from a brain tumour, has a year to live, goes out on a prolonged binge, discovers she really loves her doctor, marries him and sends him away so that she can die alone and courageously. In *The Old Maid* (39) she is the heroine who, in her youth, loved well but not wisely, found herself – horror, shock! – an unmarried mum, and brought up her daughter to believe that she is her spinster aunt. In *The Great Lie* (41) she is a second wife who fights to adopt her husband's child by his wicked first wife (a marvellous performance by Mary Astor which won her an Oscar). But the finest example is prob-ably *Now, Voyager* (42), which has been given the accolade of five-Kleenex weepie.

Now, Voyager is a dreadful picture. Correction: *Now, Voyager* should be a dreadful picture. Just look at the plot: dowdy duckling becomes elegant swan, finds impossible love with married man (Paul Henreid), worsts harridan mother (Gladys Cooper), who dies during violent row, enters sanatorium and befriends disturbed child who turns out to be the daughter of guess who, im-possible love rekindled. He wants her on any terms but she settles for what they have had and what they have got and tells him so in one of the great, terrible lines: 'Don't ask for the moon. We have the stars.'

Davis's other great strength was as a scheming bitch, a part she played to best effect in *The Letter* (40) and *The Little Foxes* (41), both directed by William Wyler, who had also brought out the best of her talents in *Jezebel* (38). Wyler was at the height of his considerable powers in the decade. He was already known as one of the great 'women's directors' and his touch was never surer than with subjects which stirred the emotions and moved the heart. His strength was in pulling back stories that, under a lesser man, could easily have slipped into bathos. He won an Oscar for *Mrs Miniver* (42) and then made two war documentaries, of which *The Memphis Belle* (44) is most notable; it follows the fortunes of a Flying Fortress bomber on its missions over Germany, missions which Wyler flew. Next came probably the finest film about men returning from war, *The Best Years of Our Lives* (46).

Three men come home after the fighting; each in

his own way will never be the same. The most obviously affected is the young sailor who has lost both his hands. Harold Russell, whose hands were amputated as a result of injuries received, played this part in his only picture and won two Oscars,

opposite
Bette Davis in (*top*) *All This and Heaven Too* with Charles Boyer (*left*) and Richard Nichols, director Anatole Litvak (Warners, 40), and with Claude Rains (*bottom*) in *Now, Voyager*, director Irving Rapper (Warners, 42)

Davis as bitch: (*top*) with Gale Sondergaard in *The Letter*, director William Wyler (Warners, 40), and (*above*) with Herbert Marshall and Teresa Wright in *The Little Foxes*, director Wyler (RKO, 41)

one for his fine supporting performance, the other an honorary award 'for bringing courage and hope to his fellow veterans'. In contrast Dana Andrews has had 'a good war' but returns to a menial job in a drug store and sluttish, unfaithful war bride, Virginia Mayo. Fredric March has, on the face of it, less to contend with. Yet the violence he has witnessed as a sergeant in combat zones has changed his attitudes, forced him to reassess: he has to learn to slide back into his safe rut. His readjustment is the least dramatic but the most typical. Plenty of opportunity here for sentimentality, but Wyler is too sure, too strong for that. The film was awarded the Best Picture Oscar, Wyler won the directorial prize, Fredric March was Best Actor and, in addition to these and Harold Russell's awards, the movie garnered three other Oscars, including one which went to Robert E. Sherwood for his original screenplay.

A tribute to Wyler's stature as a director came from Bette Davis after making *The Letter* (40). She fought Wyler about their different views of the character she was playing and for once her will did not prevail. 'I lost a battle,' she later announced, 'but I lost it to a genius. So many directors were such weak sisters that I would have to take over. Uncreative, unsure of themselves, frightened to fight back, they offered me none of the security that this tyrant did.' Wyler drew a fine performance from his star in this Somerset Maugham story of the wife of a rubber planter in Malaya who murders her lover, lies desperately to protect herself, and pays a fortune to the dead man's wife to buy the letter which will prove her guilt. Davis is at her best, hyper-tense, overwound, close to hysteria, a performance that needed strong directorial control.

The Little Foxes (41) had Davis at her most vixenish as a dominating, overbearing woman whose will, drive and ambition allow no gainsaying. The clashes between Davis and Wyler were even more resounding than before and she felt she gave 'one of the worst performances of my life'. Certainly she doesn't manage to control her celebrated mannerisms and too often she becomes La Davis at her most imperious.

The Forties gave Bette Davis her best body of work. She was also notably successful playing light comedy in *The Man Who Came to Dinner* (41) and as the schoolmistress who spots and nurtures her pupil's genius in *The Corn Is Green* (45), but with the end of the decade the supply of Davis-type pictures seemed to run out. She was still big but, as Gloria Swanson said so memorably in *Sunset Boulevard* (50), the pictures got small. She was brilliant in a brilliant film, *All About Eve* (50), as Margo Channing, a star of 'certain years' who is elbowed aside by the cunning machinations of her young protégée. But after that, the right roles eluded her until she undertook a most unlikely piece of grand guignol – *Whatever Happened to Baby Jane?* (62), in which she was paired with another of the screen's great and formidable ladies, Joan Crawford.

Joan Crawford had been a movie star since 1925. Not a movie actress, but a star. Her face, though undoubtedly beautiful, was not particularly mobile (except, perhaps, when registering anger) but her eye could transfix like the basilisk's. She was not a popular lady in Hollywood and, apparently, far from being the most likeable human being. Nonetheless, she weathered the sound revolution and scrabbled her way up to the top during the Thirties, although she barely made a movie that has lasted with any credit. At the end of the decade her career was in a perilous position, but, undeterred, she saw a chance and took it. George Cukor was making a movie with an all-female cast called, appropriately, *The Women* (39): a catty comedy full of spats, backbiting and bitchiness. Among the chief bitches was Crystal, who Crawford described as 'the hard-boiled perfume clerk who uses every wile to catch another woman's husband'. It was right up her back alley and she seized the opportunity, virtually

Charlie Chaplin
in The Great DICTATOR
Produced, written and directed by CHARLES CHAPLIN
with PAULETTE GODDARD
JACK OAKIE · HENRY DANIELL
REGINALD GARDINER · BILLY GILBERT
MAURICE MOSCOVITCH
Released thru United Artists

Fred Astaire and Rita Hayworth—dancing and singing together!

FRED ASTAIRE ★ RITA HAYWORTH
in
"YOU WERE NEVER LOVELIER"
A COLUMBIA PICTURE

opposite, top left
Moira Shearer in *The Red Shoes*, directors Powell and Pressburger (GFD, 48)

opposite, top right
Esther Williams in *Ziegfeld Follies*, director Vincente Minnelli (MGM, 46)

opposite bottom and above
Lobby cards for Chaplin's *The Great Director* with Chaplin and (centre) Jack Oakie (United Artists, 40) and *You Were Never Lovelier*, director William A. Seiter (Columbia, 42)

right
Vera-Ellen and Gene Kelly in *On The Town*, directors Kelly and Stanley Donen (MGM, 49)

Joan Crawford: (*top*) with Osa Massen in *A Woman's Face*, director George Cukor (MGM, 41), and with Ann Blyth (*above*) in *Mildred Pierce*, director Michael Curtiz (Warners, 45)

stops short of murder, and her career seemed to be back on top but following it there were some stinkers and by 1944 she was forced to admit 'the concensus of opinion among the top brass was that I was washed up'. She left MGM for Warners, where Davis reigned supreme, and her doldrums continued until she pounced on a script Davis discarded.

Mildred Pierce (45) was a part Crawford could sink her teeth into. It had respectable blood-lines – adapted from a James M. Cain novel and directed by Michael Curtiz, it was a classy prospect. Viewed dispassionately, however, it's a nasty little tale of a mother who is so determined to do the best by her daughter that she marries a man she does not love for the wealth and security he can give her and her brat. The daughter (Ann Blyth) has a squalid affair with her step-father (Zachary Scott) and then murders him. Crawford is overwhelming as the tigress, eyes glittering with misplaced devotion, who will do anything to protect her cub, and her taut performance copped that year's Oscar as Best Actress. It was her finest hour and although she never achieved such heights again (the latter part of her career was frittered on rubbishy horror flicks, with the notable exception of *Whatever Happened to Baby Jane?* in 1962) she remained, by dint of looking and acting the part, one of the legendary movie stars, perhaps the most enduring of them all.

A Woman's Face was a remake of the Swedish film, made in 1938, which had turned Ingrid Bergman into Sweden's most popular star. In the meantime one of her earlier films, *Intermezzo* (36), had reached New York and was brought to the attention of David O. Selznick who, after initial doubts, decided to sign her and put her into a remake of this story of adulterous love between a celebrated violinist (played in this version by Leslie Howard) and a pianist. *Intermezzo, A Love Story* (39, *Escape to Happiness* in GB) was a success, as was the female lead, whose Nordic, freshly-scrubbed beauty caused a minor sensation.

Selznick was indecisive about where she should go next and loaned her to other studios for rather routine pictures – *Adam Had Four Sons* and *Rage in Heaven* (both 41) – until she made a further impression in the Tracy version of *Dr Jekyll and Mr Hyde* (41). And then came *Casablanca*! She was new, she was different and, now, she was immensely popular. *For Whom the Bell Tolls* (43), a rather heavy film from the Hemingway novel, did her no harm. The critics adored her, the public loved her and the moguls were falling over each other to get her. Next came *Gaslight* (44, *The Murder in Thornton Square* in GB), in which she plays the wife of Charles Boyer, driven to the edge of insanity by him so that she won't discover his murderous past. It is pure Victorian melodrama but her attempts to hang on to sanity were so impressive that she won that year's Oscar as Best Actress.

She did seven more films in the decade. Three were for Hitchcock – the tricksy, over-elaborate *Spellbound* (45), the infinitely better *Notorious* (46), in which she was well-teamed with Cary Grant,

shoplifting the movie from under the noses of such experienced scene-stealers as Norma Shearer, Rosalind Russell, Paulette Goddard, Joan Fontaine, Marjorie Main and Margaret Dumont.

She challenged Davis at her own game with *A Woman's Face* (41), in which she played a beautiful woman, horribly scarred, who turns to crime but

magnificently threatened by Claude Rains, and treated to the Old Master's finest thriller touches, and then *Under Capricorn* (49), which seems to achieve the impossible – a boring Hitchcock film! Hitchcock confided to François Truffaut many years later that he would not have made it at all if it had not been for Bergman: he thought it would be a tremendous coup if he could capture her for a picture against all the competition.

Of the other four, *Saratoga Trunk* (45) was a second, and less successful, reteaming with Gary Cooper (they first worked together in *For Whom the Bell Tolls*); *Arch of Triumph* (48) was a second, and far less successful, reteaming with Charles Boyer, part of the reason possibly being that she played a prostitute, far too abrupt a change from one of her best-loved roles of the period, as Sister Benedict, the laughing, child-loving, boxing nun who wins Father O'Malley's affections (in the most chaste way, of course) in *The Bells of St Mary's* (45), the immensely popular sequel to Bing Crosby's immensely popular first outing as the priest, *Going My Way* (44). And that leaves *Joan of Arc* (48). When she eventually achieved her near-obsessive desire to play the Maid of Orleans on screen, she seemed to have reached the apex of her ambition. Unfortunately, it became quickly evident that her ambition exceeded her ability. Although worthy, if far too glossy, *Joan of Arc* was not liked and, indeed, some critics positively loathed it.

This setback, together with the failures of *Arch of Triumph* and *Under Capricorn*, checked her seemingly inexorable rise. Such a hiccough need not have been insuperable. Both Davis and Crawford had weathered such troughs but they never made the terrible blunder which Bergman now committed. She had long been an ardent fan of the work of Roberto Rossellini, the director whose picture *Rome – Open City* (45) played an important part in the wave of neo-realism sweeping Europe in the late Forties. They had corresponded and,

after much planning, she went to Italy to make *Stromboli* (50), fell in love with him, and had an affair. This in itself was not so unusual in Hollywood. What was intolerable, in Hollywood's eyes (and, perhaps to a lesser extent, the eyes of the public), was that Bergman abandoned her husband and child, had a baby by Rossellini, and appeared to be unrepentant.

Ingrid Bergman: (*top left*) with Gary Cooper in *For Whom the Bell Tolls*, director Sam Wood (Paramount, 43); (*top right*) with Charles Boyer in *Gaslight*, director George Cukor (MGM, 44); and (*above*) with Bing Crosby in *The Bells of St Mary's*, director Leo McCarey (RKO, 45)

85

The reaction verged on the hysterical and was compounded when reports appeared stating that Bergman was seeking a divorce. Joseph Breen, director of the Production Code Administration (in effect the watchdog of Hollywood morals), begged Bergman to issue a firm denial, his primary concern being for the effect on Bergman's commercial value and thus the investment of the Hollywood moguls.

Bergman could not deny the rumours and press stories: they were true. And her career was very nearly destroyed. The Forties gave way to the Fifties as she struggled to little avail to regain her position and make her marriage to Rossellini work. The latter finally broke and it was not until 1956 that Hollywood 'forgave' her and summoned her to play in *Anastasia*. Next came a rather thin comedy which she and Cary Grant just about managed to put some flesh to, *Indiscreet* (58), and the better *Inn of the Sixth Happiness* (58), in which she played missionary Gladys Aylward, who lavished her love on orphaned children in China. Subsequently she started a successful career in the theatre, returning to the screen for occasional outings, most notable of which were *Cactus Flower* (69) and *Murder on the Orient Express* (74).

It is unusual, even by Hollywood's idiosyncratic standards, for a star to rise and fall so spectacularly in the course of one decade, but Ingrid Bergman's zenith and eclipse were almost as nothing compared to that of Orson Welles. At 24 Welles was hailed as a 'boy genius'; at 36 one critic described him as 'possibly the youngest living has-been'. Whatever is said about Orson Welles, there is no getting away from the fact that, at 24 and at his very first attempt, he made a film which regularly appears on discerning critics' lists as one of the 10 best films ever made. *Citizen Kane* (41) has been hailed as a work of genius, one of the landmarks in cinematic art, a masterpiece. All these judgements may be true, as may critic Pauline Kael's assertion that it is 'a shallow work, a *shallow* masterpiece'.

Technically it is brilliant. It has immense grandeur; it has magnificent photography, full of deep blacks pierced by slanting shafts of light, thanks to Gregg Toland's matchless mastery of camera technique. It has excellent performances (not least Welles's own as Charles Foster Kane) from 'craftsman' actors like Joseph Cotten, Dorothy Comingore, Agnes Moorehead, Everett Sloane and George Colouris, most of whom were new to pictures. And it has moments that remain in the memory, most of which are telling pieces of cinematic business that make their plot points succinctly. For example, the failure of Kane's mistress, who he has bullied into an operatic career for which she has no talent, is summed up by one camera movement, rising from her nerve-ridden entrance on stage, right up above the proscenium to the lighting gantry, high in the roof, where one stagehand turns to another and pinches his nose with his thumb and forefinger. Her performance stinks and not a word need be said. (Curiously, the fact that we recall these bravura effects may indicate a weakness in the film. In a true work of art, the techniques are not noticed; they combine harmoniously to contribute to the whole.)

If one is being picky – and a film that is held up as among the best ever made should be subjected to detailed scrutiny – one can claim that too much is made of the mystery of 'Rosebud' – the dying word which sets a reporter researching into Kane's life. (It transpires in the last scene that Rosebud

Everett Sloane (with cup), Orson Welles and Joseph Cotten in *Citizen Kane*, director Welles (RKO, 41)

was the name of Kane's boyhood sled.) This, however, does not detract from *Citizen Kane*'s strengths, not least of which is its storyline, which is so strong it compels viewing.

Although Welles – who directed, produced and starred in the film – took half the credit for writing it, subsequent research has revealed that the majority of the work (if not all of it) was done by Herman J. Mankiewicz, a screenwriter of enormous talent and experience. It is a remarkable story which tells of the rise of an energetic young man who builds up a newspaper empire and then tries to use and abuse the power it gives him for his own ends. His wealth is prodigious but it never buys him the things he really wants – stardom for his mistress and political office for himself.

Welles issued a long statement shortly before the premiere of *Kane*. In part it said : '*Citizen Kane* was not intended to have nor has it any reference to Mr Hearst or to any other living person . . . *Citizen Kane* is the story of a wholly fictitious character.' Despite the disclaimer, it is difficult not to see strong parallels between Charles Foster Kane and William Randolph Hearst, the American press baron, and the Hearst press was instructed to do all it could to ensure that *Citizen Kane* was a flop. Among the courses it took was to refuse RKO all

advertizing and either to ignore their releases in review columns or to pillory them mercilessly. This put the ailing RKO in a hazardous position and earned Welles the disapproval of Hollywood, which needed both Hearst's money and the beneficial power of his papers.

RKO got cold feet and deferred the picture's release. Even though the film had been almost unanimously hailed by critics (excepting, of course, those working for Hearst), when it finally reached the cinemas, the public were apathetic and it did not do good business. Nor did it win the recognition from the Academy of Motion Picture Arts and Sciences that it undoubtedly deserved. Although nominated in nine categories (including Best Picture and Best Actor), it received only one Oscar – for the screenplay.

Hollywood had turned not only against the film but also against Orson Welles. His fall from grace was swift and terrible. His next film, *The Magnificent Ambersons* (42), was wrested from his creative grasp before it was finished; although an admirable (and in parts – probably the parts Welles directed – brilliant) film, it cannot be truly called an Orson Welles movie. It too failed financially and Welles, it seemed, had been given his come-uppance.

As a director we can really only talk of Welles in

terms of what might have been. His showing in *Kane* suggests he might have become one of the finest, most innovative directors in cinema history. On the other hand, the later films he was allowed to make using other people's money tend towards the overwrought and theatrical. *The Stranger* (46) has been described as 'sub-Hitchcock', although it is exciting enough; *The Lady from Shanghai* (48) splutters with visual fireworks but is virtually incomprehensible; and in the same year he made a version of *Macbeth*, which was filmed in 21 days and looked it. Another attempt at Shakespeare, *Chimes at Midnight* (66), based around Falstaff and taken from the two parts of Henry IV was more successful artistically but the main canon of his directorial work makes one look back to *Kane* and ponder if only . . .

As an actor Welles has been . . . well, powerful, looming and, more often than not, Orson Welles. Usually he has been wasted in highly-paid cameos (the proceeds from which he ploughs back into his own projects) but occasionally he has shown glimmerings of the talent that made his reputation in the Thirties – as Harry Lime in *The Third Man* (49), as Clarence Darrow, the advocate in the Leopold/Loeb murder trial, *Compulsion* (59), and as Cardinal Wolsey in *A Man for All Seasons* (66).

The abiding impression of Welles is of size: of his physical size and presence, the undoubted size of his ego, the size of his talent, the size of his

ambition. The cinema is, essentially, a collaborative art. Perhaps he is just too big for it. He was, it seems, too big for Hollywood.

Welles's 1946 movie *The Stranger*, a thriller with a serious underlying theme – the aftermath of war – is about an escaped Nazi and his attempt to merge

The Lost Weekend (above) with Ray Milland (left) and Howard da Silva, director Billy Wilder (Paramount, 45), and (below) *The Ox-Bow Incident* (GB: *Strange Incident*), director William Wellman (20th Century-Fox, 43)

Mercedes McCambridge (with cup), John Ireland and Broderick Crawford (centre) in *All The King's Men*, director Robert Rossen (Columbia, 49)

into a small American township. The war years and after provoked some rather more thoughtful movies. John Ford was in the vanguard with *The Grapes of Wrath* (40) about the Joad family, who are forced off the land and into a wandering exile by the disaster of the Dustbowl in the Thirties and their subsequent fight to survive. The celebrated last speech of the indomitable Ma Joad offered hope to audiences facing a decade that was to be as bleak as the Thirties had been: 'Can't lick us. Can't wipe us out. We'll go on forever. 'Cause we're the people.' The social concern continued after the war ended. *The Lost Weekend* (45) was a gripping, unsentimental portrayal of alcoholism, for which Billy Wilder and Ray Milland won Oscars as Best Director and Actor respectively. Previously such a theme might have been handled whimsically, or with a redeeming happy ending, but by now Hollywood could treat it with stark realism.

Even genre films would occasionally venture outside their good guy/bad guy format and explore a wider issue. In 1943 *The Ox-Box Incident* (*Strange Incident* in GB) became a vehicle for William Wellman's attack on the atrocity of lynching. And by

1949 the corruptive influence of politics was being handled more directly. Robert Rossen stayed close to reality in *All The King's Men*, which, taking the career of Huey Long as its base, showed how a man of sincerity could be perverted by power. Willie Stark (Broderick Crawford) is an honest man with a genuine reforming zeal who goes into politics. But along the way he succumbs to graft, inclines increasingly towards a fascist outlook, and covets the presidency on any terms. His seemingly inexorable rise is halted by an assassin. A worthy movie which would usually make Hollywood feel uncomfortable, it garnered Oscars for Crawford (Best Actor), for Mercedes McCambridge (Supporting Actress) and for Best Film.

The horrors revealed when the Allies reached the concentration camps of Europe jolted Hollywood's awareness of anti-Semitism and two films sought to show that it was not confined to Nazi Germany, nor was it always expressed in the barely thinkable terms of extermination. Elia Kazan's *Gentleman's Agreement* (47) handled the theme in a grimly unadorned manner. Gregory Peck played a WASP journalist who posed as a Jew to discover how discrimination was at work in American society. Today the movie seems rather stodgy but at the time it was startling enough to bring Kazan an Oscar. In the same year Edward Dmytryk placed the theme in a thriller context in *Crossfire*. A policeman (Robert Young), trying to solve the murder of a Jew, discovers that it is a racialist killing by anti-Semitic Robert Ryan (in one of the most telling and convincing performances by this sadly underrated actor). In the original Richard Brooks novel, 'The Brick Foxhole', the victim had been a homosexual but Hollywood was not yet ready to cope with *that* subject.

Inevitably, the movies had to deal with a prejudice that was deeper ingrained, wider spread in the United States. In 1949 three movies appeared about the plight of American blacks. In *Home of the Brave* the oppressed hero was changed from a Jew to a Negro but the main plot, about his disgraceful treatment by the rest of the men in his army platoon, is retained. Elia Kazan, always a director to meet controversial subjects head on, focussed on colour prejudice with *Pinky*, the dilemma of a black girl who passes for white, and the theme of mixed blood was dealt with in *Lost Boundaries*, in which a highly-respected doctor and his wife are discovered to be part-negro. Two years later, Clarence Brown linked the race and lynch problems in *Intruder in the Dust* (51), which is set in the bigoted South and tells of a desperate attempt to save a black man from the mob.

Such films gave actors a fine chance to prove their abilities. One who benefited, particularly

from a fruitful collaboration with John Ford, was Henry Fonda. He had been in Hollywood since 1935, playing light comedy and rather routine roles as fairly dull heroes, but a change came in 1939, when he was cast opposite Tyrone Power in the historically unfaithful *Jesse James*; Power as Jesse was built into a Robin Hood character and Fonda caught attention as his brother Frank. But Fonda was born to be clean-cut heroes rather than whitewashed villains. He, like Gary Cooper and his longtime friend James Stewart, seemed to epitomize

Jeanne Crain (left) and Ethel Waters in *Pinky*, director Elia Kazan (20th Century-Fox, 49)

Walter Pidgeon, Donald Crisp and Anna Lee (right foreground) with John Loder (centre) in *How Green Was My Valley*, director John Ford (20th Century-Fox, 41)

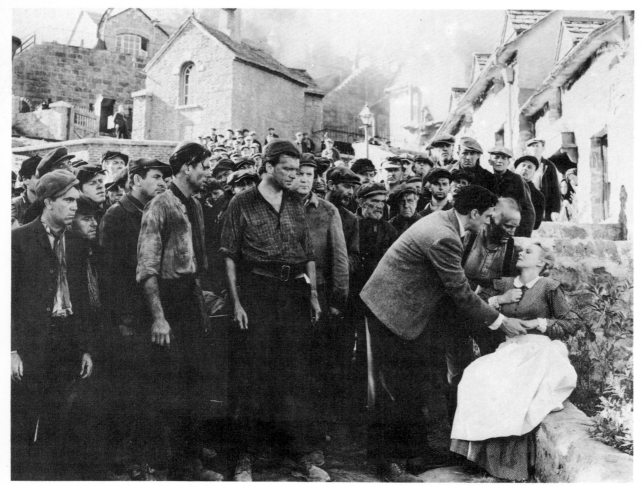

certain facets of the American character which
movie-makers like to celebrate. Fonda is particularly good in presidential mould. In 1939 Ford cast
him as *The Young Mr Lincoln*, a likeably romantic
view of the great man, and Fonda was excellent as
the rangy, honest hick with his eyes on the stars.
He returned to the political arena later in his career
with *Advise and Consent* (61), *The Best Man* (63),
and as a president faced with the threat of nuclear
war in the 1964 film *Fail Safe*.

Ford then put him in an epic Western, *Drums
Along the Mohawk* (39) and showed that the genre
suited his rather earnest persona. Over the next
few years he returned to the trail whether it was to
convey a message or not. He was excellent in *The
Ox-Bow Incident* (43) and as Wyatt Earp in *My
Darling Clementine* (46), Ford's version of the events
at the OK Corrall. He was even better as a stiff-
necked, by-the-book lieutenant-colonel of cavalry
whose inflexibility leads to disaster in *Fort Apache*
(48), and his Western roles extended, not usually
so successfully, beyond the decade with, among

others, *The Tin Star* (57), *Warlock* (58), *How the
West Was Won* (62), *The Rounders* (65) and a couple
with old pal Stewart, *Firecreek* (68) and *The
Cheyenne Social Club* (70).

The Grapes of Wrath (40) gave him the opportunity to extend himself and, although he has a
long and often honorable body of work behind
him, he has not always been given such chances,
perhaps because he is so a likeable man and therefore not presented with the opportunity for acting
fireworks. He was dependably amiable in *Mister
Roberts* (55), during which he argued with John
Ford, and they never worked together again, but
perhaps too worthy in Hitchcock's *The Wrong Man*
(56, one of the Old Master's least successful efforts
financially). He shone in *Twelve Angry Men* (56), at
his best as the conscientious voice of reason who
wants to be fair and will not be swayed from his
conviction whatever the pressure, and later in his
career was convincing as honest cops under duress,
notably in *Madigan* (67) and *The Boston Strangler*
(68), the latter based on recent real-life events.

Fonda's greatest assets were his durability and his dependability. He walked tall through his films, that patrician head with the intense eyes gazing towards some goal, showing others the way. But after the Forties he seldom had the roles which would have made him among the best, rather than the best-loved, actors in Hollywood.

Although Fonda and James Stewart both typified American virtues, Stewart specialized in more halting, bumbling, less articulate, slightly incredulous men who nonetheless have their principles. His cracker-barrel charm and sly, sometimes devious, wit get him by. He once summed his characterization up by saying: 'I'm always the plodder, the inarticulate man who tries. . . . I don't have all the answers; I have very few but I make it in the end.'

Stewart's secret was that he was so extraordinarily ordinary! He seemed to speak for all the perplexed, dogged, set-upon people confronted with the confusions of life. His early Hollywood career was ordinary in the extreme until Frank Capra noted his shambling integrity and cast him in *You Can't Take It With You* (38) and *Mr Smith Goes to Washington* (39). These showed he had an equal ability to play comedy and a certain type of tailor-made drama and fixed him successfully on his course.

His talent for comedy flowered brilliantly in George Cukor's *The Philadelphia Story* (40). It's a marvellous film with an excellent cast headed by Katharine Hepburn (as Tracy Lord, the heiress who is marrying for the second time, to a stuffy banker) and Cary Grant (as her ex, with whom she is still in love). Stewart manages the near-impossible. He steals the film from them and his witty performance as the tough newspaperman who is there to dish the dirt but falls in love with his victim (Hepburn) cannot be faulted.

After this high point, he decamped into the Air Force, flying many missions over Germany and winning the DFC. On his return to Hollywood he found the right parts weren't so easy to land. He worked again with Capra on *It's a Wonderful Life* (46), as a small-town bank manager who attempts to commit suicide because his business is ruined. He is prevented by an angel who shows that he is not the failure he felt himself to be. It is a charming, weepy fable that today is either loved for its whimsy and truth or hated for its treacly sentimentality. At the time, it failed to connect with the current mood.

He cast around for new areas and, like Fonda, found himself a niche in the Western. He was more loyal to the genre than Fonda and, indeed, is largely remembered by the post-war generation as a Westerner. In fact, he had flirted with cowboy pics before the war, appearing in the musical *Rose Marie* (36) and the jokey *Destry Rides Again* (39) opposite Dietrich. Now, thanks to director Anthony Mann, he took the Western more seriously and started strongly with *Winchester 73* (50), going on to Delmer Daves's sympathetic view of the Apache, *Broken Arrow* (50), and later working with Mann on *Bend of the River* (52, *Where the River Bends* in

John Ford directs Henry Fonda: (*opposite top*) *The Grapes of Wrath*, (left to right) Jane Darwell, Shirley Mills, Darryl Hickman, Russell Simpson, Frank Sully, Eddie Quillan, Frank Darien, Doris Bawden, Fonda, O.Z. Whitehead and John Carradine (20th Century-Fox, 40); (*opposite centre*) *My Darling Clementine*, Fonda (right) with Russell Simpson, Victor Mature, Ward Bond and Roy Roberts (20th Century-Fox, 46); (*opposite bottom*) *The Fugitive* with (kneeling) J. Carrol Naish (RKO, 47); (*right*) Fonda vs John Wayne (right foreground) in *Fort Apache* (RKO, 48)

James Stewart (left), Cary Grant and Katharine Hepburn in *The Philadelphia Story*, director George Cukor (MGM, 40)

Walt Disney Productions:
(*above*) 'The Sorceror's
Apprentice' sequence from
Fantasia (40); (*left*) *Dumbo*
(41); and (*opposite, top left*)
Bambi (42)

opposite, top right
National Velvet with (left to
right) Donald Crisp,
Mickey Rooney, Anne
Revere and Elizabeth Taylor,
director Clarence Brown
(MGM, 44)

opposite bottom
Victor Mature and Hedy
Lamarr in *Samson and
Delilah*, director Cecil B.
DeMille (Paramount, 49)

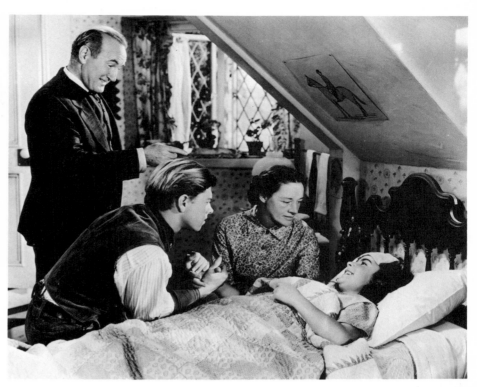

GB), *The Naked Spur* (53), *The Far Country* (55) and, best of the collaboration, the highly-rated *Man from Laramie* (55).

He was most successful when playing a peaceable man who is pushed into taking up a gun, a man who abhors violence but is driven to seek revenge. This was probably exhibited at its finest in Ford's *The Man Who Shot Liberty Valance* (62), in which he played Ransom Stoddart, a peace-loving lawyer who loathes guns but is faced with criminal violence in the shape of Liberty Valance (Lee Marvin at his most menacing). Eventually he has to go out and face Valance down, not knowing he is being backed up by his friend Doniphon (John Wayne). Although Wayne and Stewart had co-billing and it was nominally a Wayne vehicle, Ford recognized that Stewart had most of the pivotal scenes and it is remembered today as one of his finest Westerns.

Stewart tended towards the idiosyncratic. He had, for example, a particular stetson which he wore in every Western but to which Ford strongly objected as it was in a state of disintegration. The director tried to insist that Stewart wear one of Wayne's cast-offs. In the end, faced with his star's intransigence, Ford growled: 'If you ever work for me again – which I doubt – have a "hat approval" clause written into your contract.' Stewart took him at his word!

The Western restored Stewart's popularity and allowed him to spread. He had a comparatively happy collaboration with Alfred Hithcock. Stewart and Cary Grant were favourites of the director and during the Fifties he used them both, Grant in the lighter, more humorous films, Stewart in those with more emotional plots. The first teaming of star and director was *Rope* (48). Based on a stage play which, in turn, had been based on the Leopold and Loeb murder case, it is the story of two young homosexuals who murder a boy for kicks and hide his body in a trunk. The action takes place during the course of a social evening in which the guests gather around the trunk not knowing the grisly secret it contains. Only the young men's former college professor, Stewart, gets an inkling of the truth, which he finally uncovers before the night is out. Hitchcock decided to break every rule in the cinematic grammar book and recorded all the action in very long, 10-minute takes, the only time this has ever been done. It was an interesting exercise which the director admitted was not entirely successful.

More typically, Stewart was seen in *Rear Window* (54), as a photographer confined to a wheelchair who thinks he sees a murder committed across the street, in *The Man Who Knew Too Much* (56), playing the role of the title and trying to stop an assassination, and in *Vertigo* (58) as a detective with a terror of heights who, having failed to stop the woman he loves from throwing herself from a tower, then meets her double.

In addition to Westerns and thrillers Stewart also developed a sideline in biopics, scoring very strongly in *The Glenn Miller Story* (54) and as Charles Lindbergh in *The Spirit of St Louis* (57). In a long and unusually successful post-war career James Stewart became one of the most endearing of all movie stars (also carving a successful stage career for himself in the late Seventies), the only regret being that on film he seldom undertook the comedy roles with which he had previously scored such triumphs.

Undoubtedly the most successful and popular

Bing Crosby (left), Dorothy Lamour and Bob Hope in *Road to Singapore*, director Victor Schertzinger (Paramount, 40)

comedy team of the period was Bob Hope and Bing Crosby. An unusual team too, in that both achieved the topmost echelons of movie fame individually. And, of course, both were top-liners before they went to Hollywood, Hope in vaudeville and on Broadway, Crosby as the first crooner and idol of the big-band fans. In addition, of course, both were hugely popular radio stars.

Crosby made shorts before his first feature, *The King of Jazz* (30), and achieved solid success in the Thirties in light musicals, lighter comedies and featherweight musical-comedies. Hope also made a few shorts but concentrated on radio until *The Big Broadcast of 1938*, which brought radio to pictures and in which he first sang his signature tune, 'Thanks For The Memory'. In *The Cat and the Canary* (39), a comedy thriller, he delineated the major trademark of his screen persona, cowardice.

In 1940 the two came together for the first of a seven-film series, *Road to Singapore*. It was a happy accident; the movie was intended for Fred MacMurray and George Burns, but the deal fell through so Paramount offered it as a quick cheapie to three of their contract players, the third being that exotic adornment in a clinging sarong, Dorothy Lamour. Somehow everything clicked, particularly the easy-going, gag-cracking, ad-libbing relationship between Crosby and Hope: Crosby the smart one who got the girl, Hope the chiseller, the boaster, the coward, who thought he was God's gift to women and yet never got the girl. The fact that they were friends off-screen seemed to radiate through the film.

The success of *Singapore* took everyone by surprise; it made a fortune and the next year they were off on the road again, this time to *Zanzibar*. In 1942 it was *The Road to Morocco* and the title song with the unforgettable line 'like Webster's dictionary we're Morocco bound'. There was a four-year break before *The Road to Utopia* (46), and then came *To Rio* (47) and *To Bali* (52), by which time the magic was flagging and they went their own ways until meeting on the *Road to Hong Kong* (62), which was the last of them. Hope ascribes the success of the movies to the way in which he and Crosby worked together. Crosby, he said, was '. . . a very fine light comedian. A comic makes the best straight man for another comic because he knows how to play a laugh and that's why the *Road* pictures were so popular and so much fun to make.'

In between, the pair took on individual film work. Crosby naturally continued with musicals, which were generally bigger and better than the ones he made pre-*Singapore*. *Holiday Inn* (42) also had Fred Astaire and a song which went around the world as an anthem for homesick GIs – 'White Christmas' became the biggest-selling record in history. But he also tried out his muscles as a straightish actor, donning a dog collar for an unashamedly sentimental but no less winning movie about an old Irish priest (Barry Fitzgerald) who at first clashes with and then comes to admire and respect a young Irish-American colleague. *Going My Way* (43) avoided the sickeningly sugary largely because of the performances of Fitzgerald

and Crosby, and the certainty with which Leo McCarey directed. Crosby copped the Best Actor Oscar, Fitzgerald (who was also nominated in that category) got Best Support, the movie was Best Film, McCarey Best Director (and won another for his original story) and one of the songs, 'Swinging On A Star', was similarly honoured.

Its success demanded a sequel and this was very nearly as good as the original having, as it did, the considerable advantage of Ingrid Bergman as a nun. *The Bells of St Mary's* (45) just missed doing the double – the film and the two stars were all nominated for Oscars but lost out to *The Lost Weekend*, Ray Milland and Joan Crawford.

Crosby had proved his worth as an actor. He was to reinforce it in 1954 with his role as a washed-up star in *The Country Girl*; he was pipped to an Oscar but it won one for Grace Kelly and the next year they teamed again for the much lighter, and very enjoyable, *High Society* (56), which had a cracking Cole Porter score and did not disgrace *The Philadelphia Story*, on which it was based. (Crosby took Cary Grant's original role, Kelly updated Hepburn, and Sinatra had Stewart's part.) After his death – a fitting one for such a genuinely likeable man (he died on a golf course, two days after delighting a concert audience, in 1977) – Bob Hope was asked if he missed his sometime partner. 'The whole world misses him,' he replied. It was true.

Bob Hope never achieved the award-winning heights of his friend. Without Crosby to spark off, his films seldom reached the comic heights of the *Road* series, and while movies like *Monsieur Beaucaire* (45) and *Fancy Pants* (50), amongst many, are fun it is only on rare occasions that Hope hits his potential. *The Paleface* (48) shows him at his best as craven dentist Painless Potter, who is mistaken for Wild Bill Hickok (imagine his terror) and

Bob Hope with Nestor Paiva in *Paleface*, director Norman Z. McLeod (Paramount, 48)

Bud Abbott (left) and Lou Costello in *Africa Screams*, director Charles Barton (Universal, 49)

Danny Kaye in *The Secret Life of Walter Mitty*, director Norman Z. McLeod (RKO, 47)

marries Calamity Jane, in the unmistakable shape of Jane Russell. He cowers and quivers manically and his comic brilliance is gloriously sustained. A sequel, *Son of Paleface* (52) again with Russell, was not up to the mark, but he showed an empathy with the extraordinary characters who inhabited Damon Runyon's seedy New York world and appeared to effect in *Sorrowful Jones* (49).

Crosby and Hope were the most popular film comedy team since Laurel and Hardy. Although others tried to emulate their success, few got within a mile of them. Abbott and Costello started promisingly with *Buck Privates* (40) and enjoyed a good following, but their humour was always coarser and by the end of the Forties they seemed to be running out of ideas. *Abbott and Costello Meet Frankenstein* (48) provided a boost which sparked a series of encounters – . . . *The Killer* (49), . . . *The Invisible Man* (51) etc – but degenerated into tired formula. Jerry Lewis and Dean Martin paired in the late Forties, a partnership which lasted until the mid Fifties in tepid songs-and-laughter movies, commencing with *My Friend Irma* (49). They were subsequently far more successful as individuals, Lewis with manic, rather juvenile comedies like *The Delicate Delinquent* (57), *The Sad Sack* and, more interestingly (because he barely spoke throughout), *The Bellboy* (60). Martin was more versatile, not only a wildly-successful crooner, but also a dramatic actor of some power, in *The Young Lions* (58) and *Rio Bravo* (59), and a pleasing comedian, particularly in Billy Wilder's sadly underrated *Kiss Me Stupid* (64).

For a while in the Forties and Fifties it looked as if Danny Kaye might eclipse Bob Hope as the screen's best-loved comedian. He made an instant impact with a service comedy, *Up in Arms* (44), in which he showed his range of abilities, but his screen career stumbled subsequently until *The Secret Life of Walter Mitty* (47) and an excellent performance as the inveterate daydreamer. Although an increasingly popular stage entertainer, his movie success was spasmodic and it wasn't until *Hans Christian Andersen* (52), as an inaccurately lovable story-teller (Andersen, it seems, was a

morose individual) with a handful of good songs ('The Ugly Duckling', 'Thumbelina', 'Inch Worm' etc), that he appeared to live up to his early promise. He had a hit playing opposite Bing Crosby in *White Christmas* (54) and did well in and as *The Court Jester* (56) but, whereas Hope found a screen persona which fitted him well, Kaye never seemed to feel comfortable in movies and eventually abandoned them.

'There's a lot to be said for making people laugh. . . . It isn't much, but it's better than nothing in this cockeyed caravan.' So says the hero of *Sullivan's Travels* (41). The writer/director who put those words into the mouth of the director hero (Joel McCrea) was Preston Sturges who, for 10 years from 1940, turned out some of the wittiest and pithiest comedies ever produced in Hollywood. It was an extraordinary streak of creativity which, ultimately, burned out in 1950, when Sturges retired to France. Sturges was a satirist; he lampooned institutions and human foibles. In many respects he was similar to Capra but whereas Capra tended towards the sentimental, Sturges was cynical.

His first film as writer and director was *The Great McGinty* (40), which covers much the same ground as *All The King's Men* (49) but shows the rise of a political grafter in hilarious terms – 'If it wasn't for graft,' one of the characters declares, 'you'd get a very low type of people in politics.' Such was Sturges's view of the world – sardonic, laconic, beady-eyed – and he showed it to his audience, making his points with shafts of barbed laughter. *Christmas in July* (40) followed, about a young couple who win a competition, and then *Sullivan's Travels* and *The Lady Eve* (both 41), the latter a marvellously breakneck story of a con lady (Barbara Stanwyck) who tries to bilk a simple young millionaire (Henry Fonda) and ends up hoist by her own petticoat.

In 1942 came *The Palm Beach Story*, which is so full of marital (and other) complexities as to con-

found synopsis but is probably Sturges at his very finest. Blessed, as ever, with a fine star cast – Claudette Colbert, Joel McCrea, Mary Astor and Rudy Vallee, who sends himself up wonderfully as a crooner whose singing drives women away – it also has the Sturges madhouse of support players, who are never more manic than as the Ale and Quail Club, a group of dipsomaniac hunters who shoot up the train on their way to Palm Beach. This is one of the funniest scenes in talkies.

The Great Moment (43) is an oddity, a biography about the inventor of anaesthetics, but form was restored with *The Miracle of Morgan's Creek* (44),

top left
Franklin Pangborn (left) and W.C. Fields in *The Bank Dick*, director Eddie Cline (Universal, 40)

Preston Sturges's comedies: (*top right*) Henry Fonda (seated) and Barbara Stanwyck in *The Lady Eve* (Paramount, 41) and (*above*) Eddie Bracken and Betty Hutton in *The Miracle of Morgan's Creek* (Paramount, 44)

which was a comedy treading dangerous ground for the time as it revolved around wartime romance and marriage. Miss Kockenlocker (Betty Hutton) gets drunk and marries a soldier whose name she thinks in Ratskywatsky but whom she subsequently cannot trace. It's unfortunate she cannot prove her marital state for she is pregnant. A dumb but well-meaning hick (Eddie Bracken) tries to help and consequently is pitched into a crazy, desperate situation which knocks everything America and the censors hold dear – virginity, motherhood, patriotism. To cap it all, the girl winds up a national heroine when she is delivered of sextuplets! Next Sturges turned his jaundiced eye on another deeply-cherished institution – the returning war hero – in *Hail the Conquering Hero* (44). Eddie Bracken again, this time as the boy for whom the hometown goes *en fête*. The only problem is he isn't a hero at all – indeed the army wouldn't have him!

This marked the end of Sturges's most fertile, inventive, imaginative period. He made three further but generally inferior movies before bowing out – *Mad Wednesday* (46), *Unfaithfully Yours* (48) and *The Beautiful Blonde from Bashful Bend* (49). Although the latter films declined, Preston Sturges had performed a feat probably unmatched in Hollywood history – in a handful of notable films (and, moreover, magnificent comedies) he had eviscerated just about every sacred cow in the American pasture – and got away with it!

Sturges had recognized the public's need for release and relief, but in the Forties Hollywood developed a type of entertainment that was pure escapism, virtually inventing a genre that no other film industry has ever matched for sheer excitement, colour, verve, skill and panache. Although Hollywood had produced musicals before, indeed they had been early talkie staples, they do not begin to compare with the brilliance of the Forties' output.

Many of the major studios produced musicals in the decade. 20th Century-Fox usually draped theirs around a stunning blonde – Alice Faye and Betty

top
Hail, The Conquering Hero with Eddie Bracken (centre), director Preston Sturges (Paramount, 44)

Two Howard Hawks comedies: (*above*) Kenneth Tobey (left), Cary Grant and Ann Sheridan in *I Was a Male War Bride* (20th Century-Fox, 49), and (*right*) Gary Cooper (centre) and Barbara Stanwyck in *Ball of Fire* (Samuel Goldwyn, 41)

Two moods of Howard Hawks: (*left*) Cary Grant and Rosalind Russell in *His Girl Friday* (Columbia, 40), and (*below*) John Wayne in *Red River* (United Artists, 48)

Swashbucklers!: (*far left*) Basil Rathbone and Tyrone Power (right) in *The Mark of Zorro*, director Rouben Mamoulian (20th Century-Fox, 40); (*left*) Power and Mamoulian team up again for *Blood and Sand* (20th Century-Fox, 41); (*bottom left*) Maureen O'Hara, Power, Anthony Quinn and George Sanders in *The Black Swan*, director Henry King (20th Century-Fox, 42); and (*right*) Errol Flynn in *The Sea Hawk*, director Michael Curtiz (Warners, 40)

Grable were their biggest female stars – and occasionally, as in *Alexander's Ragtime Band* (38), added their male heart-throb, Tyrone Power. (The musical wasn't Power's true forte; he was better in action roles like *Jesse James* (39), *The Mark of Zorro* (40), *Blood and Sand* (41) or *The Black Swan* (42). He was the studio's swashbuckling answer to Errol Flynn but lacked the latter's *joie de vivre* and spring-heeled athleticism.)

Fox also had the quite extraordinary and most extravagant Carmen Miranda, The Brazilian Bombshell, who sang and danced while dressed like a greengrocer's shop in a series of spectacular but silly movies with exotic locations – *Down Argentine Way* (40), *That Night in Rio* (41) and *Weekend in Havana* (41) among others. These were essentially lightweight films which had musical interludes and not the true musical we know today, in which the music is integrated into the plot and helps progress it. The studio that developed this to a minor art form was MGM and it was the MGM musicals of the Forties that had most impact.

Arthur Freed – a successful lyricist who worked with Nacio Herb Brown on many songs including 'Singin' In The Rain' – was the man who attracted the finest talents to MGM and set them working on a revolutionary style of musical. He started his producing career with the Garland/Rooney outing *Babes in Arms* in 1939, but before that had been instrumental in casting Judy Garland as Dorothy in *The Wizard of Oz* (39). *Oz* had confirmed Garland as a star; *Babes* forged Garland and Rooney into a

team which continued through a couple of Andy Hardy pics and in musicals through two Freed productions, *Strike Up the Band* (40) and *Babes on Broadway* (41), after which she had her name above the credit on *For Me and My Gal* (42), in which she was supported by George Murphy and a newcomer to movies, Gene Kelly.

With this movie little Judy was finally allowed to grow up and in 1944 she had a reasonably adult role – one of the best she ever landed – in one of the best musicals ever made. That last point may be arguable, but there is surely no contest that *Meet Me in St Louis* is the most graceful, charming, heart-warming, endearing musical ever produced. A large loving family live in St Louis at the time of the World's Fair. Father wants to move to a job in New York; everyone else opposes him. Not least of the opposition results from the romantic involvement of the two eldest girls; Garland plays Esther, in love with the boy next door. The disagreement comes to a head at Christmas, when the youngest child is near hysterical at leaving all she loves. Father is persuaded and they stay on, and, in time, all go together to see the opening of the fair. Slight the plot may be but it is fleshed out by a superb cast (Leon Ames, Mary Astor, Margaret O'Brien, Lucille Bremer, Harry Davenport, Margaret Main, and Tom Drake), an excellent integrated score without any awkward cues for song (in addition to the title number there is 'The Boy Next Door', 'The Trolley Song', 'Skip To Ma Loo' and 'Have Yourself A Merry Little Christmas'), magnificent sets (an

103

entire street of imposing mansions was constructed at enormous cost) and tasteful, meticulous direction from Vincente Minnelli.

Judy Garland is marvellous. This is the Garland we like to remember, the singing, dancing actress who brought such freshness and sincerity to her films. Contrasting sadly with the raddled, ill, neurotic woman who was to lead such a tempestuous and painful life in her later years. After *St Louis* she went into a non-musical, *The Clock* (45), also directed by Minnelli, whom she later married and by whom she had a daughter, Liza, who would also make her mark on the film musical.

Next came *The Harvey Girls* (46), a good, but not remarkable, musical, and then she re-teamed with Gene Kelly (and with Minnelli and Freed) in a spoof of the Errol Flynn bounding-main pictures, *The Pirate* (48), which is probably better thought of today than it deserves to be. *Easter Parade* in the same year was wholly delightful. Garland was at her best, Astaire at his most inventive, and the Irving Berlin score full of winners – 'When The Midnight Choo-choo Leaves For Alabam', 'Steppin' Out With My Baby', the hilarious 'Couple Of Swells' routine between Astaire and Garland and, of course, the title song.

This was the last we were to see of the radiant,

irrepressible Garland. Another match with Astaire was shelved due to her ill-health, said, by the studio, to be exhaustion but actually a dependence on sleeping and pep pills which she took to meet the pressures that MGM were loading on her. In fact, their insensitivity to her fears, her crippling self-doubt and her fragility, both mental and physical, would eventually break her.

She made other movies – *In the Good Old Summertime* (49, which had charm but few flashes of brilliance) and *Summer Stock* (50) – but the lustre was missing. Had she been well she would have starred in *Annie Get Your Gun* (50, replaced by Betty Hutton), *Royal Wedding* (51, Jane Powell got the part opposite Astaire) and *Show Boat* (51, it went to Kathryn Grayson but was inferior to the 1936 version, which had Irene Dunne in the lead). All three were produced by Freed.

By 1951 Hollywood had just about finished with her even though she was barely 28. She came back in 1954 for *A Star Is Born*, in which her edgy, tense personality suits the part, after which there were only three more movies – *Judgement at Nuremburg* (60), *A Child Is Waiting* (62) and *I Could Go On Singing* (63) – before her death in 1969. Garland was a tragic victim of Hollywood's grinding demands, a brilliant, beautiful talent wasted years before its

time. Best to remember her as Dorothy and Esther, full of energy, song and vibrancy.

When Fred Astaire performed 'The Babbitt And The Bromide' duet in *Ziegfeld Follies* (46), another Freed MGM musical, he must have been aware that his crown was in danger from the man dancing beside him. Gene Kelly was the new young lion of musicals, very different from the musical-comedy tradition from which Astaire sprang. Kelly had learnt his trade in modern dance and, particularly, modern ballet; he was athletic, muscular, chunky; he had ambitions to push forward the boundaries of the musical.

As it turned out, there was room for both of them and Astaire was far from finished. Great musicals still demanded his featherlight touch and he scored hits well into the Fifties with *Holiday Inn* and *You Were Never Lovelier* (both 41), *Blue Skies* (46),

Musicals: (*opposite top*) Carmen Miranda in *That Night in Rio*, director Irving Cummings (20th Century-Fox, 41); (*opposite bottom*) James Cagney in *Yankee Doodle Dandy*, director Michael Curtiz (Warners, 42); (*above*) Fred Astaire and Eleanor Powell in the 'Begin The Beguine' number from *Broadway Melody of 1940*, director Norman Taurog (MGM); and (*left*) Judy Garland in 'The Boy Next Door' from *Meet Me in St Louis*, director Vincente Minnelli (MGM, 44)

Easter Parade (48), *Daddy Long Legs* (55) and *Funny Face* (57) among several others. Indeed he was so secure that he could send himself up; in *The Band Wagon* (53) he plays an ageing musical-comedy star who is on the wane and registered one of his best ever performances in this hilarious, lively and immensely likeable spoof of Broadway.

Meantime, Kelly scored well in *For Me and My Gal* (42), abandoned his pumps for a couple of acting parts, and was billed under Red Skelton in *Du Barry Was a Lady* (43) before returning strongly with *Cover Girl* (44), partnered by Rita Hayworth. Not content with starring, he also undertook the choreography on this one and brought in a Broadway pal to help – Stanley Donen. Together they would achieve a breakthrough in the movie musical by co-directing/choreographing the revolutionary *On the Town* (49) and then make one of the most cherished of all musicals, *Singin' in the Rain* (52). Donen later went on to make *Seven Brides for Seven Brothers* (54), *Funny Face* (57) and *The Pajama Game* (57).

Kelly loved experimenting: in *Anchors Aweigh* (45) he not only teamed up with Frank Sinatra but also performed a dazzling dance routine with Jerry, the cartoon mouse! In *The Pirate* (48) he brought his balletic grace to swashbuckling – no one ever swung from a mainsail with more elan, and he continued in like vein in the non-musical remake of *The Three Musketeers* (48), arguably the best of several versions of the story. By 1949 he was ready to put most of what he'd learned into practice.

On the Town is frequently hailed as one of the great musicals, if not the greatest. What it certainly *can* be called is a great pioneering musical. It took the musical out of the studio and into the streets. It used New York as a giant set around which three sailors on shore leave (Kelly, Sinatra and Jules Munshin) and the girls they pick up (Betty Garrett, Vera-Ellen and Ann Miller) cavort and prance, their steps seemingly in rhythm with the traffic, bustle and life of the metropolis. It had a tremendous, heady, revolutionary impact. But it is not truly one of the best musicals ever made; the score was not outstanding and the dancing, while energetic and full of verve, inclines too much towards the balletic. One of Kelly's faults was pretentiousness, particularly in his later films, when ballet for its own sake is introduced, slowing the pace and sometimes detracting from the narrative thrust.

Having progressed this far, he went a step farther with *An American in Paris* (51), a slender story of a GI who stays on in the city after the war, tries to become a painter, and falls in love with Leslie Caron. The climax was a ballet to Gershwin music; at 20 minutes it was the longest dance number ever to be included in a musical and it is a minority voice which says it was just too long. The majority opinion is that the ballet and the film are triumphs for Kelly. It was the first musical to win the Best Picture Oscar since *The Great Ziegfeld* (36), and it all but swept the board that year with five technical awards, plus The Irving Thalberg Memorial Award to its producer, Arthur Freed (well-

Kelly and Astaire: (*opposite top*) Fred with Judy Garland in the 'A Couple of Swells' number from *Easter Parade*, director Charles Walters (MGM, 48); (*opposite bottom*) together in 'The Babbitt And The Bromide' number from *Ziegfeld Follies*, director Vincente Minnelli (MGM, 46); (*above left*) Astaire in the 'Shoes With Wings On' number from *The Barkleys of Broadway*, director Charles Walters (MGM, 49); (*above*) Kelly and Sinatra in 'If You Knew Suzy' from *Anchors Aweigh*, director George Sidney (MGM, 45); and (*left*) Kelly with (left to right) Alice Pearce, Sinatra, Betty Garrett, Ann Miller and Jules Munshin in *On the Town*, directors Kelly and Stanley Donen (MGM, 49)

deserved as this was just one of the many peaks in his incomparable career), and a special statuette to Kelly 'in appreciation of his versatility as an actor, singer, director and dancer, and specifically for his brilliant achievements in the art of choreography on film'.

Still not content, Kelly followed with what is undoubtedly one of the very favourite musicals ever made. And, as proof, one sequence must rate as one of the most instantly recognizable pieces of choreography. When Gene Kelly starts singing – and dancing – in the rain everyone knows it is Gene Kelly in *Singin' in the Rain* (52). They may even remember that the film is about the early days

of talkies, that it also starred Debbie Reynolds and Donald O'Connor (and, of course, lovely Jean Hagen as silent queen Lena Lamont), that it is gloriously funny, and that there are several other excellent songs, including 'Good Mornin'' and 'Make 'Em Laugh'. That, in effect, it was the very highest point of the American, the MGM, musical, the culmination of all the talents who had conspired during the Forties to turn the genre into something vivid, alive and trail blazing.

With such a wealth of expertise and talent in every department, with the musical riding high and its exclusive property, Hollywood seemed to be entering the Fifties without a qualm or worry.

40s Oscars

YEAR	BEST FILM	BEST ACTOR	BEST ACTRESS
1940	*Rebecca*/ Selznick-UA	James Stewart/ *The Philadelphia Story*	Ginger Rogers/ *Kitty Foyle*
1941	*How Green Was My Valley*/ 20th Century-Fox	Gary Cooper/ *Sergeant York*	Joan Fontaine/ *Suspicion*
1942	*Mrs Miniver*/ MGM	James Cagney/ *Yankee Doodle Dandy*	Greer Garson/ *Mrs Miniver*
1943	*Casablanca*/ Warner Brothers	Paul Lukas/ *Watch on the Rhine*	Jennifer Jones/ *The Song of Bernadette*
1944	*Going My Way*/ Paramount	Bing Crosby/ *Going My Way*	Ingrid Bergman/ *Gaslight*
1945	*The Lost Weekend*/ Paramount	Ray Milland/ *The Lost Weekend*	Joan Crawford/ *Mildred Pierce*
1946	*The Best Years of Our Lives*/ Samuel Goldwyn-RKO	Fredric March/ *The Best Years of Our Lives*	Olivia de Havilland/ *To Each His Own*
1947	*Gentleman's Agreement*/ 20th Century-Fox	Ronald Colman/ *A Double Life*	Loretta Young/ *The Farmer's Daughter*
1948	*Hamlet*/ Universal-International	Lawrence Olivier/ *Hamlet*	Jane Wyman/ *Johnny Belinda*
1949	*All the King's Men*/ Columbia	Broderick Crawford/ *All the King's Men*	Olivia de Havilland/ *The Heiress*

opposite left
Oscar-winner Greer Garson with Walter Pidgeon and child-actors Christopher Severn and Clare Sanders in *Mrs Miniver*, director William Wyler (MGM, 42)

opposite right
William Wyler's *The Best Years of Our Lives*, with (left to right) Teresa Wright, Dana Andrews, Myrna Loy and Fredric March (RKO, 46)

left
Ginger Rogers takes the Best Actress award for *Kitty Foyle*, director Sam Wood (RKO, 40) with Gladys Cooper and Dennis Morgan

40s Oscars

BEST DIRECTOR	BEST SUPPORTING ACTOR	BEST SUPPORTING ACTRESS	YEAR
John Ford/ *The Grapes of Wrath*	Walter Brennan/ *The Westerner*	Jane Darwell/ *The Grapes of Wrath*	1940
John Ford/ *How Green Was My Valley*	Donald Crisp/ *How Green Was My Valley*	Mary Astor/ *The Great Lie*	1941
William Wyler/ *Mrs Miniver*	Van Heflin/ *Johnny Eager*	Teresa Wright/ *Mrs Miniver*	1942
Michael Curtiz/ *Casablanca*	Charles Coburn/ *The More the Merrier*	Katina Paxinou/ *For Whom the Bell Tolls*	1943
Leo McCarey/ *Going My Way*	Barry Fitzgerald/ *Going My Way*	Ethel Barrymore/ *None But the Lonely Heart*	1944
Billy Wilder/ *The Lost Weekend*	James Dunn/ *A Tree Grows in Brooklyn*	Anne Revere/ *National Velvet*	1945
William Wyler/ *The Best Years of Our Lives*	Harold Russell/ *The Best Years of Our Lives*	Anne Baxter/ *The Razor's Edge*	1946
Elia Kazan/ *Gentleman's Agreement*	Edmund Gwenn/ *Miracle on 34th Street*	Celeste Holm/ *Gentleman's Agreement*	1947
John Huston/ *Treasure of the Sierra Madre*	Walter Huston/ *Treasure of the Sierra Madre*	Claire Trevor/ *Key Largo*	1948
Joseph L. Mankiewicz/ *A Letter to Three Wives*	Dean Jagger/ *Twelve O'Clock High*	Mercedes McCambridge/ *All the King's Men*	1949

the Fifties

'Why should people go and pay money to see bad films when they can stay at home and see bad television for nothing?' Sam Goldwyn put his finger on the problem that faced Hollywood all through the Fifties. The industry feared and despised TV – 'I'm delighted with it because it used to be that films were the lowest form of art. Now we have something to look down on.' (Billy Wilder) – but it could not ignore it. Box-office receipts were hit very badly. The industry had grown fat during the war. Millions flocked to the movies, prepared to queue for whatever tripe the studios offered. Now they didn't need cinemas: a box in the corner would relay tripe to them without effort. The rise of TV was inexorable. By 1959 36 million homes in the US had sets; the next year the figure had risen to 85 million.

At first the studios tried to fight. Moguls forbade their contract players to appear on TV. This had little effect. Stars returning from the war were no longer willing to be bound by restrictive contracts and, when their terms of employment were over, many, like James Stewart and Clark Gable, went freelance, hiring themselves out to the top bidder or setting up, with varying but mostly small degrees of success, their own production companies. And, in any case, TV did not need movie stars; it made its own.

Hollywood's answer was the gimmick. The first idea was to make it easier to see films and this led to a craze for building drive-in cinemas, the next best thing to sitting in your parlour and being entertained. Then it came up with bigger, if not better.

On 30 September, 1952, *This Is Cinerama* opened on Broadway and ran for 122 weeks – three projectors threw three synchronized films at a huge screen. The result was a 146-degree vista and some rather strange effects where the three reels seamed together on the screen. It was certainly a novelty; audiences thrilled as the cameras plunged them down roller coasters or sped them by plane across the continent. But the process was a 10-year wonder: few theatre owners could afford to convert to the dimensions it required and, anyway, they weren't getting very much product to show. Most of the output was massive travelogues – *Cinerama Holiday* (54), *Seven Wonders of the World* (55) and such ungripping pap; the first feature was *How the West Was Won* (62), which was a big

subject but still not large enough to fill the screen *and* thrill the audience.

Next came CinemaScope, a wide-screen process using a single lens, which was less complex and far more successful for feature films. The method was pioneered by 20th Century-Fox in 1953 with a biblical epic, *The Robe*. It was popular enough for others to rush out their own versions – Paramount had VistaVision, Mike Todd had Todd-AO, etc., and before too long certain exhibitors saw enough profit in it to convert at least one cinema in major towns to the huge screen needed to take it.

Still Hollywood cast about for new technology to woo armchair viewers. During the decade they introduced stereophonic sound, which was a reasonably welcome innovation, and 3D, which was not.

Three-dimensional films had been made, briefly, in the Thirties. Now audiences were issued with polaroid glasses, through which it seemed as though the action was leaping out of the screen. That was the theory. In reality, the technical problems resulted more in farce than horror, thrills or excitement. The first of the new 3D movies was *Bwana Devil* (53, the less said about which, the better) and then came a spate of larger, occasionally much worthier, ventures. At their worst, 3D sequences were ludicrous; in *House of Wax* (53, directed by André de Toth, who was blind in one eye and therefore could not see the effects he was creating!) a reasonably thrilling Vincent Price horror story was held up occasionally to allow some totally unnecessary business to exploit the process.

Like the other desperate attempts, 3D failed. The movies were not going to beat TV so they had to find a way of living alongside it. Indeed, it is some measure of the speed with which the movies fell to the upstart that, by 1958, every major studio had sold its entire pre-1948 output to TV companies.

Hollywood movies of the Fifties were oddly schizophrenic in their attempts to carve a niche in the audience's affections. The crisis caused them to become even more spectacular (and frequently much sillier) or to return to a quality of film-making and story-telling that hadn't been seen since the heydays of the Thirties.

It's difficult to say which came first – the big screen or the trend towards epics which could not be comfortably encompassed on conventional screens. Whichever, the epic flourished in the decade, commercially if not artistically, and much of the credit for this must go to Cecil B. DeMille.

DeMille had been making big pictures for years but in the Fifties with big screen *and* colour he could go right over the top. His specialist subject was the biblical epic, which he treated with a mixture of reverential awe and tasteless vulgarity, but he would stray, when he found a topic massive enough, into other areas. He approached the decade with *Samson and Delilah* (49); Victor Mature had his locks (looking like an oil slick) cut by Hedy Lamarr and the film is principally notable for his destruction of the temple. (Mature had Neanderthal good looks that suited the genre, although his acting seldom ascended above the woeful; other excursions back into history included *Androcles and the Lion* (53), *The Robe* (53), and two 1954 efforts, *Demetrius and the Gladiators* and *The Egyptian*.) Next DeMille essayed a huge and lumpen movie in which several plots came together under the big top, *The Greatest Show on Earth* (52), which he packed with stunts and stars – Betty Hutton, Cornel Wilde, Dorothy Lamour, James Stewart and Charlton Heston.

In Heston, DeMille found an actor who could almost match his physique with his acting ability. He was built in epic mould, adamantine and commanding. It is to DeMille's credit that he was first to spot this; through most of the decade Heston played in routine adventure actioners – *Pony Express* and *Arrowhead* (both 54), and *The Secret of the Incas* (54) – and seemed destined to go the same way as Mature. But DeMille had him in mind for the epic which would make all others look like programme fillers – he saw Heston as Moses in *The Ten Commandments* (56).

This was not just to be big, but the BIGGEST: years – as they say – in the making and, at $7,500,000, the most costly movie ever. It was huge, it was incredibly successful, it was – on occasions – eye-bogglingly spectacular, and it was also amazingly boring for much of its length. No matter, it proved that if you make films big enough, lavish enough, colourful enough, outrageous enough, you'll pull folks away from the tube.

The Ten Commandments made millions and a huge star out of Heston, who went on to even bigger and more expensive movies, including one of the best biblical epics – at least of the Fifties – *Ben Hur* (59). Now it was William Wyler's turn to show what he could do with spear carriers and horsemen. If anything, *Ben Hur* is more reverential than DeMille's excursion and also, mercifully, less vulgar. It is no coincidence that the movie is best remembered for its chariot race. It used the wide screen to great effect and all credit must go to Yakima Canutt, who staged it. The rest of the movie, though occasionally moving, tends to be rather leaden. Nonetheless, it was an astonishing success at the box office (it *had* to be to recoup MGM's $15 million investment) and scooped the Oscar pool – a record 11 awards, including Best Picture, Best Actor (Heston), Best Supporting Actor (Hugh Griffith as a rascally Arab sheikh), Best Director and seven others in the various technical categories.

above
Victor Mature (standing) and Richard Burton (third from right) in *The Robe*, director Henry Koster (20th Century-Fox, 53)

left
Stewart Granger and Rita Hayworth in *Salome*, director William Dieterle (Columbia, 53)

The trend to historical and biblical epics had been set. In 1950 Mel Ferrer had won an Oscar for his portrayal of *Cyrano de Bergerac*, a film which was well above the average. *Quo Vadis* (51) was about Nero's oppression of the Christians. Mervyn LeRoy's only insight into the motivation of the character was that he was a 'son of a bitch' who 'plays with himself'! Not all the Bible pics were so garish. *David and Bathsheba* (51) was a worthy attempt to redress the balance with worthy Gregory Peck in the title role. The film eschewed hokum and vulgarity and was as dull as watching a loaf go stale. *Salome* (53) had the distinct advantage of Charles Laughton as Herod and Rita Hayworth as the biblical stripper but that did not save it. Nor did the fact that, according to this version, she is a heroine who attempts to save John the Baptist!

There were some brave efforts. You can't look to Roman history and ignore Julius Caesar. Joseph Mankiewicz made a version of *Julius Caesar* in 1953

The chariot race from *Ben Hur*, staged by Yakima Kanutt, director William Wyler (MGM, 59)

James Mason (top) and Brando in *Julius Caesar*, director Joseph Mankiewicz (MGM, 53)

that was faithful to Shakespeare's original, even though the casting was startling. John Gielgud made a fine Cassius, as expected; Louis Calhern was an acceptable Caesar, James Mason a surprisingly good Brutus; Deborah Kerr played Portia and Greer Garson was Calphurnia. But the controversy really settled around the casting of Mark Antony. That part went to Marlon Brando.

In the event Brando confounded the doubters and, if his portrayal of Mark Antony was not definitive in the classical sense, it *was* different. And powerful. 'Friends, Romans, countrymen' is delivered as rabble-rousing rhetoric and with it, and the rest of the performance, Brando electrified an otherwise dull but respectful film.

He was nominated for an Oscar. His third nomination as best actor in only his fourth film! That tells something of the impact Brando made on Hollywood. And what is also telling is that he was passed over each time. Brando conformed to nobody's image of a movie star. He loathed Hollywood and said so. He despised the press and said so. Hollywood and the press decided they disliked him too. But neither could ignore his talent. Yes, he looked, acted and dressed like a bum and, as often as not, he played a bum. But, hell, what an actor! Yes, he mumbled and he sought motivation and he was devoted to the so-called Method school of acting but when he slouched on screen he took it over.

Brando had made his reputation on Broadway and, although strenuously courted by all the major studios, held out until tempted by an independent producer, Stanley Kramer, who put him in a film directed by new-wave director, Fred Zinnemann.

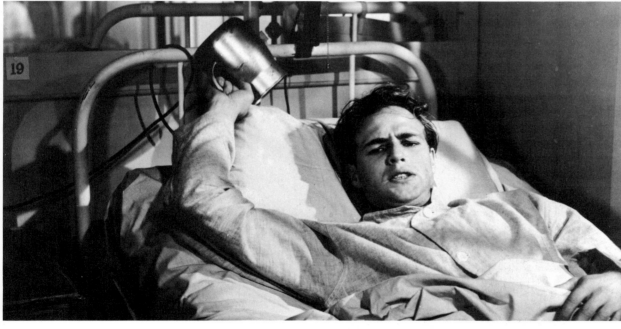

Marlon Brando in *The Men*, director Fred Zinnemann (United Artists, 50)

Zinnemann, Nicholas Ray, Elia Kazan and others were veering away from the typical Hollywood film with its high gloss, its distance from reality, its dependence on stars rather than stories, its belief in the primacy of entertainment. They had learned a lesson from a handful of films coming out of the Italian industry: Roberto Rossellini's *Rome – Open City* (45) and *Paisa* (46), Giuseppe de Santis's *Bitter Rice* (49), and Vittorio de Sica's *Bicycle Thieves* (48, for which he won an Oscar). Between them these men revolutionized European cinema, creating a 'neo-realist' school in which stories of ordinary, simple, often oppressed people could be told, using

all the eloquence of cinematic art. These were not lavish, star-packed productions in glowing colour – they were made in monochrome on modest budgets, using actors rather than stars (and frequently people who had never acted before). They generally had strong narratives with an underlying message, and, most important of all, they were firmly embedded in reality. They were about real people in real situations.

Determined to create that kind of cinema, the American new-wave directors required a different type of actor to the one that had dominated Hollywood in the Thirties and Forties. And the new

WARNER BROS. BRING YOU THE FIRST FEATURE PRODUCED BY A MAJOR STUDIO IN 3D!

NATURAL VISION

COLOR BY WARNERCOLOR

3 DIMENSION "HOUSE OF WAX"

STARRING **VINCENT PRICE · FRANK LOVEJOY · PHYLLIS KIRK**

above
Lobby card for *House of Wax,* director André de Toth (Warners, 53)

left
Laurence Olivier's *Richard III* (Lopert, 56)

right
Yul Brynner (left), Charlton Heston and Henry Wilcoxon (far right) in *The Ten Commandments*, director Cecil B. DeMille (Paramount, 56)

below
Peter Ustinov and Patricia Laffan in *Quo Vadis*, director Mervyn LeRoy (MGM, 51)

breed of actor, who had trained in New York's Actors' Studio and worked on the dark plays of writers like Tennessee Williams, was not particularly interested in the razzmatazz of Hollywood. It was entirely in keeping, then, that an actor like Brando should prefer Kramer's offer of *The Men* (50), directed by Zinnemann, to the blandishments of Louis Mayer and others.

In *The Men* Brando played a paraplegic confined to a wheelchair as a result of war wounds. It was a performance of great power, and 'powerful' is the commonest description of his work. He brought power, pain and intensity to everything he did in his early years. Who can forget him as the inarticulate, highly-sexed slob, Kowalski, in Tennessee Williams's *A Streetcar Named Desire* (51)! Elia Kazan directed and later said Brando was 'the only genius I've ever met in the field of acting'. It was a *tour de force* for everyone concerned, and all the major parts won their performers Oscars – Vivien Leigh as Blanche Dubois, Karl Malden as the rough fellow who loves her, Kim Hunter as Kowalski's wife, Stella – all except Brando, who was beaten to the award by Bogart.

Next came *Viva Zapata!* (52, Elia Kazan directed again), in which Brando vividly played the Mexican revolutionary in a film that gave new respectability to biopics, which had become trite, inaccurate and self-serving. Anthony Quinn won a Best Supporting Oscar; Brando was nominated for Best Actor, but it went to Gary Cooper. Then an entire change of role, if not necessarily style, in *Julius Caesar* (53); another nomination, but William Holden got it for his performance in *Stalag 17*.

115

Brando broody: in *The Wild One* (*top*), director Elia Kazan (Columbia, 54), and (*above*) with Thomas Handley and Eva Marie Saint in *On the Waterfront*, director Kazan (Columbia, 54)

As if his impact had not been great enough, he next took a role which became a stereotype for disaffected youth: Johnny the leader of a motorcycle gang which terrorizes a small town in *The Wild One* (54). This was felt to be so alarming that it had a rough ride and was banned for years in Britain where, it was feared, its glamorization of violent hoodlums would inflame audiences into emulation. Seen today, it is nowhere near as disturbing as it was made out to be. In fact, it is often laughable and Brando seems too moody, much too resentful for credibility.

On the Waterfront (54) was perhaps his best role of the decade. He plays Terry Malloy, an ex-boxer who, if he had many brains to start with, has not had them improved by the pounding he's taken in the ring. Despite his claim 'I could've been a contender', it is patently obvious that he could not. He earns his living as a longshoreman and is drawn into the fringes of political corruption by his brother Charlie (Rod Steiger) who is a minion of a grafting union boss. Duped into unwittingly contriving the death of an idealistic docker, he falls in love with the murdered man's sister (Eva Marie Saint) and is torn apart by love of her and loyalty to his brother. It is a strong subject, strongly directed by Kazan and brilliantly acted by Brando, who is magnificent as the stumbling hero. The movie's power was recognized with a Best Picture Oscar, as was Eva Marie Saint for Best Support and, at last, the Academy could ignore Brando no more, he was unequivocally Best Actor of the year.

He was also, and despite his best efforts, the biggest movie star in Hollywood. So the studios lined him up for a biblical epic, *The Egyptian*. He

ducked out, quite rightly because it was a stinker, and was inadequately replaced by Edmond Purdom. So, instead of the Bible, Fox looked to costume drama and he played Napoleon, quite effectively, in *Desirée* (54). For the rest of the decade he seemed intent on showing his versatility. He did a musical next, *Guys and Dolls* (55), then played a Japanese in *The Teahouse of the August Moon* (56), an air force hero who falls for a Japanese girl in *Sayonara* (57) and lastly, and rather more strongly, an idealistic Nazi in *The Young Lions* (58).

They were parts in which he could thrill and excite an audience less than in the early years. Nonetheless, Marlon Brando was *the* male star of the Fifties, the one who seemed to sum up its doubts and tensions, its violence and frustration.

There was another actor who, had he lived, might have been a contender. It was Elia Kazan who spotted James Dean's potential. 'There was value in Dean's face,' he said later. 'His face is so desolate, lonely and strange.' Dean had the vulnerability of a wounded animal, and, like a wounded animal, he would spit and kick out and fight back. Even more than Brando in *The Wild One*, Dean seemed to represent the youthful side of the generation gap.

He was typecast from the start. Kazan put him into *East of Eden* (55) to kick against parental authority, to be misunderstood, to be – in the phrase

of the day – the Crazy Mixed-up Kid. He was disturbed, he was confused, he was surly and he was very beautiful.

His truculence on screen was a projection of his real-life resentment, his unease with life, his wilful rebelliousness and seeming intent on self-destruction. Nicholas Ray channelled all this into a film that seemed to be the definitive statement on the mood of a generation, *Rebel Without a Cause* (55). Dean was a mixed-up kid, a bad boy, but not as bad as the punks who cruise around looking for trouble.

Dean's real problem is that he despises his father for his weakness and seems unable to relate to anyone except Judy (Natalie Wood), who, like him, is essentially nice but misunderstood. He is redeemed by his attempt to save his friend Plato (Sal Mineo), by the love of a good woman, by his rejection of the punks, and by a reconciliation with his father.

Rebel had enormous impact when it was released but today it looks contrived and the acting, particularly of the young people, is far from subtle. Dean himself frequently overdoes the moodiness. But kids aren't critics and they saw in the film and, particularly in Dean, an exaggerated image of their own emotions.

It was time for Dean to show he had range as an actor. George Stevens cast him in *Giant* (56) and asked him to age, to develop from a young ranch hand (with a chip, of course) to a wealthy middle-aged playboy (with a bigger chip). *Giant* was a cinematic 'Dallas', chronicling two generations of a Texan ranching family; it was packed with stars – Rock Hudson and Elizabeth Taylor as well as Dean and an unusually strong supporting cast, including Mercedes McCambridge, Carroll Baker and Chill Wills – and it sprawled like the landscape in which it was set. It was not a bad film but it was by no means a very good film. Dean, as Jet, was not dis-

graced. He was nominated for an Oscar (as he had been for *East of Eden*) but was rightly passed over; the nomination probably owed more to the fact that he killed himself in a car crash shortly after he had completed work on the film.

It's impossible to say whether Dean would have matured into an actor of stature. He was promising but, unlike Brando, he was a star who projected part of his own personality. Could he ever have grown out of his resentful young man identity? To his own generation it did not matter, Dean died young and that was enough to raise him to cult status. He remains forever the embodiment of Fifties frustration.

Although George Stevens showed in *Giant* that he was prepared to give stories the big-screen treatment, he could also match Zinnemann and Kazan for grittiness. With *Shane* in 1953 he handled the Western in a new way. Alan Ladd plays a stranger with a clouded past who comes to the aid of decent homesteaders terrorized by a magnificently evil Jack Palance, but this is not the West of common Hollywood myth: it is a violent, muddy, bloody place where good and bad are not clear cut. Ladd is not all good, and the righteous, in the shape of little Elisha Cook Jr, are brutally gunned down.

Henry King had suggested a new way of handling

James Dean and Elizabeth Taylor in *Giant*, director George Stevens (Warners, 55)

opposite, top left
Alan Ladd and child-actor Brandon de Wilde in *Shane*, director George Stevens (Paramount, 53)

opposite, top right
Gary Cooper in *High Noon*, director Fred Zinnemann (United Artists, 52)

opposite, bottom left
Alex Nichol (left) and James Stewart (second from right) in *The Man from Laramie*, director Anthony Mann (Columbia, 55)

opposite, bottom right
Ernest Borgnine (left), Burt Lancaster and Cooper in *Vera Cruz*, director Robert Aldrich (United Artists, 54)

118

the Western in 1950 with his downbeat *The Gunfighter*, in which an ageing quickdraw artist who wants to hang up his pistols, is pursued by young hotheads out to make a name for themselves. The title role gave Gregory Peck one of his better roles. Enviably handsome and a steady actor, he could not seem to break away from being rather stolid, even dull on screen. Although in numerous admirable and sometimes successful films – *The Keys of the Kingdom* (44), *Gentleman's Agreement* (47), *Twelve O'Clock High* (49), and *The Big Country* (58) among others – it wasn't until 1962 and *To Kill a Mockingbird* that he got the part that perfectly matched his earnest decency and brought a long-strived-for Oscar as Best Actor.

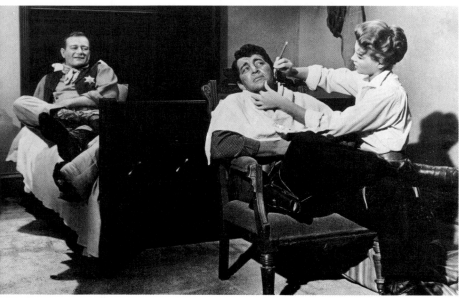

top
John Wayne leads in *The Searchers*, director John Ford (Warners, 56)

above
John Wayne, Dean Martin (centre) and Angie Dickinson in *Rio Bravo*, director Howard Hawks (Warners, 59)

right
Peter Finch and Audrey Hepburn in *The Nun's Story*, director Fred Zinnemann (Warners, 59)

Perhaps the most influential and successful of the new-wave Westerns was Zinnemann's *High Noon* (52), which some rate as highly as *Stagecoach* (39). Gary Cooper excelled amid an excellent cast as Will Kane, the marshall who is quitting to get married (to Grace Kelly) but stays on to face one more threat and, in the process, nearly loses his wife and his life and finds himself abandoned to his fate by the townspeople he is protecting. The final shoot-out is both tense and lyrical, the choreography of fear and violence.

In *High Noon* Zinnemann brilliantly expanded a small, tight incident which lasted only a few hours, was confined to one place, and involved a limited number of people. But he could also work on a bigger canvas. *From Here to Eternity* (53) is set in and around the attack on Pearl Harbor, yet it's a picture in which the characters and their troubles are never overshadowed by events around them. The film is notable for Zinnemann's deft, disciplined, sensitive touch and for its oblique use of sexuality – particularly in the affair between non-commissioned Burt Lancaster and officer's lady Deborah Kerr (their clinch on the beach as the waves erupt symbolically about them has become a classic and a cliché). It is also remembered as the movie which gave a desperately-needed boost to the flagging career of Frank Sinatra and netted him a Supporting Oscar as Private Maggio. (The film, Donna Reed and the director all won awards.)

After this, Zinnemann changed tack, going for bigger, lusher productions, like *Oklahoma!* (55) and *The Nun's Story* (58).

Elia Kazan stayed more faithful to his social-realist roots. After *A Streetcar Named Desire* (51), *Viva Zapata!* (52), *On the Waterfront* (54) and *East of Eden* (55), he returned to the work of Tennessee Williams with *Baby Doll* (56). Williams's plays had provided much film material in the decade – *The Glass Menagerie* (50), *The Rose Tattoo* (55), and

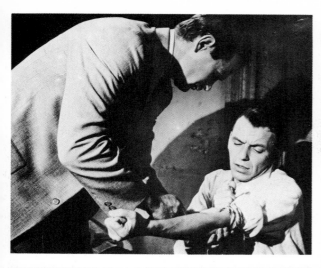

Suddenly Last Summer (59). However, producers and directors had had to fudge or obscure the sexuality which lay at the root of them. Although censorship was easing, it still was not ready to accept undiluted Williams.

Kazan, who had already incurred the censor's wrath with *Streetcar*, now invited greater disapproval with *Baby Doll* (56), which was condemned by the Catholic Legion of Decency as 'morally repellent in theme and treatment'. There's no denying that, for the time, it was strong meat. Carroll Baker is a nubile child married to an older man (Karl Malden); she sleeps in a cot wearing provocative two-piece nighties, sucking her thumb, the ripe tautness of her body – which she denies her husband until she reaches 20 – driving the man to distraction. His craving and her teasing are heightened by the steamy Southern atmosphere and aggravated by the arrival of Eli Wallach, who attempts to wreak revenge on Malden by seducing his child-wife. It was a potent stew of claustrophobic sexual tension and became a *cause célèbre*.

Kazan handled his assault on censorship with a far more artistic and artful hand than some other directors. Otto Preminger, who contributed four noteworthy movies to the decade – *Carmen Jones* (54) and *Porgy and Bess* (59), 'black' musicals, and two 'message' films, *The Man with the Golden Arm*

(56) about drug addiction and *Anatomy of a Murder* (59) about the trial of a man who killed another for allegedly raping his wife – entered the lists against the censor with *The Moon Is Blue* (53). This is a shallow story about a secretary described as a 'professional virgin' (played by Maggie McNamara), who is holding on to her maidenhead to capture Mr Right. The censor objected to the plot and to the word 'virgin'.

Only he knows why he objected to the word that described the female state he held most dear for he must surely have smiled on Hollywood's own 'professional virgin', Doris Day. Although she started as, and remained, a singer, Doris Day seldom seemed to get the plum musical roles in the Fifties, with the exception of *Calamity Jane* (53) and *The Pajama Game* (57). Somehow the big musicals of the decade, mostly by Rodgers and Hammerstein, seemed to go to others. *Oklahoma!* (55) starred

'Adult' themes: (*top left*) Darren McGavin (left) and Frank Sinatra in *The Man with the Golden Arm*, director Otto Preminger (United Artists, 56); (*top right*) Carroll Baker in *Baby Doll*, director Elia Kazan (Warners, 56); (*above left*) Diane Varsi and Orson Welles in *Compulsion*, director Richard Fleischer (20th Century-Fox, 59); and (*above right*) James Stewart in *Anatomy of a Murder*, director Otto Preminger (Columbia, 59)

121

Shirley Jones and Gordon MacRae; *The King and I* (56) featured the non-musical Deborah Kerr and, of course, Yul Brynner in his most famous role; the massively successful *South Pacific* (58) had Mitzi Gaynor and Rossano Brazzi in the main parts. All these and other big musicals – like *Carousel* (56), *Pal Joey* (57) and *Carmen Jones* (54) – were immensely popular at the time, but few were as exuberant, as boisterous and as joyfully uninhibited as *Seven Brides for Seven Brothers* (54), in which the explosive, energetic dancing was brilliantly captured and directed by Stanley Donen. Not until *West Side Story* (61) were we to see such verve in the Hollywood musical again.

Hitchcock: (*opposite, top left*) Grace Kelly and Cary Grant in *To Catch a Thief* (Paramount, 55) and (*opposite, top right*) James Stewart spies on Raymond Burr in *Rear Window* (Paramount, 54)

opposite centre
Porgy and Bess, director Otto Preminger (Columbia, 59)

opposite, bottom left
Bing Crosby and Grace Kelly in *High Society*, director Charles Walters (MGM, 56)

opposite, bottom right
Howard Keel and Kathryn Grayson (foreground) in *Kiss Me Kate*, director George Sidney (MGM, 53)

MGM musicals: (*right*) Howard Keel and tiny Betty Hutton in *Annie Get Your Gun*, director George Sidney (50); (*below*) Gene Kelly in the 20-minute ballet from *An American in Paris*, director Vincente Minnelli (51); (*bottom*) *Seven Brides for Seven Brothers*, director Stanley Donen (54); and (*below right*) Cyd Charisse and Fred Astaire in 'The Girl Hunt' ballet from *The Band Wagon*, director Vincente Minnelli (53)

left
Unmistakable! Kelly in the title number from *Singin' in the Rain*, directors Kelly and Stanley Donen (MGM, 52)

right
Leslie Caron and Astaire (at right) in the 'Dancing Through Life' number from *Daddy Long Legs*, director Jean Negulesco (20th Century-Fox, 55)

below
Mitzi Gaynor in 'Gonna Wash That Man Right Outta My Hair' from *South Pacific*, director Joshua Logan (20th Century-Fox, 58)

below right
Dorothy Dandridge and Harry Belafonte in *Carmen Jones*, director Otto Preminger (20th Century-Fox, 54)

Yul Brynner (left), Rita
Moreno, Deborah Kerr and
Rex Thompson in *The King
and I*, director Walter Lang
(20th Century-Fox, 56)

below left
Doris Day and John Raitt in
The Pajama Game, director
Stanley Donen (Warners, 57)

below
Judy Garland in *A Star Is
Born*, director George Cukor
(Warners, 54)

Perhaps Doris Day's particular charm was not
suited to these vehicles. She found her forte in a
particular type of light comedy in which she
generally played a prim career girl who sublimates
her sexual drive in her job until she comes up
against a hunk whom she at first resists, then falls
for. There is a complicated misunderstanding and
they fall out; lastly, comes the tender reconciliation
with her yielding but *within* the vows of marriage.

Teacher's Pet (58), opposite Clark Gable, provided the blueprint. In 1959 came the first biggie,
Pillow Talk, in which she pits her wits and virginity

against a quintessentially Fifties heart-throb, Rock Hudson. They teamed again for *Lover Come Back* (62) and once more for *Send Me No Flowers* (64). But Miss Day was rather promiscuous in her choice of screen partners, deserting Hudson for Cary Grant (*That Touch of Mink*, 62), James Garner (*The Thrill of It All* and *Move Over Darling*, both 63) and Rod Taylor (*Do Not Disturb*, 65).

The series probably works best when big, bashful-grinning Rock was the man in her life. He had looked set for a modest career as a cleaner-cut Victor Mature, two-fisting his way through actioners. And that's what he did, with the exception of a weepie, *Magnificent Obsession* (54), until George Stevens decided that he too might be able to stretch himself in *Giant* (56). He did stretch to almost good acting and stepped up the league; he

top
Doris Day in *Calamity Jane*, director David Butler (Warners, 53)

above
Sinatra and Kim Novak in *Pal Joey*, director George Sidney (Columbia, 57)

above right
Rock Hudson and Jane Wyman in *Magnificent Obsession*, director Douglas Sirk (Universal, 54)

right
Hudson with Doris Day and Nick Adams in *Pillow Talk*, director Michael Gordon (Universal, 59)

still made actioners but they had more class. He even took a crack at Hemingway in the remake of *A Farewell to Arms* (57) but his efforts could not match Gary Cooper's in the 1932 version. *Pillow Talk* showed he had a pleasing flair for comedy and probably saved him from going the way of many beefcake actors.

'Beefcake', that was what new stars had to be, although many of them acted like hamburgers. However, acting was usually felt to be less important than showing a well-developed set of pectorals when the script called for the male lead to take his shirt off. Some 'actors' like Steve Reeves and Jeff Chandler did not graduate above this but Robert Mitchum, Tony Curtis, Kirk Douglas and Burt Lancaster, who were all required to ripple their biceps, moved on to better things.

Mitchum was perhaps the unluckiest; he worked steadily during the decade but got bogged down in material that wasn't worthy of his talents. This was partly his own fault; he had a no-nonsense approach to his work which prompted him to look at the salary before the script. He should have followed in Bogart's footsteps and some of his earlier work like *The Story of GI Joe* (45), *Crossfire* (47) and *The Big Steal* (49) proved he was capable of it. But although he made at least 25 films in the Fifties most of them are best forgotten. He could elevate an average film when inclined to, as he proved in *Macao* (52), *River of No Return* (54) and *Heaven Knows Mr Allison* (57), but he usually felt he was doing enough by strolling through a film with that unmistakable walk.

However, one of his Fifties films, *Night of the Hunter* (55), stands out above the rest. Directed by Charles Laughton, it has Mitchum as a homicidal preacher searching for a cache of money and terrorizing the people who stand between him and it. He delivers a performance full of evil and menace in a film which is unusually dark and sinister. It's to be regretted that Mitchum didn't push himself more often. His three contemporaries did extend themselves and all became big stars and competent actors.

Lancaster was often over-ambitious as an actor as witnessed by his workmanlike but rather forced performances in *Come Back Little Sheba* (52), *The Rose Tattoo* (55) and *Separate Tables* (58); he excelled when the part suited his personality as in *From Here to Eternity* (53), *Vera Cruz* (54), a superior Western in which he flashes his amazing teeth to alarming effect as the crooked partner of Gary Cooper, and *The Sweet Smell of Success* (57), where he played a corruptible columnist. He certainly

Robert Mitchum: (*top*) with Jane Russell in *Macao*, director Josef von Sternberg (RKO, 52); (*above*) in *Night of the Hunter*, director Charles Laughton (United Artists, 55); and (*left*) with Deborah Kerr in *Heaven Knows Mr Allison*, director John Huston (20th Century-Fox, 57)

Burt Lancaster: (*top left*)
with Tony Curtis, Katy
Jurado and Sidney James
(right) in *Trapeze*, director
Carol Reed (United Artists,
56); (*top right*) in *Come Back
Little Sheba*, director Daniel
Mann (Paramount, 52);
(*above*) with Wendy Hiller in
Separate Tables, director
Delbert Mann (United
Artists, 58)

above right
Bogart in *The Caine Mutiny*,
director Edward Dmytryk
(Columbia, 54)

right
Fredric March in *Death of
a Salesman*, director Laslo
Benedek (Columbia, 52)

reached beyond himself as the director of *The Kentuckian* (55) but has fulfilled his ambitions as an independent producer.

The studios might be in decline, but the independents were flourishing. Stanley Kramer – who made *Death of a Salesman* (52), *High Noon* (52), *The Wild One* (54), *The Caine Mutiny* (54) and *On the Beach* (59) among many others during the decade – and Otto Preminger had scored well. Lancaster was quick to the trend, forming Hecht-Hill-Lancaster Productions, which not only set up several of his own movies but two that were to garner a great deal of praise, *Marty* (55) and *The Bachelor Party* (57). Both were Paddy Chayevsky scripts and both were examples of what the Americans could do in adapting the Italian neo-realist style.

The Bachelor Party follows a group of men boozing their way through a stag party, the drink stripping away the bonhomie and revealing each man's disappointments. *Marty* was about a butcher reaching his thirties and resigning himself to loveless bachelorhood before finding a girl and being torn between her and his traditional Italian roots.

Kirk Douglas: (*right*) in
The Vikings, director Richard
Fleischer (United Artists,
58); (*below*) with George
MacCready in *Detective
Story*, director William
Wyler (Paramount, 51);
and (*below right*) in *Paths of
Glory*, director Stanley
Kubrick (United Artists, 57)

Marty has been described as 'the smallest picture ever to win an Oscar'; it was made for a pittance – $350,000 – and is probably the closest the American cinema ever came to the spirit and style of the neo-realists. Ernest Borgnine won the Best Actor Oscar for his fine, warm, sensitive performance.

(Borgnine was seldom given such a chance to star. His long and fruitful career was grounded on contributing sterling supporting performances in some excellent films – *From Here to Eternity* (53), *Bad Day at Black Rock* (54) and *The Best Things in Life Are Free* (56) – and others of lesser quality but considerable success like *The Vikings* (58), *The Dirty Dozen* (67) and *The Wild Bunch* (69) among many, many others. Never quite a star, but always worth watching.)

Kirk Douglas resembled Lancaster in several respects – they both had the teeth and the dimple for starters. They appeared together fairly often and very competitively; indeed, director John Frankenheimer once said that Douglas has 'wanted to be Burt Lancaster all his life'. And Douglas, like Lancaster, set up his own production company. It was not quite so successful, although it turned out two of the better epics, *The Vikings* (58) and *Spartacus* (60).

He had also done his share of action pics but had always shown a pushy cockiness (evident on screen) in extending his career. Although he could tote a gun or thrust a broadsword with the best of them, he was also very effective as a heel – the gutter journalist in *Ace in the Hole* (51, also known as *The Big Carnival*), the obsessive cop in the excellent *Detective Story* (51, William Wyler breaking convention and showing the ambivalent, unglamorous face of police work), and the shitty film producer in *The Bad and the Beautiful* (52, in which Vincente Minnelli has a rare swipe at Hollywood mores). Occasionally he took on parts that led him riskily to the edge of his range and even beyond. He attempted too much as van Gogh in *Lust for Life* (56); the physical resemblance was remarkable and he could be crazy when needed but he lacked the subtlety to portray the agonized artist. However, he was tremendous in a truly excellent film, Stanley Kubrick's *Paths of Glory* (57).

Paths of Glory has been called the best film of the Fifties, the best war film (anti-war, actually anti-politics-of-war), and one of the best films in any category. It is powerful, moving and thought-provoking and, in its reality, its closeness to its

subject, its lack of didacticism, it is one of the most disturbing and genuinely distressing films ever made.

Set during the First World War and based on fact, it concerns a group of French generals' decision to shoot dozens of their own men following a pointless and disastrous attack on a German position. Some disgusting haggling reduces the number to three, chosen at random. Their commander, Colonel Dax (Douglas), is appalled and strenuously pleads for their lives, defending them at the court martial. It is inevitable that he loses. The men are executed with great ritual, one, who is wounded, being carried to the stake on a stretcher.

Douglas's performance, amid many in a cast of unusual excellence, could hardly be bettered.

was good in *The Outsider* (61), as Ira Hayes, the Indian Marine who helped raised the flag on Iwo Jima, and chillingly convincing as the psychopath in *The Boston Strangler* (68), but the best memory is of him sitting on a beach, overdressed in blazer and flannels, persuading in those clipped Grant tones a none-too-bright Marilyn Monroe that he not only owns the yacht moored in front of them but an oil company as well.

Curtis described making love to Marilyn Monroe

Neither the film nor the principals involved in it were nominated for Academy awards, most of which went to a glossier, less cynical film – itself excellent, often brilliant – which took an oblique view of war and its 'heroics': *The Bridge on the River Kwai*.

Tony Curtis never got a chance like that given to Douglas but he did fight his way out of a lot of dross to show that he was better than the studios would credit. He started as a 'face' actor, and for the first few years he was unrelievedly awful. To be fair, he was given some awful material. He wasn't bad as and in *Houdini* (53), did well enough in *Trapeze* (56), very well in *The Sweet Smell of Success* (57) as a toadying press agent, cut a fine figure in *The Vikings* (58), was far from disgraced by Sidney Poitier – they were escaping convicts chained together – in *The Defiant Ones* (58), and really showed what he could do right at the end of the decade in one of the funniest, fastest-paced, most enjoyable comedies to come out of Hollywood: *Some Like It Hot* (59).

It's never easy acting comedy with such a consummate artist as Jack Lemmon and both had to be at their peak if they weren't to lose the whole film to Marilyn Monroe. The glory of *Some Like It Hot* is that everything works; there are few surer writers and directors of comedy than Billy Wilder, who somehow manages to keep this manic movie within reasonable bounds.

The main joke is a drag gag – Lemmon and Curtis have to disguise themselves as women and join an all-girl band to escape the hoodlums who are out to murder them – but Curtis is even funnier when he deserts his frock, dresses as a shy, impotent playboy and, assuming a wicked impression of Cary Grant's voice, attempts to seduce Monroe. He had all too few opportunities to show his paces – he

up or making up scurrilous 'facts' about her life. She was the last and the greatest of that Hollywood star personality – the sex symbol. The Fifties were as much hers as they were Brando's, and she became probably the most famous woman of her generation.

Marilyn Monroe was one of those few people the camera loves; it could not treat her unflatteringly but it could also not disguise that every so often the eyes showed a bewildered, unloved little girl who sought affection, needed reassurance, feared rejection. She was loved by millions in public but seemed unable to find a deeper love in private. 'A sex symbol is a thing,' she said. 'I hate being a thing.'

In her brief career Monroe made 30 films from *Dangerous Years* in 1947 to *Something's Got to Give*, her last, unfinished picture. In the first dozen or so she was just one more starlet who wiggles on, is ogled and wiggles off. However, she had a small but telling part in John Huston's gripping thriller *The Asphalt Jungle* (50), and another small but reasonably telling part in Joseph Mankiewicz's elegant, caustic comedy, *All About Eve* (50, in a cast that included Bette Davis, George Sanders, Celeste Holm and a rich assortment of stalwarts at the top of their form). She was attracting notice, more, it has to be said, for her beauty than her acting ability but, at that stage, it did not matter – the publicity mills were grinding behind her. She got a chance to act – and her first co-star billing – in a drama, *Don't Bother to Knock* (52), as a deranged baby-sitter. In retrospect she shows little ability but the sight of her as a deeply confused young woman is an unhappy portent.

Hollywood now had a rising star but didn't know what to do with her. In fact, her forte was for undemanding comedy. Howard Hawks put her into *Monkey Business* (52) with Cary Grant but, although likeable and amusing enough, it was a poor example of Hawks's brilliance with crazy comedy and again she was little more than decoration. By the time of *Niagara* (52) her name and image were bigger than the demands of the part. Hawks tried again, to better effect, with *Gentlemen Prefer Blondes* (53), in which she was a diamond-digger opposite Jane Russell, another star whose success depended more on her quite phenomenal physical attributes (shown

Monroe in early roles: (*below*) with Cary Grant in *Monkey Business*, director Howard Hawks (20th Century-Fox, 52), and (*below right*) with Louis Calhern in *The Asphalt Jungle*, director John Huston (MGM, 50)

– or rather, for she steamily seduced him in the movie, being made love to by her – as 'like kissing Hitler'. A remark which, if she ever read it, must have hurt this most vulnerable, insecure and defenceless of sex symbols. So much has been said about Marilyn Monroe. Since her pathetic death in 1962 a distasteful industry has thrived on digging

Monroe emergent: (*left*) in *How to Marry a Millionaire*, director Jean Negulesco (20th Century-Fox, 53); (*below left*) with Joseph Cotten in *Niagara*, director Henry Hathaway (20th Century-Fox, 52); and (*below*) with Jane Russell in *Gentlemen Prefer Blondes*, director Howard Hawks (20th Century-Fox, 53)

to even greater effect by the bra Howard Hughes had designed for her when he literally built her into stardom in the Forties). The next, *How To Marry A Millionaire* (53), was not at all dissimilar; this time three gold-diggers – the others were Betty Grable and Lauren Bacall – try to hook wealthy men.

The River of No Return (54) would not be remembered at all were it not for the stars (her co-star was Mitchum), but *There's No Business Like Show Business* (54) does not deserve recalling. It's one of the direst musicals ever made despite the stars, who included Ethel Merman, Donald O'Connor, Mitzi Gaynor and Johnnie Ray. No matter, she was now very, very big, her popularity enhanced by her

Monroe triumphant: (*right*) in *Bus Stop*, with Don Murray, director Joshua Logan (20th Century-Fox, 56), and (*below*) in *Some Like It Hot* with Tony Curtis (left) and Jack Lemmon, director Billy Wilder (United Artists, 59)

marriage to all-American baseball hero Joe di Maggio. However, success was starting to bring its problems. She was already sick of the roles she was getting and beginning to display the neuroses that would dog her later years. There were rows on set, there were walk-outs, there were refusals to appear in what she considered unworthy films. She was, incidentally, almost certainly correct in her latter attitude.

Ironically, when she won a better role in a better film it contributed to her personal unhappiness. Billy Wilder, that sly humorist, put her into a satire on marital infidelity, *The Seven Year Itch* (55), in which she is the object of lust for Tom Ewell, a man who is feeling the restrictions of seven years of married life during a sweltering New York summer. It was funny and, although many of the jokes do use Monroe as a sex object, the lampoon is as much against the Ewell character. One scene called for her to stand over a street ventilation grill, letting the air from it blow up her skirt. When this sequence was filmed, a huge crowd gathered and gawped lovingly as MM's skirt blew up around her shoulders in take after take. Di Maggio, also on hand, was disgusted by the way his wife had become public property and stormed off. The marriage shuddered to an end.

Desperate to prove herself to herself and to others who merely regarded her as a dumb blonde, she went to the Actors' Studio in New York and married the US's foremost intellectual playwright, Arthur Miller. Briefly things seemed to be going her way. Her next movie, *Bus Stop* (56), was directed by Joshua Logan and gave her a chance to act, especially as Cherie, the small-time cabaret singer, draws parallels with her own dilemma – the object of male fantasies who is insecure and unloved.

She yearned for more control of her own career, set up a production company, and through it made *The Prince and the Showgirl* (57). Now the world's brightest sex symbol had also captured the most respected figure in the British theatre – Laurence Olivier was to direct and star. It was not a happy collaboration, and it was not a particularly successful film. A frothy Rattigan Ruritanian romance gets bogged down, as if Olivier is faintly ashamed of the material and wants to give it more significance.

It needed the touch of a Wilder. Happily, the next had that – the brimming, good-hearted, hilarious *Some Like It Hot* (59). Monroe was at her most incandescent, and, on screen at least, there is no hint of the Hitlerian qualities Tony Curtis later implied. It was a hard film to follow and *Let's Make Love* (60) was not up to the mark, her increasing unhappiness not helped by the decline in her marriage to Miller and the fact that she was reportedly besotted with her co-star Yves Montand.

Her neuroses and insecurities were now increasing and not aided by a growing dependence on various drugs to wake her up and calm her down. Her last completed film was John Huston's *The Misfits* (61) from an Arthur Miller script. It all looked so right at the start – a good part, a great director, and Clark Gable and Montgomery Clift to play against. In the event, though an excellent, rather bleak film, it was also a doomed project; Gable died shortly after shooting was finished, Monroe was shortly to take her own life, Clift was suffering from alcoholism and would be dead by the end of the Sixties.

Personal despair was beginning to overwhelm Monroe. *Something's Got to Give* was abandoned because of her ill-health. She was undergoing mental treatment, and before long she felt unequal to the struggle. She dimmed her own radiance for ever in 1962, another victim of the pressures of movie stardom.

Marilyn Monroe was the most successful, the best-loved and the most tragic of a type which flowered briefly in the Fifties. They were women judged, it seemed, by the same criteria as battery chickens – by the breasts and legs. Blonde, bounteous girls tried to emulate the Monroe magic. Some are recalled today – Jayne Mansfield, Britain's answer Diana Dors, Sweden's contender Anita Ekberg. Most of the American contingent never rose above 'B' (or 'C' or 'D') pictures and their names mean little.

Three foreign ladies made rather more impression – Brigitte Bardot, the prototype sex kitten who, in the rather more liberal atmosphere of French films, thrilled by baring her breasts but contributed little of movie interest when plucked from her native soil. Gina Lollobrigida had the figure and the temperament but failed to make the transition to being taken seriously as her compatriot and great rival, Sophia Loren, did.

A growing star in Italy by the mid Fifties, it was inevitable that Loren would make an assault on Hollywood, but her first American movies were hardly demanding. She was rather lost in a big picture, *The Pride and the Passion* (57), where she had very strong competition from Cary Grant and Sinatra. Her next co-star was not so impressive; Alan Ladd was physically no match for her and she

had little to do in *Boy on a Dolphin* (57) beyond looking very seductive in some very wet clothes. She got a stab at something meatier as the object of lust for father and son (Burl Ives and Anthony Perkins) in *Desire under the Elms* (58) but wasn't truly ready for heavy-duty acting and proved rather better against Grant in a simple comedy, *Houseboat* (58). By then she was an international star but her output for the rest of the decade was no better than average.

It wasn't until 1961 that she showed 'em what she could do as a mother who suffers terribly with her daughter in war-riven Italy. The subject of *Two Women* was close to her heart and her experience, and her portrayal convincing enough to garner her a Best Actress Oscar. She then had a brief period of satisfying work – acting comedy nicely opposite Peter Sellers in *The Millionairess* (61) and managing not to be overwhelmed by either subject or co-star Charlton Heston in *El Cid* (61), by which time she was one of the screen's first ladies and seemed to grow more beautiful as she got older. However, like others whose fame exceeds the performances they are asked to give, she was frittered away in films that never demanded more of her than her lovely presence.

One lady of the era did not conform to the buxom

Monroe imitators: (*below*) Jayne Mansfield, with Tom Ewell, in *The Girl Can't Help It*, director Frank Tashlin (20th Century-Fox 56), and (*right*) Diana Dors, with Odile Versois (left), in *Passport to Shame*, director Alvin Rakoff (United Co-productions, 59)

Sophia Loren was a foreign challenger to Monroe: (*left*) with Cary Grant in *Houseboat*, director Jack Rose (Paramount, 58), and (*below left*) in *The Pride and the Passion*, director Stanley Kramer (United Artists, 57)

below
Audrey Hepburn with Fred Astaire in *Funny Face*, director Stanley Donen (Paramount, 57)

build of other female stars. Billy Wilder said of Audrey Hepburn, 'She may make bazooms a thing of the past.' She didn't, of course, but her gamine good looks established a more chic style on screen and she garnered praise and popularity in many movies, including *Roman Holiday* (53, for which she won Best Actress Oscar), *Funny Face* (57), *The Nun's Story* (59), and *Breakfast at Tiffany's* (61), and

left
Ingrid Bergman and Yul
Brynner in *Anastasia*,
director Anatole Litvak
(20th Century-Fox, 56)

opposite top
Rita Hayworth in *Miss Sadie
Thompson* with Charles
Bronson (far right),
director Curtis Bernhardt
(Columbia, 53)

below left
Gloria Swanson in *Sunset
Boulevard*, director Billy
Wilder (Paramount, 50)

below
Bette Davis (left), Thelma
Ritter and Celeste Holm in
All About Eve, director
Joseph Mankiewicz (20th
Century-Fox, 50)

she landed the coveted part of Liza Doolittle in *My Fair Lady* (64).

Lovely ladies enjoyed their following in the Fifties but so did a very unlovely menagerie of monsters, thanks to the craze for science fiction. The sci-fi boom had two broad themes – Planet Earth threatened by a bestiary of monsters, either extra-terrestrial aliens or mighty mutants, and man's attempts to go into space.

The first school started strongly in 1951 when Howard Hawks turned his considerable talent towards the genre. *The Thing* (aka *The Thing from Another World*) is a massive vegetable (played by James Arness), which is defrosted from its space capsule tomb on the polar icecap by some scientists. The plot, like that of most sci-fi shockers, is pretty crass but Hawks's direction – particularly his use of naturalistic, overlapping dialogue – elevates the movie to the near-credible and effectively grips the audience.

Thereinafter the world was menaced by a be-wildering array of Things which had dropped from the heavens, been wakened from their slumberings, or horribly mutated by atom-bomb tests. For the first time man had the capability to wipe himself and his planet out, and the vicarious horror of rampaging dinosaurs, like *The Beast from 20,000 Fathoms* (53) or *Godzilla* (54), or massive insects such as *Them* (53), *Tarantula* (55) and *The Black Scorpion* (57) may have assuaged the fear of real holocaust by more mundane but no less horrific means. Mostly the mere titles of the junk that was served up tell enough of the quality (and, indeed, the plot) to suffice: *The Man from Planet X* (51), *Phantom from Space* (53), *Killers from Space* (54),

Katharine Hepburn in
mid-career: (*opposite left*)
with Bogart in *The African
Queen*, director John Huston
(United Artists, 51), and
(*opposite right*) with Tracy in
Pat and Mike, director
George Cukor (MGM, 52)

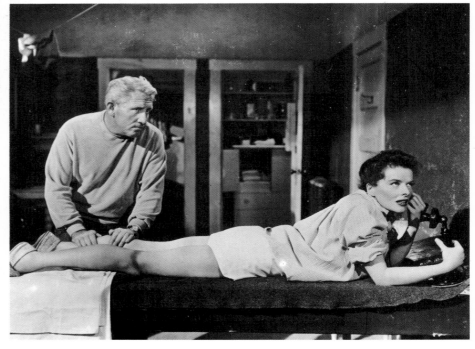

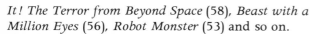

It! The Terror from Beyond Space (58), *Beast with a Million Eyes* (56), *Robot Monster* (53) and so on.

A few excursions into the genre rose above this dross. *The Creature from the Black Lagoon* (54) has its moments, and *The War of the Worlds* (53), based on the H.G. Wells fantasy but updated and translocated to twentieth-century California, grips and has a twist in that the Martians are not wiped out by man's ultimate weapon, the A-bomb, but by the common cold. Some had messages to disseminate, a few were even allegorical. Robert Wise's *The Day the Earth Stood Still* (51) has space emissaries who warn of the dangers of continued experimentation with the bomb; *The Incredible Shrinking Man* (57) shows the (fictitious) effects of radiation but proves that man, however tiny, can fight against a hostile environment. (This film is one of the best ever to use the well-worn midget/giant device, making the normal environment of the dwarfed man chillingly hostile as he fights attacks from spiders and cats.)

Perhaps the best of the bunch was *Invasion of the Body Snatchers* (56), in which Don Siegel tells a thrilling story expertly *and* makes a cleverly disguised political point. The story is of a small town where aliens have landed and planted vile seed pods which hatch out into replicas of the towns-

people; the clones destroy the real citizens, replacing them as near-automatons. It is grainy and grim, intelligently made and ends with a powerful sequence in which the hero flees town and runs towards the on-coming traffic, screaming, 'You're next! You're next!'

The political point he's making is that the American people are seemingly engaged in a headlong rush towards repressive conformity. The US was in the grip of the McCarthy witchhunts with the

Sci-fi boom: (*opposite, top left*) *The Beast from 20,000 Fathoms*, director Eugene Laurié (Warners, 53); (*opposite, bottom left*) Michael Rennie in *The Day the Earth Stood Still*, director Robert Wise (20th Century-Fox, 51); (*opposite, top right*) Julia Adams shrinks from *The Creature from the Black Lagoon*, director Jack Arnold (Universal, 54); (*opposite, bottom right*) Grant Williams as *The Incredible Shrinking Man*, director Jack Arnold (Universal, 57); (*right*) Jack Kelly (left foreground), Earl Holliman, Warren Stevens and Leslie Nielsen in *The Forbidden Planet*, director Fred M. Wilcox (MGM, 56); and (*below*) Fred Astaire and Gregory Peck (right) in *On the Beach*, director Stanley Kramer (United Artists, 59)

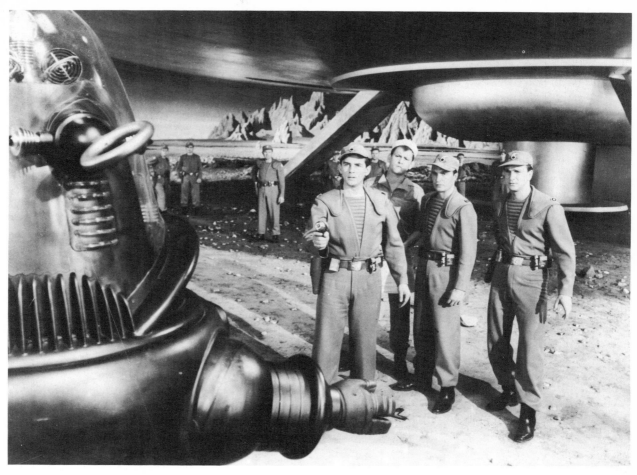

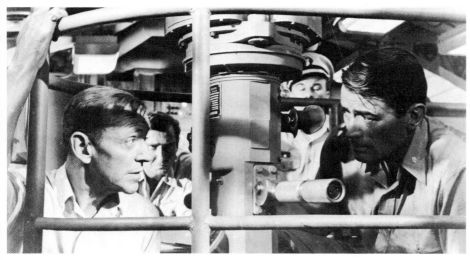

House Un-American Activities Committee investigating supposed Communist subversion in every part of American life and, especially, the movie industry. Hollywood proved its cowardice by virtually caving in and grovelling before the self-serving judges, brutally expunging anyone who was seen to be a Communist sympathizer (something that might be indicated by having a taste for, say, vodka). It also made a series of virulently anti-Communist (and very, very pro-FBI movies), which were little more than remakes of anti-Nazi films of the Forties. They scarcely deserve consideration but among the more frenetically rabid of the day were *I Married a Communist* and *My Son John* (both 49), *I Was a Communist for the FBI* (51) and *The Red Menace* (52).

Not everyone joined in the witchhunt. Many were shocked by the methods used, and Bogart and Bacall, Gene Kelly, John Huston, Danny Kaye and others chartered a plane and flew to Washington to protest. We'll never know how many fellow travellers there were in Hollywood; undoubtedly some people had sympathy for Communist ideals, many had admiration for Russia. Some, including a broken Larry Parks who had been a big hit in the *Al Jolson Story* (46), confessed, probably under extreme pressure, and were blacklisted. John Garfield, who simply refused to give names of friends who might be Communist, was outcast, and the rejection is thought to have contributed to his early death. Some went into self-exile – directors Jules Dassin, John Berry and Joseph Losey took off for the liberal atmosphere of Europe. And others, the 'Hollywood Ten', became scapegoats: these writers, producers and directors refused to say whether they were Communists and, as a result, were given prison sentences and were unable to work (except under pseudonyms or by others 'fronting' for them) for several years.

At the time, the United States and its mouthpiece, Hollywood, seemed to see threats from every corner. If it wasn't the Commies, then it was the young who were about to destroy the Land of the Free. Sometimes, of course, it was the two working in conjunction for, after all, what was rock & roll if not a Communist plot to subvert the morals of the nation's youth? Look at *The Blackboard Jungle* (55), which showed the reaction of a bunch of juvenile delinquents in a rough school to their well-meaning teacher (Glenn Ford). They smash all his jazz classics and prefer the raucous rubbish which

142

shrieks stridently over the credits. (The song was 'Rock Around The Clock', performed by Bill Haley and the Comets.)

The Hollywood moguls may not have approved of the music but they saw a few bucks in it and quickly rushed Bill Haley into his own movie called, of course, *Rock Around the Clock* (56). Shoddy it was, but for teens it had two great advantages: it was probably the first film ever made just for them and it featured rock & rollers in between the so-called plot and acting – Haley, the Platters, Freddie Bell and the Bellboys and others. Teens embraced it, some too enthusiastically if you believe press stories which reported that they rioted and smashed up cinemas.

More of the same was called for and *Don't Knock*

the Rock – cheaper, quicker, shoddier – appeared in 1957. *The Girl Can't Help It* (56) was an improvement on both. It had a reasonably strong and really quite amusing storyline revolving around Tom Ewell's attempt to make Jayne Mansfield into a star, it was in colour, and it presented its rock stars – Fats Domino, Little Richard, Gene Vincent, the Platters, Eddie Cochran, Julie London – in an even more flattering light.

In the meantime, rock & roll had created its first superstar: Elvis Presley. It was not long before he turned to Hollywood and wrung welcome dollars from the new audience it had discovered. Presley's first four movies – *Love Me Tender* (56), *Loving You* (57), *Jailhouse Rock* (57) and *King Creole* (58) – were not at all bad. They had reasonably coherent plots, were packed with good, occasionally great, songs and showed evidence of craftsmanship. It was also

opposite top
Walt Disney's *Sleeping Beauty* (59)

opposite, bottom left
Sidney Poitier (second from left) in *The Blackboard Jungle*, director Richard Brooks (MGM, 55)

Presley 'acting': (*opposite, bottom right*) in *Love Me Tender*, director Robert Webb (20th Century-Fox, 56); in (*top left*) *King Creole* with Vic Morrow (right), director Michael Curtiz (Paramount, 58); and (*above*) in *Loving You*, director Hal Kanter (Paramount, 57)

left
Elizabeth Taylor in *Cat on a Hot Tin Roof*, director Richard Brooks (MGM, 58)

Paul Newman (right) and John Dehner (centre) in *The Left-Handed Gun*, director Arthur Penn (Warners, 58)

evident that, while no Brando, Presley had considerable screen presence, prowled like a panther and could hold his own by sheer force of personality and sex appeal.

His films were big box-office and it seemed just possible that when he inevitably grew out of rock & rolling he would be a screen star of some magnitude. Unfortunately, after his return from army service in 1960, he apparently lost interest; the first few – *GI Blues* (60), *Flaming Star* (60) and *Wild in the Country* (61) – showed promise but the rest soon became production-line songs-girls-exotic-location schlock and Presley, who had looked as if he would advance the progress of rock movies, actually succeeded in setting them back several years.

Indifference halted Presley's burgeoning career, but another young man stuck to his task and even overcame a disastrous start in *The Silver Chalice* (54). Paul Newman was destined to become one of the top movie stars in the world. If not THE top movie star. By the Seventies he was one of that elite band – the 'bankable' star. These were the true rarities whose names in very difficult financial times could attract money into a motion-picture venture by virtue of their box-office appeal. He has been described as the last movie star, the last of the people who were stars first and actors only second. It's arguable; what about Redford, what about Eastwood, what about Bronson? Nevertheless, he is probably the last of a generation of stars whose popularity stretches back to the Fifties and remained unchallenged into the late Seventies.

He was described in the mid Fifties as an 'actor's actor', a new Brando. In fact, he emerged as a 'personality actor': he almost always turned in a creditable performance but his success owed a great deal to his good looks and his self-depreciating humour.

After his debacle in that biblical epic, he turned to a role which suited him far better, a biopic of the Depression boxer Rocky Graziano in *Somebody Up There Likes Me* (56). Then came a hiccough as he was miscast in three films until he found a smallish niche as young men who weren't exactly angry but

rather annoyed, starting with the steamy *Long Hot Summer* (58). He then played Billy the Kid in *The Left-Handed Gun* (58), Arthur Penn's pseudo-psychological study of the outlaw/hoodlum, and returned to the frustrated young man role in *Cat on a Hot Tin Roof* (58), in which his wife wonders why he doesn't sleep with her. He is homosexual – of course Hollywood dare not say it – but he scored another hit and by the end of the decade he was poised to reach the heights of stardom.

Exodus (60) was all-round big: big story, big box-office, big cast, among which Newman got his fair share of attention. Then came the movie that confirmed the promise. As Fast Eddie Felson, the pool-room shark in *The Hustler* (61), he shows the intense hunger of a driven man. Nothing matters more than being proved the best in his sleazy world. His performance delineated the characterization for *Hud* (63), the film that crashed him into the top echelon.

Hud Bannon was a pretty unlikeable character; he pushed too hard, he came on too strong. He was, strangely, a very typical Fifties anti-hero, who somehow had enormous appeal for the youth of the Sixties. Perhaps they recognized some truth in his philosophy: 'The world's so full of crap, a man's going to get into it sooner or later, whether he's careful or not.' Hud was an older version of the James Dean figure and Newman was very nearly exactly right for it, the only flaw being that his innate charm made him such an appealing heel.

Now there was no stopping Newman. The films that followed were so-so. *The Prize* (63) was a good Hitchcockian thriller, *Torn Curtain* (66) was a below par thriller from Hitchcock, and in between there were three which didn't make the grade. But in 1966 he hit form again in and as *Harper* (*The Moving Target* in GB), a world-weary private eye, followed with *Hombre* (67) as a half-breed Indian in a quirky Western, and then came up with another definitively Newman characterization: *Cool Hand Luke* (67). The oddball vandal – he decapitates parking meters when drunk – is sent to a brutal penitentiary and refuses to conform. His revolt starts small and escalates (as the punishments become more severe) until he breaks out and is remorselessly hunted to his death.

By the end of the Sixties he was virtually unassailable but was becoming increasingly bored with stardom and acting. He turned to directing – scoring a critical success with *Rachel, Rachel* (68), starring his wife Joanne Woodward – and, like so many others at his level, started taking control of his movies, two of which pushed him into whatever is the next magnitude of superstardom – *Butch Cassidy and the Sundance Kid* (69) and *The Sting* (73), both in happy partnership with Robert Redford. Both were amiable tales of amiable men, although *Cassidy* with its inevitably bloody ending was probably the better. *Cassidy* caught the public imagination; it was a different sort of Western, rather soft-centred, occasionally wearying (particularly the bicycling sequence), but obviously so enjoyable to make that it infected the audience.

He appeared in *The Towering Inferno* (74), one of

Burgeoning Elizabeth Taylor: (*opposite top*) with Spencer Tracy and Joan Bennett in *Father of the Bride*, director Vincente Minnelli (MGM, 50), and (*opposite bottom*) in *Suddenly Last Summer*, director Joseph Mankiewicz (Columbia, 59)

the better disaster movies, with his nearest rival for international popularity, Steve McQueen, and then did a movie that *was* a disaster, *Buffalo Bill and the Indians* (76). By the Eighties, Newman was perhaps the best actor never to have won an Oscar. It probably didn't bother him as he seemed to have gone into semi-retirement. Perhaps there was very little for him left to do.

The same might be said of Elizabeth Taylor, who was undeniably the last of the old-fashioned movie queens. Her long career is probably best remembered for its marital dramas. She started as a child star in the Forties, capturing the affection in *National Velvet* (44) and *Little Women* (49), and progressed into the Fifties and adult roles via *Father of the Bride* (50, a delightful comedy which had Spencer Tracy at his bewildered, well-meaning best). She graduated to sexier, more full-blooded roles in *A Place in the Sun* (51) and then *Giant* (56), by which time she had married Mike Todd, the extrovert showman who was one of the most successful independent producers of the day and who had cleaned up with the massive *Around the World in Eighty Days* (56). With this marriage, her third, she seemed to blossom into ripe sexuality – Burton described her breasts as 'apocalyptic' – and she was ready to take on some more challenging roles.

They came her way: Maggie the rejected wife in *Cat on a Hot Tin Roof* (58); another excursion into Tennessee Williams's world – this time less sanitized – in *Suddenly Last Summer* (59); and as a whore in *Butterfield 8* (60), for which she won her first Oscar. By now she was the world's top female screen star and attracting some attention as an actress, although there is a suspicion that her Oscar was awarded less on merit than for her life-or-death battle against pneumonia.

But even she couldn't turn *Cleopatra* (62) into a box-office hit. In the entire history of the movies there had been no greater fiasco. It should have taken weeks to make; it took years. She should have earned $125,000, which after expenses, 10% take of the gross, and other bits and bobs would have parleyed up to a cool $1 million; she earned twice that, thanks to the inordinate delays. It's doubtful whether anyone can remember the original budget but it eventually came in at $44 million (to that point the most expensive movie Hollywood had ever made). Little of this would be remarkable if it had stood any chance of recouping. Or if it had been even a halfway decent picture. It wasn't.

The public probably remember *Cleopatra* for one thing – it was the vehicle for the most publicized romance of the day, the love affair between Elizabeth Taylor and Richard Burton. For all the evident passion between the two, none of it shows on the screen. When they ultimately disengaged themselves from their partners and regularized their relationship, Burton and Taylor became the most celebrated husband and wife in movie history since Pickford and Fairbanks. And, like their predecessors, they emerged as movie royalty, progressing through the world, distributing largesse. They also made films. A couple weren't bad: *Who's*

Afraid of Virginia Woolf? (66), in which she played a vicious, blowsy, gin-soaked harridan and for which she won another Oscar, and *The Taming of the Shrew* (67) were really rather good. But *The Sandpiper* (65), *The Comedians* (67), *Boom!* (68) and *Hammersmith Is Out* (72) were totally unworthy of them and the $1 million salary they were allegedly commanding – *each*!

The on-off marriage broke up amid spectacular rows and even more spectacular reconciliations and by the end of the Seventies Elizabeth Taylor had retired from the screen and settled down with her seventh or eighth husband, declaring there would be no more movies, no more divorces.

Hollywood was not the only film industry to be in a state of financial chaos and occasional creative panic during the decade. The other major English-language industry, that in Britain, was also experiencing problems. Just after the war there had been nearly 5000 cinemas in Great Britain; by 1960 1675 of them had gone and studios had had to close their doors too.

Other changes followed. The government introduced a new system of certifying films. The two broadest categories – 'U' for universal viewing and 'A' for adults or children accompanied by adults – remained but the old 'H' certificate (for Horrific, designed to keep children out of frightening films) was changed to 'X', a larger area of restriction, which acknowledged the more 'adult' (meaning sexier) themes being introduced into films. The first couple of 'X' films did not do good business and so producers and exhibitors decided to play safe with unadventurous movies designed for a family audience.

However, the tradition of British humour was maintained. The finest exponent was Ealing Studios. 'An Ealing Comedy' was a virtual guarantee that the film would be slyly satiric, usually showing ruggedly individual, often rather eccentric, characters in a battle of wits against insensitive bureaucracy. Post-war rationing and restrictions gave excellent plots for this sort of comic confrontation. *Whisky Galore* (48) pits wily Highlanders against customs officials as they fight to keep a cargo of Scotch which has been washed ashore; *Passport to Pimlico* (49) has a London borough turning itself into a state within a state; *The Man in the White Suit* (51) looks at how vested interests conspire to suppress a new product – an indestructible suiting material; *The Titfield Thunderbolt* (53) is concerned with the fight to keep an old railway line open.

All ripe subjects for gentle irony, as were the confusions of having a boys school and girls school billeted in the same building. *The Happiest Days of Your Life* (50) gave that consummate actor Alastair Sim a chance to be marvellously worried as the headmaster, and in 1954 in *The Belles of St Trinians* he shone again, but this time as a head*mistress* in charge of a school of nubile delinquents. Sim was just one of several British comic actors and actresses who turned in brilliant performances during the period. But two were so outstanding that they moved onto the international screen.

Alec Guinness, undoubtedly one of the country's

finest actors particularly in comic and/or character roles, had a marvellous decade, starting with *eight* characters of rich invention in Robert Hamer's cherished comedy of murder and manners, *Kind Hearts and Coronets* (49). He played Disraeli in *The Mudlark* (50) and then went outside the law in *The*

Lavender Hill Mob (51, he made another excursion into comic crime with *The Ladykillers* in 1955). He was the inventor in *The Man in the White Suit* (51) and then consolidated his reputation with a series of characterizations, mostly humorous, until David Lean cast him as the unbending British officer in *The Bridge on the River Kwai* (57), which won him an Oscar and international fame.

One of his cohorts in *The Ladykillers* had been a younger man who first made his reputation in British radio, as one of the Goons, and then switched to films, where he extended his seemingly limitless cast of characters, not infrequently playing several in the same movie.

Peter Sellers was good in *The Ladykillers*, better as the aged, broken-down projectionist of an aged broken-down cinema in *The Smallest Show on Earth* (57), brilliant in several roles in *The Naked Truth* (58), and probably reached his height as Fred

Kite, the bolshy shop steward in *I'm All Right, Jack* (59), an hilarious lampoon on labour relations. In the meantime, *The Mouse That Roared* (59), about a tiny state which declares war on the US, had caused a deal of interest there and Sellers's three parts were being noticed. By the decade's end he was on the brink of an international career, by the mid-Sixties an international star.

With a few notable exceptions, British comedy was restricted in appeal to the home market. The Americans had little taste for, or did not understand, the tit-and-bum, knockabout farce of the Carry On . . . series, which began with *Carry on Sergeant* (58) and continued through 27 others for about 20 years. Nor did foreign markets warm particularly to the shenanigans of young doctors who get into scrapes. *Doctor in the House* (54) led off with Dirk Bogarde, Kenneth More and James Robertson Justice and was so successful in Britain

British comedy: (*opposite top*) *The Titfield Thunderbolt*, director Charles Crichton (Ealing, 53); (*opposite bottom*) Alastair Sim in dual roles in *The Belles of St Trinians*, director Frank Launder (Launder-Gilliatt,54); (*below*) Dirk Bogarde and Brigitte Bardot in *Doctor at Sea*, director Ralph Thomas (Rank, 55)

that they continued (with some cast changes) through *Doctor at Sea* (55), which boasted foreign import Brigitte Bardot, *At Large* (57), *In Love* (60), and *In Distress* (63). By this last one, the man who had starred as Dr Simon Sparrow in all except *Doctor in Love* was thoroughly fed-up with the whole business and quit.

Dirk Bogarde was the most distinguished graduate of the Rank 'charm school'. This curious little enterprise had been started by J. Arthur (later Lord) Rank of the Rank Organisation, which, by the Fifties, had a near-monopoly of British cinema, in film production, and distribution and exhibition. Rank had set out with the intention of promulgating Christian virtues via the medium, and, as part of his policy, he hired young, good-looking, clean-cut actors and actresses and proceeded to build them into stars, making sure they smiled nicely, acted politely in public, and kept their names free from scandal. It was an irksome and not always successful training; most of his rising stars waned quickly and many did not do their best work (Bogarde being a prime example) or achieve most fame (Joan Collins, for instance) until they had broken away from its strictures.

But, by the end of the decade, there was a new spirit abroad in British and European films. No longer were film-makers content to keep their material safely within the bounds of the 'U' and 'A' certificates. They wanted to explore the adult themes that the 'X' category was invented to accommodate.

One British studio, Hammer, were not concerned so much with reflecting social trends as scaring the pants off people. Previously their principal product had been modest 'B' features and 'musical featurettes' showcasing pop stars, but they tried their hand at sci-fi with *The Quatermass Xperiment* (55, *The Creeping Unknown* in US) and then decided to return to a genre which had been largely neglected since the war – the good old horror pic. The first outing revived one of the great monsters and, with *The Curse of Frankenstein* (57), two new stars were brought into the chills-&-thrills business: Peter Cushing and Christopher Lee.

This was so successful that the next year they resuscitated the other arch-villain, Dracula (*Horror of Dracula* in US), again with Cushing and Lee. Before long Hammer were ringing every possible change: Frankenstein's monster and the vampire Count were frequently killed off and miraculously reappeared; *The Mummy* (59) walked again, once more with Lee and Cushing; the werewolf roamed in *Curse of . . .* (60) and so on and on, mostly in colour, through the Sixties, adding as they went more explicit sexuality and, occasionally, tempting declining stars to their roster – Tallulah Bankhead in *Fanatic* (65, *Die! Die! My Darling!* in US), Bette Davis in *The Nanny* (65) and *The Anniversary* (68), and Joan Fontaine in *The Witches* (66, *The Devil's Own* in US). They also captured some of the younger sex symbols, notably Ursula Andress for *She* (65) and Raquel Welch for the ludicrous *One Million Years BC* (66).

Hammer films were, by and large, cheap and

More British comedy:
(*opposite top*) *The Ladykillers*
with (left to right) Cecil Parker,
Danny Green, Herbert Lom,
Peter Sellers and Alec Guinness,
director Alexander Mackendrick
(Ealing, 55); (*opposite centre*)
I'm All Right, Jack with (left
to right) Sellers, Irene Handl,
Ian Carmichael and Liz Fraser,
director John Boulting (British
Lion, 59); (*opposite bottom*)
Genevieve with Kay Kendall and
Kenneth More, director Henry
Cornelius (Rank, 54); and (*left*)
Carry On Nurse with Kenneth
Connor (third from left),
Leslie Phillips and Kenneth
Williams, director Gerald Thomas
(Anglo-Amalgamated, 59)

Hammer horror: (*centre left*)
The Curse of Frankenstein, with
Christopher Lee and Peter
Cushing, director Terence Fisher
(57) and (*centre right*) Lee as
Dracula, director Fisher (58)

good at returning their investments, even attracting
a cult following in the States. The days were gone
when the British film industry attempted to gain a
foothold there by lavish spending. It was not
money that was going to recharge British films and
have an effect on Hollywood in the Sixties. It was
a new feeling, one which had started in London
with a stage play called 'Look Back in Anger' in
1956. The ripples from that were going to spread
wide in the next decade.

Angry young men: (*bottom left*)
Laurence Harvey and Simone
Signoret in *Room at the Top*,
director Jack Clayton (Remus,
58), and (*bottom right*) Mary Ure
(left), Richard Burton and Claire
Bloom in *Look Back in Anger*,
director Tony Richardson
(Woodfall, 59)

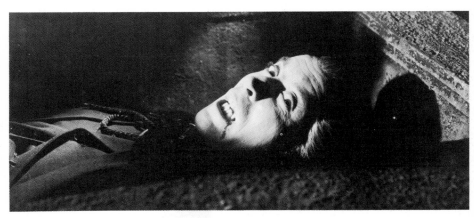

50s Oscars

YEAR	BEST FILM	BEST ACTOR	BEST ACTRESS
1950	*All About Eve/* 20th Century-Fox	Jose Ferrer/ *Cyrano de Bergerac*	Judy Holliday *Born Yesterday*
1951	*An American in Paris/* MGM	Humphrey Bogart/ *The African Queen*	Vivien Leigh/ *A Streetcar Named Desire*
1952	*The Greatest Show on Earth/* DeMille-Paramount	Gary Cooper/ *High Noon*	Shirley Booth/ *Come Back, Little Sheba*
1953	*From Here to Eternity/* Columbia	William Holden/ *Stalag 17*	Audrey Hepburn/ *Roman Holiday*
1954	*On the Waterfront/* Columbia	Marlon Brando/ *On the Waterfront*	Grace Kelly/ *The Country Girl*
1955	*Marty/* Hecht-Lancaster-UA	Ernest Borgnine/ *Marty*	Anna Magnani/ *The Rose Tattoo*
1956	*Around the World in 80 Days/* Todd-UA	Yul Brynner/ *The King and I*	Ingrid Bergman/ *Anastasia*
1957	*The Bridge on the River Kwai/* Columbia	Alec Guinness *The Bridge on the River Kwai*	Joanne Woodward/ *The Three Faces of Eve*
1958	*Gigi/* MGM	David Niven/ *Separate Tables*	Susan Hayward/ *I Want to Live!*
1959	*Ben Hur/* MGM	Charlton Heston/ *Ben Hur*	Simone Signoret/ *Room at the Top*

50s Oscars

BEST DIRECTOR	BEST SUPPORTING ACTOR	BEST SUPPORTING ACTRESS	YEAR
Joseph L. Mankiewicz/ *All About Eve*	George Sanders/ *All About Eve*	Josephine Hull/ *Harvey*	1950
George Stevens/ *A Place in the Sun*	Karl Malden/ *A Streetcar Named Desire*	Kim Hunter/ *A Streetcar Named Desire*	1951
John Ford/ *The Quiet Man*	Anthony Quinn/ *Viva Zapata!*	Gloria Grahame/ *The Bad and the Beautiful*	1952
Fred Zinnemann/ *From Here to Eternity*	Frank Sinatra/ *From Here to Eternity*	Donna Reed/ *From Here to Eternity*	1953
Elia Kazan/ *On the Waterfront*	Edmond O'Brien/ *The Barefoot Contessa*	Eva Marie Saint/ *On the Waterfront*	1954
Delbert Mann/ *Marty*	Jack Lemmon/ *Mister Roberts*	Jo Van Fleet/ *East of Eden*	1955
George Stevens/ *Giant*	Anthony Quinn/ *Lust for Life*	Dorothy Malone/ *Written on the Wind*	1956
David Lean/ *The Bridge on the River Kwai*	Red Buttons/ *Sayonara*	Miyoshi Umeki/ *Sayonara*	1957
Vincente Minnelli/ *Gigi*	Burl Ives/ *The Big Country*	Wendy Hiller/ *Separate Tables*	1958
William Wyler/ *Ben Hur*	Hugh Griffith/ *Ben Hur*	Shelley Winters/ *The Diary of Anne Frank*	1959

Award winners: (*opposite left*) Marlon Brando and Vivien Leigh in *A Streetcar Named Desire*, director Elia Kazan (Warners, 51); (*opposite right*) David Niven and Cantinflas in *Around the World in 80 Days*, directors Michael Anderson and Kevin McClory (United Artists, 56); (*above*) Burt Lancaster and Deborah Kerr in *From Here to Eternity*, director Fred Zinnemann (Columbia, 53); (*right*) Ernest Borgnine in *Marty*, director Delbert Mann (United Artists, 55)

the Sixties

below
Richard Harris and Rachel
Roberts in *This Sporting Life*,
director Lindsay Anderson
(Rank, 63)

bottom
Elsie Wagstaff, Frank Pettet
and Albert Finney (right) in
*Saturday Night and Sunday
Morning*, director Karel Reisz
(Bryanston/Woodfall, 60)

The ripples became a wave, the 'new wave' or *nouvelle vague*, a journalist's phrase devised to describe a movement of young directors in France. It started with a group of young cinema lovers who put together a magazine called Cahiers du Cinema, in which they overpraised the directors they admired – Hitchcock, Fritz Lang, Preminger, Nicholas Ray and others – and castigated those they thought were swept up by the impersonal, commercial grind of size and extravagance.

Simplicity was the key word: 'cheap films on simple subjects'. They scrounged the money to put their philosophy into action, and produced a string of films which returned to the basics. They were personal, they were spare, they were usually monochrome and they set great store on the creation of mood and ambiance.

The most influential members of the French new wave were François Truffaut, Jean-Luc Godard, Claude Chabrol, Louis Malle and Alain Resnais. But, although the French cinema may have been the most experimental and revolutionary of the period, it was not the only industry turning out fascinating, very cinematic (as opposed to blatantly commercial) work. Italy had commanding, sometimes perplexing, directors in Michelangelo Antonioni and Federico Fellini. And new forms of cinema had been erupting almost everywhere except Hollywood – in Sweden, in Poland, and in Japan, for example. All these film-makers eventually had an influence on the major film industry in the world, Hollywood. But the most direct input came, rather surprisingly, from Britain.

John Osborne's play, 'Look Back in Anger' had revolutionized British theatre, throwing out middle-class drawing-room comedy and replacing it with so-called 'kitchen-sink' dramas about so-called 'angry young men'. In fact, the plays – and novels and, later, films – followed many of the precepts of the French new wave. There were also young directors, some coming on in TV, who wanted to show 'the significance of the everyday' and, in the words of Lindsay Anderson, who directed *This Sporting Life* (63) set in the grimy North of England and centred around the life of a Rugby League player (Richard Harris) and his jagged relationship with his landlady (Rachel Roberts): they wanted '. . . to make people – ordinary people, not just Top People – feel their dignity and their importance.' A new breed of actors and actresses was emerging too, people like Harris, Albert Finney, Tom Courtenay, Rita Tushingham and Alan Bates, who came from working-class backgrounds and had not had the orotund training of the classical theatre. The people, the subjects, the style all converged at the same time.

Tony Richardson's *Look Back in Anger* (59, with Richard Burton as the original 'angry young man', Jimmy Porter) and Jack Clayton's *Room at the Top* (58, in which Laurence Harvey was the pushy grammar-school boy who was not beyond using his sex appeal to get ahead) led the way. Karel

Reisz continued the trend with *Saturday Night and Sunday Morning* (60), in which Finney as a raw factory lad, kicking against his dreary fate, conducts a disastrous affair with a married woman.

The major themes centred around youth, class and sex; they were franker, grittier, more intimate films than the British were wont to see but audiences recognized the reflection of their own lives. The cinema was not just an entertainment medium now; it could also be a chronicle of the times. In Richardson's *A Taste of Honey* (61) Rita Tushingham is an unmarried mother, got pregnant by her black boyfriend and helped by a young homosexual: three themes that were earlier unacceptable. In *Loneliness of a Long Distance Runner* (63) Richardson centres on a Borstal boy whose only talent is as an athlete – nobody would have put up a penny for such a 'depressing' story a few years before.

However, the grimness of the early Sixties in Britain quickly gave place to Swinging London, and before long directors were finding their subject matter elsewhere. Success breeds success and it is usually accompanied, at least in the film industry, by money. The men who had done so well on very little were soon being given bigger budgets to tackle wider subjects.

Tony Richardson, for example, came up with a dazzling, licentious costume comedy, *Tom Jones* (63), which equalled, nay outstripped, in vigour, beauty and bravado anything Hollywood could do. Schlesinger made a film about the morals of a permissive dolly bird – *Darling* (65) – which won its star, Julie Christie, an Oscar. He then put her into costume for a big, good-looking but patchy version of Thomas Hardy's classic novel *Far from the Madding Crowd* (67).

Soon Hollywood felt that British directors had something to offer. Schlesinger went off to make a

uniquely American film about homosexual hustlers in New York, *Midnight Cowboy* (69). And before long others were following him. Peter Yates, after a fairly short career in Britain which included a pop movie, *Summer Holiday* (62), helped change the American cop movie with *Bullitt* (68). John Boorman also started with a pop vehicle – *Catch Us If You Can* (65), built around the Dave Clark Five – and issued in a new era of brutality with Lee Marvin in *Point Blank* (67).

Although most directors defected to the West, one travelled the other way. Joseph Losey, an exile from the McCarthy era, hit brilliant form in Britain and made some outstanding films with a star who had long been waiting for such an opportunity – Dirk Bogarde, graduate of the Rank charm school.

Julie Christie and Dirk
Bogarde in *Darling*, director
John Schlesinger (Anglo-
Amalgamated, 65)

right
Albert Finney and Joyce
Redman in *Tom Jones*,
director Tony Richardson
(United Artists/Woodfall, 63)

far right
Noel Howlett and Dirk
Bogarde in *Victim*, director
Basil Dearden (Rank, 61)

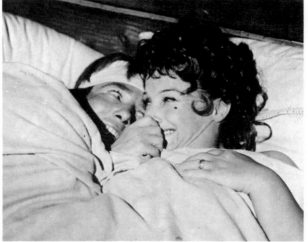

Bogarde had made a personal breakthrough into meatier material as a homosexual being blackmailed in *Victim* (61), one of the first films to look at the subject with a reasonable degree of honesty. The homosexual theme was more subtly treated in Losey's *The Servant* (63), an enigmatic film in which Bogarde played an ambivalent manservant who leads his master, James Fox, into decadent dependence on him. Director and star re-teamed for *King and Country* (64), which covered some of the same territory as *Paths of Glory* (57) and had Bogarde as an officer defending Tom Courtenay on a charge of desertion.

Bogarde then worked with Schlesinger on *Darling*, as one of Julie Christie's lovers, and helped Losey in a spoof of the comic-strip heroine *Modesty*

Blaise (66), which also starred Monica Vitti as Modesty and that archetypal British star of the decade, Terence Stamp. It was not one of their better collaborations. However, *Accident* (67) was worthier of both, though with a Harold Pinter script it tended towards the oblique. Bogarde as a university professor, one of whose students is killed, showed the ability to act through stillness – appearing to do little but conveying much – which won him such plaudits for *Death in Venice* (70). Their last venture of the decade, *The Damned* (69), was another of Losey's examinations of decadence, this time in Nazi Germany, but it lacked discipline and rather wasted Bogarde.

Although some of Losey's work was controversial, it did not meet the near-hysterical reaction accorded to the most idiosyncratic director of the period, Ken Russell. He, like Schlesinger, started in TV. His first try at cinema features was entirely untypical, a bawdy seaside comedy called *French Dressing* (63). Four years later he did a flashy, confusing job on Len Deighton's *Billion Dollar Brain* and returned to TV before going back to the big screen with a loving, very sensual, rather too prosey film of D.H. Lawrence's *Women in Love* (69), which garnered much attention for its explicit love scenes and the nude wrestling match between Alan Bates and Oliver Reed.

Next came *The Music Lovers* (70), a rampant, raunchy, disturbing and occasionally salacious view of the life and homosexuality of Tchaikovsky. There were several lapses of taste in it but nothing as compared to *The Devils* (71), which was a veritable orgy of visual outrageousness. All hell broke loose (no pun intended) and the critics were baying for Russell's blood. It was violent, tasteless, occasionally repellent, immensely thrilling and, in the director's own words, 'a harsh film about a harsh subject': the diabolic possession of a convent of nuns in seventeenth-century France.

Ever perverse, Russell turned for his next subject to a lightweight little musical by Sandy Wilson, *The Boyfriend* (71). A backstage musical of the old school which he glammed up with Busby Berkeley-type setpieces, it was a joyful, affectionate evocation of the Twenties and a loving spoof on Hollywood. On Russell went into the Seventies with *The Savage Messiah* (72), *Mahler* (74), a film version of The Who's rock opera *Tommy* (75), the supposed life of Liszt, *Lisztomania* (75), which was savaged even more than most of his work, and *Valentino* (77). More often loathed than loved, Russell was always extraordinary, one of the most daring directors of a daring period.

Billion Dollar Brain, Russell's second film, was but one in a welter of movies about spies, a subgenre that was immensely popular in the Sixties. The progenitor of the cult was, of course, James

Bond. The series based around the Ian Fleming novels and starring Sean Connery (in six) was a phenomenon. Bond was a hero of the time, smooth,

Male relationships: (*above*) Dirk Bogarde and James Fox in *The Servant*, director Joseph Losey (Elstree, 63); (*far left*) Bogarde and Michael York in *Accident*, director Losey (London Independent Producers, 67); and (*left*) Oliver Reed and Alan Bates (right) in *Women in Love*, director Ken Russell (United Artists, 69)

suave, sophisticated but given to flashes of sadism and sexual amorality of a prodigious order. He could cope in any situation and usually emerged from whatever threat – be it potential disembowelling by a laser beam or decapitation by a steel-brimmed bowler – with a laconic sense of humour and a beautiful, busty bird on his arm.

Dr No (62) commenced the run and many carped that Connery was entirely miscast as the public-school clubman hero. His strong working-class Scottish burr and burly physique seemed to be at odds with the upper-crust, discerning, rather willowy character of the books. The critics may have been right but the public did not agree. They

took to Connery/Bond instantly and followed him devotedly through *From Russia with Love* (63), *Goldfinger* (64), *Thunderball* (65) and *You Only Live Twice* (67), each grossing more than the one before and making an enormous impact in the States.

Connery wearied of the typecasting and ducked out of *On Her Majesty's Secret Service* (69), his hand-crafted shoes being inadequately filled by ex-model George Lazenby. Connery returned, at a massive fee said to be $1,200,000, to do *Diamonds Are Forever* (71) and was replaced, somewhat more effectively, by Roger Moore, who debuted with *Live and Let Die* (73). By now the series, although still incredibly successful, had lost its style, the

James Bond: (*right*) Sean Connery and Harold Sakata in *Goldfinger*, director Guy Hamilton (United Artists/Eon, 64), and (*below*) Connery and Ursula Andress in *Dr No*, director Terence Young (United Artists/Eon, 62)

Rival spies: (*below right*) Richard Burton and Oskar Werner (right) in *The Spy Who Came in from the Cold*, director Martin Ritt (Paramount, 65); (*opposite top*) Michael Caine in *The Ipcress File*, director Sidney J. Furie (Rank, 65), and (*opposite, bottom right*) James Coburn in *In Like Flint*, director Gordon Douglas (20th Century-Fox, 67)

opposite centre
Caine as lecher with Shelley Winters in *Alfie*, director Lewis Gilbert (Paramount, 66)

156

producers turning Bond into a puppet Actionman surrounded by increasingly unlikely villains and overwhelmed by ever more complex technology. Bond continued through the Seventies but remained, essentially, a hero of the Sixties.

No other spy ever touched Bond for popularity, although Harry Palmer had a good stab. He was the hero (nameless in the novels) created by Len Deighton and the antithesis of stiff upper-lipped Bond. Palmer, excellently played by Michael Caine, who had just broken through from almost total anonymity in *Zulu* (63), was bolshy and working class, viewing his job through jaundiced eyes and heavy spectacles. *The Ipcress File* (65) was tougher and more realistic than the Bond films, far less glamorous and more sardonic. It really established Caine, who went on to cement his cocky Cockney persona (this time as a heel who loves and leaves women) in a risqué morality tale, *Alfie* (66). Less gimmicky than the Bond series, the Palmer sagas only ran to two other, less satisfying, outings, *Funeral in Berlin* (66) and *Billion Dollar Brain* (67).

One British spy story of the time was outstanding – *The Spy Who Came in from the Cold* (65) – based on John Le Carré's superior novel and starring Richard Burton (at his best and commendably restrained) as the disillusioned agent, Leamus. This was even more realistic than *The Ipcress File*, showing espionage to be dirty work in which the spy is a pawn never knowing who he is betraying and, more important, who is betraying him. Unfortunately, Le Carré was not as well served by two other films from his novels: *The Deadly Affair* (67) and *The Looking Glass War* (69).

It wasn't long before the Americans attempted to clamber aboard the Bond-wagon with two spy heroes, Helm and Flint, who owed everything to their British counterparts, especially girls and technological gimmicks. Matt Helm was played by Dean Martin in *The Silencers* (66), *Murderer's Row*

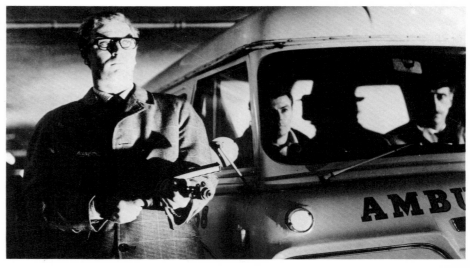

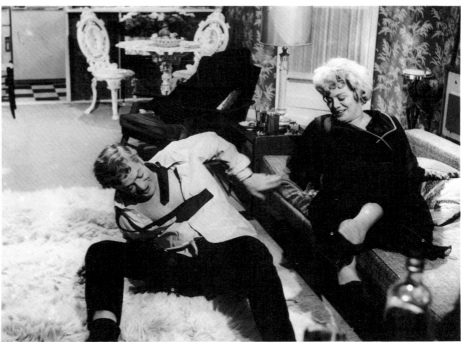

(67), *The Ambushers* (67) and *The Wrecking Crew* (68). Flint was James Coburn in *Our Man Flint* (66) and *In Like Flint* (67), but neither could tell whether a Martini had been shaken or stirred.

Altogether, Hollywood was having a poor time of it. The best thrillers were coming out of Britain and the best Westerns (holy cow!) were coming out of Italy. Sergio Leone was the director who brought a whole new style to the Western and started a sub-genre instantly dubbed 'The Spaghetti Western'. These began as cheap rip-offs, using a cut-price American star, surrounding him with European actors (mostly playing Mexicans, thanks to their swarthy Mediterranean looks) whose dialogue was dubbed into English, and set in a desolately bleak landscape to cut down on expensive set building. Add to this an insatiable appetite for violence, an eerie, menacing score (preferably by Ennio Morricone), and a blurring of good and evil and you have a potent brew. Leone's strength was in bringing a certain elan to the format and creating in Clint Eastwood's 'Man With No Name' an enigmatic, ruthless, unheroic but immensely capable central character.

Eastwood had made his name as Rowdy Yates in the long-running, but fast-fading, TV series 'Rawhide'. During a summer break in the schedule Leone offered him peanuts for a few weeks' work, pinched a plot from Kurosawa's *Yojimbo* (61) and turned out *A Fistful of Dollars* (64). The film was a slow burn; it did reasonably well in Europe and then, unexpectedly, caught the public imagination and cleaned-up financially. Next year Eastwood was back, again as the mysterious, avenging stranger, for *A Few Dollars More* (65) and a bigger budget also stretched to a splendid villain, Lee van Cleef. This, too, hit the jackpot and in 1966 the third movie followed, bigger, not necessarily better, undoubtedly more ingenious in its portrayal of

Spaghetti Eastwood: (*above*) in *A Fistful of Dollars*, director Sergio Leone (United Artists, 64), and (*right*) with Lee van Cleef (left) and Gian Maria Volonte in *For a Few Dollars More*, director Leone (PEA, 65)

violence, with Eastwood and van Cleef *and* Eli Wallach as *The Good, The Bad and The Ugly* (though not necessarily in that order).

Leone had hit a goldmine and soon American stars were ready to add their names to films which, a few years previously, they would not be seen dead (or dealing out death) in for directors they'd never heard of. Leone remained the father of the trend, though, and perhaps his greatest coup was in bagging Henry Fonda for *Once Upon a Time in the West* (69) and persuading him to play a particularly nasty and effective villain!

All did well out of the Spaghetti Western but none as well as Eastwood. It turned him into a star and, with careful management of his career and, particularly, his loner image, a superstar. He now applied what he had learned in an American effort that aped the style, *Hang 'Em High* (68). Next for Eastwood was a Western in an urban setting – *Coogan's Bluff* (68). A hick sheriff pursues an unusually unpleasant criminal through Manhattan, meeting contempt and ridicule for his frontier methods from the local cops. It had the distinct advantage of being directed by Don Siegel, who had already proved his ability to create suspense *and* build good characterization in such films as *Riot in Cell Block 11* (54), *The Invasion of the Body Snatchers* (56), *Baby Face Nelson* (57), *The Killers* (64), and *Madigan* (67).

With *Coogan's Bluff*, Siegel and Eastwood took parts of The Man With No Name characterization, built on Eastwood's naturally deadpan style, and cast everything in a modern mould to create a cool, utterly self-assured man who is capable of coping with any situation, does not flinch from meeting violence with violence, has a measure of self-

mockery, and a rather ambivalent (some have called it fascist) attitude to the methods he uses to achieve his ends.

Together Eastwood and Siegel honed this persona in an off-beat Western co-starring Shirley Maclaine, *Two Mules for Sister Sara* (69), a strange piece of grand guignol set in the Civil War, *The Beguiled* (71), and *Dirty Harry* (72). In between Eastwood appeared in an epic, boyish war caper with Richard Burton, *Where Eagles Dare* (69), a most unlikely version of the musical *Paint Your Wagon* (69), in which he and Lee Marvin were surprisingly competent, and another war actioner, *Kelly's Heroes* (70), about a looting expedition behind enemy lines.

He had also set up his own production company, Malpaso, and decided to try his hand at directing. He got some help from Don Siegel in a horror/thriller *Play Misty For Me* (71) and proved he had an aptitude. He also took over for a period on *Dirty Harry* when Siegel fell ill. Harry Callaghan was the

top left
Henry Fonda in *Once Upon a Time in the West*, director Sergio Leone (Paramount, 69)

Don Siegel directs: (*top right*) Angie Dickinson and Ronald Reagan in *The Killers* (Universal, 64), and (*above*) Eastwood in *Coogan's Bluff* (Universal, 68)

159

distillation of the characterization he'd been refining over the years and the film shot Eastwood to the top, making him one of the 'bankable' stars. This cop of unswerving determination but dubious methods reappeared twice more, in *Magnum Force* (73) and *The Enforcer* (76), but his virtues were being lost amid a welter of gratuitous violence.

Eastwood displayed his sense of humour (at his own expense) in *Thunderbolt and Lightfoot* (74), *Every Which Way But Loose* (78, co-starring with an ape) and *Bronco Billy* (80) but perhaps his best film – certainly the best he directed – was a lovingly

'The Duke' in *El Dorado*,
director Howard Hawks
(Paramount, 67)

evoked, rather beautiful Western, *The Outlaw Josey Wales* (76), which confirmed that he could, if he wished, aspire to the stature of Gary Cooper.

The Western, thanks in no small part to Italy, was enjoying a boom, one which Hollywood was swift to note. But the Westerns in the early decade were largely disappointing, unable to match quality to quantity. A prime example is John Wayne's directorial effort, *The Alamo* (60). Wayne had a less than usually successful decade, apart from *The Man Who Shot Liberty Valance* (62), but he more than made up for it in 1969 with his splendid performance as the one-eyed, paunchy old fighter Rooster

Cogburn in Henry Hathaway's immensely likeable *True Grit*, for which he finally and, it must be said, deservedly won his Oscar.

Perhaps the comparative lull in Wayne's career was a reflection of the running down of John Ford's activity. Nonetheless, the old fox had a couple of good shots left – *Liberty Valance*, of course, and *Cheyenne Autumn* (64), a film which was, for Ford, absolutely huge. It was also untypical in that it was a sympathetic hymn to the Indian – 'I've killed more Indians than Custer,' he once said. It was a decent and respectful movie but overlong and the master's touch only truly showed in the

Julie Christie and Terence Stamp in *Far from the Madding Crowd*, director John Schlesinger (MGM, 67)

Jon Voight (left) and Dustin Hoffman in *Midnight Cowboy*, director John Schlesinger (United Artists, 69)

above
Tom Courtenay in *Billy Liar*,
director John Schlesinger
(Continental, 63)

right
Mary Ure and Richard Burton
(right) on set for *Where
Eagles Dare*, director
Brian Hutton (MGM, 69)

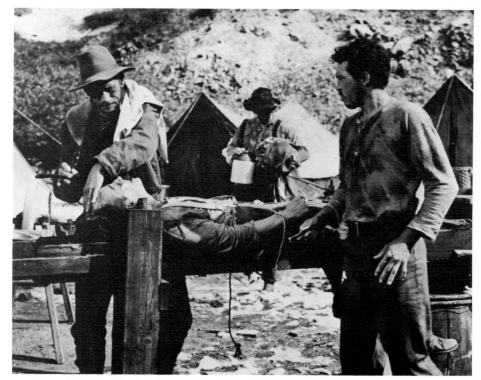

The changing face of the Western: (*opposite*) Paul Newman in *Butch Cassidy and the Sundance Kid*, director George Roy Hill (20th Century-Fox, 69); (*left*) Warren Oates (foreground) and Ben Johnson in *The Wild Bunch*, director Sam Peckinpah (Warners, 69)

below
Ride the High Country (GB: *Guns in the Afternoon*), with (left to right) John Anderson, John Davis Chandler, L.Q. Jones and Warren Oates, director Sam Peckinpah (MGM, 62)

bottom
Yul Brynner, Steve McQueen, Horst Buchholz, Charles Bronson, Robert Vaughn, Brad Dexter and James Coburn in *The Magnificent Seven*, director John Sturges (United Artists, 60)

hilarious Dodge City parody of Western movies.

It was not until the end of the decade that Hollywood came to terms with the new style of Western and turned in some fresh views like *Butch Cassidy and the Sundance Kid* (69). And the man who assisted the change was cheered by some and condemned by others. Sam Peckinpah had already contributed to the genre with the admirable *Ride the High Country* (62, *Guns in the Afternoon* in GB) about a couple of saddle-sore old veterans and starring a couple of the same, Joel McCrea and Randolph Scott, and the bigger, rougher, not so admired *Major Dundee* (65), starring Charlton Heston.

However, certain elements in this, particularly the bloody hounding-down of Indians, *might* have prepared audiences for Peckinpah's next effort, *The Wild Bunch* (69). Again the main characters are past their peak but, more important, it is 1914 and cars are appearing in the West; the days of freebooting banditry are over. The film is an elegy for a passing breed and brilliantly handled. However, its two episodes of violence caused a furore because of the blood-spurting, slow-motion, repetitive detail in which they are shown. Peckinpah claimed the realism (and the action replays) were necessary to condemn violence. The debate went on endlessly and it is for each individual to decide. Certainly *The Wild Bunch* started something of a vogue for gruesome violence (carried on in the Western in Seventies films like *Soldier Blue* – where it seems to make a point – and *Lawman* – where it does not).

If Hollywood was slow to note the changing mood of the Western, it had no excuse because one at the very start of the decade pointed the way. John Sturges's *The Magnificent Seven* (60) contained much that Sergio Leone would put to good use. It was set in Mexico, it was about bounty hunters of doubtful moral probity, it was very fast and furious, and it had a tremendous score and thrilling gunplay. What the industry did, however, recognize was that of the seven there was one established

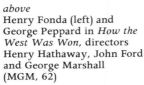

above
Henry Fonda (left) and George Peppard in *How the West Was Won*, directors Henry Hathaway, John Ford and George Marshall (MGM, 62)

right
John Wayne and Robert Mitchum (right) in *El Dorado*, director Howard Hawks (Paramount, 67)

above centre
Paint Your Wagon, director Joshua Logan (Paramount, 69)

Steve McQueen: (*right centre*) with Tuesday Weld in *The Cincinatti Kid*, director Norman Jewison (MGM, 65); (*above, far right*) in *The Great Escape*, director John Sturges (United Artists, 63), and (*far right*) with Faye Dunaway in *The Thomas Crown Affair*, director Norman Jewison (United Artists, 68)

star – Yul Brynner – and three who were potentially stars. To deal with the three that did not make it: they were Brad Dexter, Horst Buchholz and Robert Vaughn (who was to do very nicely, thank you, on TV in 'The Men From UNCLE' spy spoof, and contributed some silkily serpentine politicos, notably in *Bullitt* in 1968 and, again on TV, in 'Washington – Behind Closed Doors'). The three who broke through to movie superstardom were – in reverse order of magnitude – James Coburn, Charles Bronson and Steve McQueen.

All three were heroes for the time, ruggedly handsome, good in action, but with an off-beat individuality that made them rather more interesting than the beefcake men of the previous decade. And all three were brought together again by John Sturges in 1963 for his blockbuster POW story,

The Great Escape, in which McQueen was the indefatigable Hilts who so nearly makes it on a motorbike, Bronson was Velinski the tunneler who breaks with claustrophobia at the last moment, and Coburn was a less-than-convincing Australian, Sedgwick. This film pushed McQueen and Bronson up several rungs but somehow Coburn never achieved the promise he'd shown.

Coburn made a big impression in *The Magnificent Seven* as Britt, the man who can outdraw a gun with his knife-throwing. He spoke only 55 words in the whole movie but his ranginess, his looks and his brooding, coiled aura of violence said more than dialogue. He made a splendid thug in *Charade* (63), was okay in the poor pair of Flint films, and then seemed content to stroll through modish but empty movies. He took the trip to Europe for Leone's *A Fistful of Dynamite* (71) and was in Peckinpah's much-vaunted but deeply-flawed *Pat Garrett and Billy the Kid* (73). In 1975 he came together again with Bronson for *The Streetfighter* (aka *Hard Times*); they worked well but Bronson had done so much better for himself.

Charles Bronson didn't have to act much; his stone face, blasted from a quarry, his hard body, and his scarcely moving lips, from which threats fell more easily than endearments, were enough. It took him a long time to reach stardom. If you look carefully at the credits of many lesser films made through the Fifties, you'll see the name Charles Buchinski – Bronson served his apprenticeship before he hit gold in *The Seven* (60). He built on the success, hitting another peak with *The Great Escape* (63), dipped slightly again before another upward blip in *The Dirty Dozen* (67), and just kept on working, mostly abroad for good money and the star billing which was still continuing to elude him in Hollywood.

Leone's *Once Upon a Time in the West* (69) opposite Fonda helped but he really broke through when he was taken up by British director Michael

Newman in *The Hustler*,
director Robert Rossen
(20th Century-Fox, 61)

Newman directs his wife:
Joanne Woodward in *Rachel,
Rachel* (Warners, 68)

Winner, who put him in a series of meretricious, nastily violent films, starting with *Chato's Land* (72), a Western. Next he was a hitman in *The Mechanic* (72), which had a neat if brutal twist, and was fast becoming 'bankable'. *The Valachi Papers* (72) and *The Stone Killer* (73) continued the ice-cold, rock-hard image and his success. *Mr Majestyk* (74), as a vengeful farmer who takes on the racket and bloodily wins, kept him typecast and then came *Death Wish* (74), another Winner film. In it he is a peaceable businessman whose wife and daughter are brutally raped (shown with unnecessary and vicarious detail) who sets about cleaning up the streets of New York single-handed. The message, if there was one, was ambivalent and, although *Death Wish* was, regrettably, hugely successful, it's possible that the public's appetite for such rubbish was sated because as the decade went on Bronson's popularity waned and he was no longer able to guarantee a return on his films.

McQueen's popularity did not suffer such a dip;

he just seemed to get bored with being a star. However, during the Sixties and into the Seventies he was one of the few serious contenders for Paul Newman's No. 1 position. Where McQueen differed from Coburn and Bronson was in his ability to step outside his hunky, macho mould and act. He started in films in the Fifties and dawdled through such forgettable numbers as *The Blob* (58) before earning fourth credit (after Sinatra, Lollobrigida and Peter Lawford) on John Sturges's war film *Never So Few* (59). Then Sturges put him into *The Magnificent Seven* (60) and people were really taking notice. He was squandered in a couple of routine movies until Sturges used him in *Escape* (63) and gave him the best sequence, the motorbike break-out.

He then broke type in *Love with a Proper Stranger* (63), idled for a while, and came back strong as *The Cincinatti Kid* (65), which did for him and poker-playing what *The Hustler* (60) had done for Newman and pool. *Nevada Smith* (66), a diluted strand from Harold Robbins's novel 'The Carpetbaggers' followed, and then came *The Sand Pebbles* (66), a popular war film. He was on the brink of super-stardom and it came with the next two, *The Thomas Crown Affair* (68), a stylish, tricksy caper film with Faye Dunaway, and *Bullitt* (68). This was one of the memorable films of the decade. McQueen was excellent as the dogged cop in what was a very superior – in story, casting and direction – police thriller. He was nearly, but not quite, overshadowed by an exceptionally thrilling car chase which showed everybody else how such sequences should be handled; most directors made the mistake of subordinating plot and character to the chase.

After *Bullitt* McQueen was among the biggest of the big; a so-so Western, *The Reivers* (70), couldn't dislodge him; he lavished love and care on *Le Mans* (71) – motor racing was his obsession and this was one of the best features on the subject. *Junior Bonner* (72) didn't match up even though he was, as usual, excellent, one of the true professionals who could carry a film. During *The Getaway* (72) his marriage, one of the longer and better established in Hollywood, broke up; he later married his co-star Ali McGraw and, seemingly assured pro-fessionally and personally, he went into two monsters – *Papillon* (73) and *The Towering Inferno* (74), the latter with his 'rival' Newman. They showed the others how a couple of pros can make their mark even against a blazing skyscraper.

And then . . . well, it seemed to fall apart for

McQueen. The marriage to McGraw broke up, he put on a great deal of weight, became a recluse and virtually retired. He longed, it was said, for more challenging roles, did Ibsen's *An Enemy of the People* (76), which got roasted critically, and went into a decline due, sadly, to contracting cancer, of which he died in 1980.

Stars like McQueen helped Hollywood wrest back the dominance it had lost but in the early Sixties the industry was still working on the often mistaken premise that the more you spend, the more you get back. Certain films of epic proportion were worth the trouble and expense – David Lean's *Lawrence of Arabia* (62) and *Dr Zhivago* (65) gained critical and financial success – but most of the big war films, like *The Longest Day* (62, the film seemed to last longer than the actual Normandy landings and the cast list was just a Who's Who), *The Guns of Navarone* (61), *The Blue Max* (66, which mingled sex with flying stunts) and *The Battle of the Bulge* (66), were little more than big, very noisy, very impersonal war films.

However, these were, by and large, better than some of the epics based on an original idea from the Bible. *King of Kings* (61) was incredibly dull, inexplicable as it was directed by Nicholas Ray, but preferable to George Stevens's *The Greatest Story Ever Told* (65), another Who's Who. And Then There Was *The Bible* (66), in which another good director, John Huston, came an awful cropper. The

opposite top
Paul Newman in *Cool Hand Luke*, director Stuart Rosenberg (Warners, 67)

far left, top
Robert Redford (right) in *The Downhill Racer*, director Michael Ritchie (Paramount, 69)

Epics from David Lean: (*far left, bottom*) *Lawrence of Arabia*, with (left to right) Peter O'Toole, Claude Rains, Jack Hawkins (second from right) and Anthony Quayle (Columbia, 62), and (*left*) Geoffrey Keen and Omar Sharif (left) in *Dr Zhivago* (MGM, 66)

above
George Peppard in *The Blue Max*, director John Guillermin (20th Century-Fox, 66)

right
Walter Gotell, Gia Scala, Irene Papas, James Darren, Stanley Baker, Anthony Quinn, David Niven and Gregory Peck in *The Guns of Navarone*, director J. Lee Thompson (Columbia, 61)

project got bogged down around Abraham and,
according to one critic, 'may have set religion back
a couple of thousand years'.

The historical epic staggered on. *Spartacus* (60)
was lively; *El Cid* (61) exciting in parts (especially
if you spot a truck making its anachronistic way
behind the medieval Moors!). *Exodus* (60) was
turgid and provoked Mort Sahl to stand up after
several gruelling hours at the premiere and plead
to Otto Preminger, 'Let my people go!'.

There were a couple of honourable exceptions.
Fred Zinnemann's *A Man for All Seasons* (66) stood
out like a good deed in a naughty world, faithful to
Robert Bolt's excellent script, which gave a superb
cast fine opportunities to shine. Paul Scofield won
the Oscar for his playing of Thomas More, and the
film and director each got one, as did Bolt and
cameraman Ted Moore for his beautiful, restrained
colour photography. *The Lion in Winter* (68) gave
Peter O'Toole a vehicle in which to rant and spark,
showing a form which he seldom chose to display
on film, appearing in movies rather less than his
contemporaries. After his great success in *Lawrence
of Arabia* (62), he followed up as a young Henry II
in the interminable version of *Becket* (64) and then
made infrequent appearances, more notably in
Goodbye Mr Chips (69) and the disappointing *Man
of La Mancha* (72). *The Lion in Winter* has him at his
best as an older but no less rumbustious Henry II,
spatting with his cast-off queen, Eleanor of
Aquitaine. Everybody had enormous fun but
Hepburn, sly and consummate as ever, walked off
with the Oscar, her third and the first actress ever
to achieve this feat.

Furthermore, it was the second year running she
had won the award! In 1967 she took it for her role

right
Gregory Peck (centre) and
James Anderson (right) in
To Kill a Mockingbird,
director Robert Mulligan
(Universal, 63)

Sidney Poitier: (*below*) with
Rod Steiger (right) in *In The
Heat of the Night*, director
Norman Jewison (United
Artists, 67), and (*bottom*)
with Katharine Houghton
and Spencer Tracy in *Guess
Who's Coming to Dinner,*
director Stanley Kramer
(Columbia, 67)

below right
Tracy again, in *Judgement at
Nuremberg,* director Stanley
Kramer (United Artists, 61)

as the liberal mother who is confronted by her
daughter's marriage to a black man in *Guess Who's
Coming to Dinner*? Had the Academy exercised its
usual sentimentality, Spencer Tracy, whose last
film this was and who was outstanding, would also
have won one but that went to Rod Steiger for his
performance as a bigoted, racist small-town cop
who chafes against a smart black detective in *In the
Heat of the Night*.

Both films confronted the question of colour in
the States and both inevitably starred Sidney
Poitier as the black protagonist. Inevitably because,
apart from Harry Belafonte who was an infrequent
movie actor, Poitier was the only black star in
Hollywood. He had made his first movie in 1950
and scored well in Joseph Mankiewicz's essay on

173

174

opposite top
Sophia Loren and Charlton Heston in *El Cid*, director Anthony Mann (Allied Artists, 61)

opposite, bottom left
Robert Shaw (left) and Paul Scofield in *A Man for All Seasons*, director Fred Zinnemann (Columbia, 66)

opposite, bottom right
Katharine Hepburn in *The Lion in Winter*, director Anthony Harvey (Avco Embassy, 68)

above
Audrey Hepburn in the 'Wouldn't It Be Luvverly' number from *My Fair Lady*, director George Cukor (CBS/Warners, 64)

above right
Jack Wild and Ron Moody in *Oliver!*, director Carol Reed (Columbia, 68)

right
Anne Bancroft and Dustin Hoffman in *The Graduate*, director Mike Nichols (United Artists, 67)

racialism, *No Way Out* (50); he was excellent as a near-delinquent in *Blackboard Jungle* (55), but was mostly bogged down playing Africans and token Negroes until he and Tony Curtis were chained convicts on the run in *The Defiant Ones* (58), an oblique look at prejudice. He *had* to be in *Porgy and Bess* (59) but, with the exception of *Lilies of the Field* (63), as an uppity-boy-tamed-by-nuns for which he won an Oscar, he wasn't getting parts worth a damn until he went to England to make a rather slender story of a West Indian teacher in a slum school, *To Sir with Love* (67). It did reasonably well in Britain but was a big and very unexpected hit in the States, the first of three that year to star him.

The other two, *Guess Who* and *Heat*, were more significant. The first looks rather wishy-washy in retrospect but for the time it was honest and decent, if rather sentimental, and was undoubtedly the most successful film on racial prejudice ever made. The second was good on several levels. It was a good thriller, tense, exciting and, especially where Poitier as the Northerner Virgil Tibbs gets beaten up by young white racists, disturbing. It also had considerable performances from Poitier and Steiger. And it manages to make its point without capsizing the story AND have a rattling good story that doesn't fudge the message. *Heat* beat *Guess Who* to the Best Film Oscar, but it also won over two other movies that have remained, if not classics of the decade, then at least quintessentially Sixties films – *The Graduate* and *Bonnie and Clyde*.

Bonnie and Clyde (67) was breathtaking on first viewing. Somehow director Arthur Penn – who had previously made a mark directing Newman in *The Left-Handed Gun* (58) and extracted high-key performances from Anne Bancroft (who won an Oscar) and Patty Duke as the teacher and blind, deaf and dumb child in *The Miracle Worker* (62) – managed to hit a mood. His hero and heroine (Warren Beatty and Faye Dunaway) were beautiful, their exploits made amusing, and the whole thing shot through a glossy, luscious lens. Only on second viewing is it revealed as slick, empty and rather dishonest. Bonnie and Clyde are not heroes: they are sordid, psychopathic killers, and the violence that seemed balletic at first becomes sickening. However, the film was hailed as a masterpiece and made a fortune. It didn't much harm the careers of Dunaway, Michael J. Pollard and Gene Hackman. And it positively rocketed the career, and the fortune (he produced), of Warren Beatty.

Oddly, Beatty is better known and more popular than most of his movies have deserved him to be. Before *B&C* he had made an impact on his debut, as a frustrated young lover in *Splendor in the Grass* (61), and then did little of any value although he'd worked consistently. After *B&C* he did rather less: three comparative turkeys in *The Only Game in Town* (69), *McCabe and Mrs Miller* (71) and *$* (or *Dollars*, 72). But he had two very good shots in the Seventies in films he also produced (guaranteeing himself an even bigger fortune) – *Shampoo* (75), a raunchy view of California's sexual morals which was sharp and funny and in which he was good as

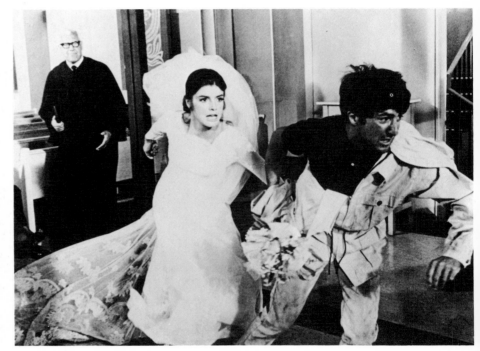

The cult of youth: (*opposite top*) Warren Beatty and Faye Dunaway in *Bonnie and Clyde*, director Arthur Penn (Warners, 67); (*opposite centre*) Katharine Ross and Dustin Hoffman in *The Graduate*, director Mike Nichols (United Artists, 67); (*opposite bottom*) Arlo Guthrie (in hat) in *Alice's Restaurant*, director Arthur Penn (United Artists, 69); (*above*) *Pajama Party*, director Don Weis, (American International, 64); The Beatles in *Help!* (*centre*) and *A Hard Day's Night* (*bottom*), director Richard Lester (United Artists, 65 and 64)

graphed direction, for the wincingly true and hilarious observations, particularly when smart, sophisticated Mrs Robinson (Anne Bancroft) seduces Hoffman, for the performances (Hoffman excels at bumbling hesitancy), or for the Simon and Garfunkel score. In any other year it would have copped the major Oscars; as it was only Nichols picked one up for his masterly direction.

The success of *The Graduate* took the Hollywood establishment by surprise; it had not realized there was a market for sophisticated, intelligent movies aimed at young people. It had failed to notice that youth was having one of its periodic revolutions – the hippies in their beads, bells and kaftans were rather peacefully trying to change the world. Slowly the movie capital awakened to it. Arthur Penn made a hippy-ish film about and starring Woody Guthrie's son, Arlo – *Alice's Restaurant* (69), which was a step in that direction – and *Monterey Pop* (68) was a glossy documentary of a huge music festival, but before these, the films put out for teens had been fairly rubbishy features, in which a pop group plays a few numbers and mumbles its way through a skeleton of a story.

The Beatles were the exceptions. Richard Lester transformed the genre in 1964 with an off-beat, dizzy-paced, almost surreal comedy, *A Hard Day's Night*, and then burst into colour with a comic strip featuring our heroes in *Help!* (65). But, by and large, pop musicals remained fairly firmly in the Fifties.

This was something of a surprise because the conventional movie musical had been given a new direction with *West Side Story* in 1961. The first half is explosive and liberating, the streets coming alive with bounding, athletic young dancers; the second half is for various reasons, not least cost, confined mostly to the studio and not as satisfactory. This, surely, was an indication (as *On the Town* had been in 1949) that the form must move away from the restrictions of the sound stage. It did not happen. Musicals like *The Music Man* (62), *Gypsy* (62) and *The Flower Drum Song* (62) may have served their stars and scores well enough but they were still rather stagey. *My Fair Lady* (64) and *Oliver!* (68) may have been immensely popular and won their

a thick but libidinous hairdresser, and a likeable comedy lifted from the 1941 movie *Here Comes Mr Jordan*, updated and retitled *Heaven Can Wait* (78). Both were big hits.

The other outstanding film of 1967 was *The Graduate*. This too made a remarkable impact but for a different reason: it was a comedy that hit slap on target for the mood of young people. Benjamin Braddock (Dustin Hoffman) was a bit of a rebel; he wasn't a hippy, he was a nice clean-cut lad, but he felt there must be more to life than his parents' generation had settled for.

Doesn't sound like much but that says nothing for Mike Nichols's very witty, ravishingly photo-

left
Russ Tamblyn (centre) in *West Side Story*, directors Robert Wise and Jerome Robbins (United Artists, 61)

below left
Barbra Streisand and Louis Armstrong in the title song from *Hello Dolly*, director Gene Kelly (20th Century-Fox, 69)

below
Fred Astaire (second from left) and Petula Clark (right) in the 'Look To The Rainbow' number from *Finian's Rainbow*, director Francis Ford Coppola (Warners, 68)

above
Paula Kelly and Chita Rivera (second and third from left) in the 'Hey, Big Spender' number from *Sweet Charity*, director Bob Fosse (Universal, 68)

above right
Chitty Chitty Bang Bang, director Ken Hughes (United Artists/Warfield/DFI, 68)

right
Barbra Streisand in *Funny Girl*, director William Wyler (Columbia, 68)

Julie Andrews: (*top*) in *The Sound of Music*, director Robert Wise (20th Century-Fox, 65), and (*above*) doing 'The Tapioca' with James Fox in *Thoroughly Modern Millie*, director George Roy Hill (Universal, 67)

ever equalled *The Sound of Music* (65). Whatever anybody says about the film – and few critics have any good to say of it – the public *adored* it. And they were the ones to make it not only the most successful musical in history, but the biggest money-taker of all time. (It was only knocked off the top of Variety's All-Time Film Rental Champs by *The Godfather* (72), and only one musical – *Grease* (78) – has beaten its $79 million take in rentals. Indeed, it is the only Sixties film to be in the 1980 Top Ten.)

For a while, Julie Andrews was the golden girl of the Sixties. She got there with her first film – Disney's charming children's tale, *Mary Poppins* (64); not only was it a monster hit, it also got her the Oscar as Best Actress. She next did a straight-ish, non-singing part in *The Americanization of Emily* (65) and, if she hoped to break her goody-goody image by being bedded by randy James Garner, she was disappointed. Then came *The Sound of Money* . . . sorry . . . *Music* and Hollywood was fawning on her. It's doubtful whether anyone had ever achieved so much in commercial terms with only three movies.

A routine epic, *Hawaii* (66), came next, followed by one of Hitchcock's least satisfactory efforts, *Torn Curtain* (66), but that didn't matter, it had Andrews AND Paul Newman. Then it was back to musical comedy with the likeable, but undemanding *Thoroughly Modern Millie* (67). She couldn't keep it up, of course. After the heights came a plunge into the depths – both her next two, *Star!* (68) and *Darling Lili* (69), were commercial catastrophes. Indeed, *Star!* very nearly caused the total collapse of 20th Century-Fox. Buoyed by the success of *The Sound of Music*, it had put a fortune into that film, as well as *Doctor Dolittle* (67), *Hello Dolly* (69), *Patton* (70) and *Tora! Tora! Tora!* (70), but public taste had turned sharply away from these over-stuffed movies, which were so inflated in price they never had a hope of recouping their investment.

Julie Andrews's star waned just as another's ascended. Barbra Streisand had starred in *Hello Dolly* but her career could stand the knock because she was still riding high off the success (and Oscar) gained with *Funny Girl* (68). She went into the Seventies reasonably confident but her next, *On A Clear Day You Can See Forever* (70), fared no better and it looked as if her personality and, according to many, her ego were bigger than her box-office appeal.

The Owl and the Pussycat (70) was better, she was good as a brassy prostitute who disrupts the life of mild George Segal, but *What's Up Doc?* (72) didn't have the charm or deftness of the Thirties crazy comedies it was saluting. *The Way We Were* (73) opposite Redford was a biggie. There was another comedy, *For Pete's Sake* (74), and an unnecessary follow-up to her debut, *Funny Lady* (75). By which time she wanted control of her career and, it seemed, just about everything else. She did yet another remake of *A Star Is Born* (76), this one in a rock setting, which was violently disliked by everyone except the public, which must prove she knows something other people don't.

share of awards but they did not compare with the sheer exuberance, vivacity, and energy of Bob Fosse's *Sweet Charity* (68). The latter had its flaws, not least a jerky plot, but when Shirley Maclaine, Chita Rivera *et al* get dancing it lifts the roof.

However, for sheer profit nothing in history had

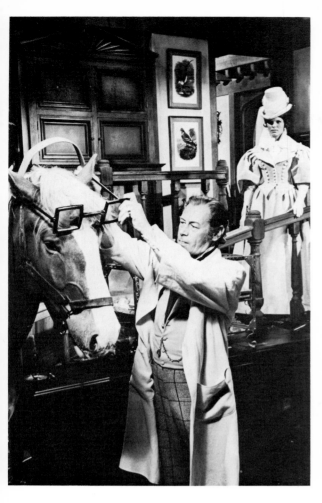

The Sixties were not a particularly good time for female stars; the meaty roles were being handed out to men and few had the chance to rise like Bette Davis and others had before her. (The Seventies were to prove even thinner.) Sex symbols were in decline, although Raquel Welch enjoyed some success. She was mainly an adornment in *Fantastic Voyage* (66) and the entirely preposterous *One Million Years BC* (66). She was massively upstaged by Mae West in the lamentable *Myra Breckinridge* (69), and there was little improvement in the next decade when she sought to prove she was more than a body, *Hannie Caulder* (71), *Fuzz* (72), and even the successful *Three Musketeers* (73) hardly advancing her ambition.

Nonetheless, a good actress *could* still land a good part. Shirley Maclaine's many talents had been displayed in *The Apartment* (59) and *Irma La Douce* (63) but then frittered in trivia until *Sweet Charity* (68), in which she was magnificently explosive. But the lack of good material kept her mainly on the stage and writing books, occasionally reappearing in unworthy films, until she and Anne Bancroft were brought together as ageing ballet dancers in the justly acclaimed movie *The Turning Point* (78).

Glenda Jackson had a more fruitful time, commencing in 1969 with *Women in Love*, for which she won an Oscar the following year. She was the antithesis of glamour as represented diversely by Welch and Maclaine, shrewdly allowing that 'I came up on the wave that allowed people to look like people.' She was neurotic in *The Music Lovers* (70) and very, very funny opposite George Segal in

A Touch of Class (72), which brought her a second Oscar. After that there were some so-so efforts – *The Romantic Englishwoman* (75) opposite Michael Caine, a re-teaming with Segal for *Lost and Found* (79), which did not repeat the success of *Class*, and *House Calls* (78), using Matthau as the comic foil – and some mistakes like a biography of Bernhardt, *The Incredible Sarah* (76).

She found it difficult to land parts as good as she'd had in *Sunday Bloody Sunday* (71). But this was not a problem exclusive to women. Peter Finch, her co-star in *Sunday* (they were tremendous together), had suffered from a lack of worthy parts in

top left
Rex Harrison and Samantha Eggar in *Dr Dolittle*, director Richard Fleischer (20th Century-Fox, 67)

top right
John Richardson and Raquel Welch in *One Million Years BC*, director Don Chaffey (Hammer, 66)

above
Glenda Jackson (left) and Jennie Linden in *Women in Love*, director Ken Russell (United Artists, 69)

above
John Phillip Law and Jane Fonda (second from left) in *Barbarella*, director Roger Vadim (Paramount, 68)

left
Brigitte Bardot and Jeanne Moreau (right) in *Viva Maria*, director Louis Malle (United Artists, 65)

below left
Peter O'Toole and Ursula Andress in *What's New Pussycat?*, director Clive Donner (United Artists, 65)

right
Elizabeth Taylor in *Butterfield* 8, director Daniel Mann (MGM, 60)

Taylor and Burton: in (*opposite top*) *The Taming of the Shrew*, director Franco Zeffirelli (Columbia, 67), and (*opposite, bottom right*) in *Cleopatra*, director Joseph L. Mankiewicz (20th Century-Fox, 62)

above
Clark Gable and Marilyn
Monroe in *The Misfits*,
director John Huston
(United Artists, 61)

above centre
Sophia Loren and Eleanora
Brown (right) in *Two
Women* (*La Ciociara*),
director Vittorio de Sica
(Champion, 61)

right
Peter Finch in *The Trials of
Oscar Wilde* (US: *The Man
with the Green Carnation*),
director Ken Hughes
(Warwick, 60)

his long career. However, when he had a good role
he matched it with a powerful performance; wit-
ness his work in *A Town Like Alice* (56), *The Nun's
Story* (59), *The Trials of Oscar Wilde* (60), *The
Pumpkin Eater* (64) and, of course, his stunning
performance in *Network* (76), which gained him an
Oscar nomination. The prize would almost certainly
have gone to him even if he had not died of a heart
attack in early 1977.

But, in the late Sixties, individual actors were
being swamped by the sheer size of productions.
Even comedy was becoming monstrously overblown. *It's a Mad, Mad, Mad, Mad World* (63),
Those Magnificent Men in Their Flying Machines (65)
and *The Great Race* (65) did get a few laughs between
them. Far more reliable, though, was the work of
Billy Wilder, who had a productive decade, starting
with *The Apartment* (60), which satirized sex and
the office and offered Jack Lemmon and Shirley
Maclaine a marvellous chance as a pair of outsiders
who find love. Then came a Cold War comedy, *One,
Two, Three* (61), the demusicalized version of *Irma
La Douce* (63), and a much underrated, very funny,
very saucy sex-comedy, *Kiss Me Stupid* (64), in
which Dean Martin sent himself up rotten, and a
terrific, abrasive lampoon on insurance frauds,
The Fortune Cookie (66, *Meet Whiplash Willie* in GB),
which gained Walter Matthau a hugely deserved
Supporting Actor Oscar.

above
Peter Finch and James Mason in *The Pumpkin Eater*, director Jack Clayton (Columbia, 64)

left
Sarah Miles and Stuart Whitman in *Those Magnificient Men in Their Flying Machines*, director Ken Annakin (20th Century-Fox, 65)

below
Ray Walston, Dean Martin (centre) and Kim Novak in *Kiss Me Stupid*, director Billy Wilder (United Artists, 64)

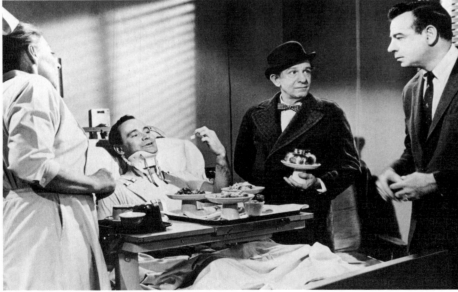

top left
Milton Berle and Terry-Thomas (right) in *It's a Mad, Mad, Mad, Mad World*, director Stanley Kramer (United Artists, 63)

Jack Lemmon: (*above*) with Walter Matthau (right) in *The Fortune Cookie* (GB: *Meet Whiplash Willie*), director Billy Wilder (United Artists, 66), and (*right*) with Lee Remick in *Days of Wine and Roses*, director Blake Edwards (Warners, 62)

This was his breakthrough from reliable back-up roles to name above the credit and his first teaming with Jack Lemmon (who'd also had a marvellous decade with *The Apartment* and the tragi-comic *Days of Wine and Roses* (62) among much other estimable work). The two were re-united in 1968 for one of the funniest comedies of the period, *The Odd Couple*, from Neil Simon's play in which two divorced men, one a slob (Matthau), the other obsessively tidy, attempt to share an apartment. Simon himself was enjoying a good run: he had also contributed the script for *Sweet Charity* and had a massive hit with a gentle comedy about a pair of

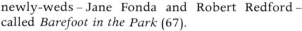

newly-weds – Jane Fonda and Robert Redford – called *Barefoot in the Park* (67).

One of the unlikeliest comedy hits of the time also starred Jane Fonda but, although she was good, it was a man who had been a supporting player and classic heavy in movies since 1951 who stole the film from her and went on to snatch the Best Actor Oscar of 1965 from Burton, Steiger and Olivier. In *Cat Ballou* Lee Marvin was quite outrageous but then look at the part he had. Correction, the parts. Not only was he the broken-down drunk gunslinger (with a broken-down drunk horse), who can scarcely uncross his eyes, let alone raise his pistol. He *also* played his twin brother, a mean, vicious gunslinger with a metal nose!

Marvin had not been a support player for all those years and in all those films – including some crackers like *The Wild One* (54), *The Caine Mutiny* (54), *Bad Day at Black Rock* (54), *The Man Who Shot Liberty Valance* (62, as the eponymous baddie) and *The Killers* (64) – not to seize his chance. Despite his

iron-grey hair and beat-up features, he became the most macho man around in *The Professionals* (66), *The Dirty Dozen* (67), Boorman's *Point Blank* (67) and *Hell in the Pacific* (68, a two-hander in which he and Toshiro Mifune fight their own Battle of the Pacific). He also became a recording star with his extraordinary gravel-voiced rendition of 'I Was Born Under A Wandering Star' from *Paint Your Wagon* (69).

One of the people Marvin beat to the award in 1965 was Rod Steiger who had been nominated for his performance in and as *The Pawnbroker* (65). It was a laudable piece of acting in a serious and

top centre
Robert Redford and Jane Fonda in *Barefoot in the Park*, director Gene Saks (Paramount, 67)

top right
Jack Lemmon and Walter Matthau in *The Odd Couple*, director Gene Saks (Paramount, 68)

above
Lee Marvin in *Point Blank*, director John Boorman (MGM, 67)

Lee Marvin: (*top*) reviewing *The Dirty Dozen*, director Robert Aldrich (MGM, 67); (*above left*) with Jane Fonda in *Cat Ballou*, director Eliot Silverstein (Columbia, 65), and (*above right*) in *The Professionals*, director Richard Brooks (Columbia, 66)

moving film, but the film was more noted at the time for a row about its content, the outcome of which was to alter the American movie radically.

Throughout the Sixties the moral climate had been changing. Hollywood had been slower into the new, 'adult' territories than the European and British industries, mostly because it was still rigidly overseen by powerful lobbies whose disapproval

could mean, Hollywood believed, disastrous box-office losses. The most powerful of these bodies was the National Legion of Decency (which in 1965 became the National Catholic Office for Motion Pictures – NCOMP). NCOMP fought a vigorous rearguard action against one aspect of screen sexuality: the depiction of nudity.

Many producers were increasingly irked by the

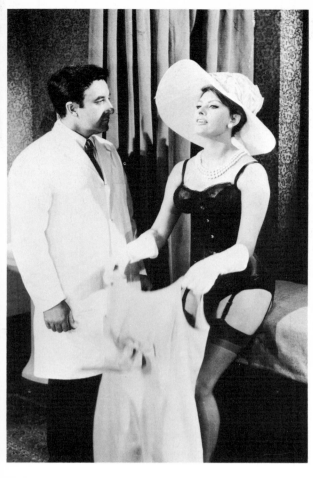

undue influence of the Legion. It was becoming ever more ridiculous that a serious producer had to fudge vital story elements because he could not show the naked human body. It was also ludicrous that the human body could and was being shown violated in various ways by explicit violence but could not be depicted in an act of love.

Undoubtedly the Legion had a point in suspecting that once the barriers were down, exploitative producers would include gratuitous scenes of nakedness in their films. However, the charge of exploitation could not fairly be levelled against Sidney Lumet, one of the new generation of independent directors, whose work to that point included such serious (if occasionally rather worthy) works as *Twelve Angry Men* (57), *The Fugitive Kind* (60), *A View from the Bridge* (61), *Long Day's Journey into Night* (62) and *Fail Safe* (64), and

Peter Sellers: (*above left*) with Sophia Loren in *The Millionairess*, director Anthony Asquith (20th Century-Fox, 61); (*above*) with Graham Stark in *A Shot in the Dark*, director Blake Edwards (United Artists, 64), and (*left*) with John Le Mesurier in *The Pink Panther*, director Blake Edwards (United Artists, 63)

(Left to right) Ralph Richardson, Dean Stockwell, Katharine Hepburn and Jason Robards Jr in *Long Day's Journey into Night*, director Sidney Lumet (20th Century-Fox, 62)

189

top left
Beryl Reid (second from right) and Susannah York in *The Killing of Sister George*, director Robert Aldrich (Cinerama, 69)

Two by Sidney Lumet: (*top right*) Harry Andrews and Sean Connery (right) in *The Hill* (MGM, 65), and (*above*) Thelma Oliver and Rod Steiger in *The Pawnbroker* (Landau, 65)

body reawakens his constant nightmare as the scene flashes to Auschwitz, where he had been forced to watch the sexual humiliation of his wife at the hands of the guards. The naked whore and his naked wife become one. There is nothing in the scene that can remotely be described as erotic. It simply makes its point and is pivotal in illustrating the roots of Nazerman's despair and disgust. Lumet decided to fight the censure and, eventually, won.

The floodgates did not instantly give way – there were still a number of wrangles – but throughout the decade new 'firsts' were notched up. Nudity, although by no means as common as it was to become in the Seventies, was now not at all uncommon. And an increasing variety of sexual subjects was explored: lesbianism in Lumet's *The Group* (65) and then *The Fox* (68, including the suggestion of female masturbation), the hints of oral sex in *Bonnie and Clyde* (67) and others, and homosexual fellatio in Schlesinger's *Midnight Cowboy* (69), in which Jon Voight as the big, blond country boy who goes to New York to earn his fortune as a stud servicing rich women meets with so little success he is forced to take on squalid gay tricks to keep him and runty, crippled friend Ratso (Dustin Hoffman). Before the end of the decade, the last taboo, the showing of 'full frontal nudity', had gone. For the record, in Britain flashes of pudenda were seen in Antonioni's controversial (mostly because it was so puzzling) British film *Blow-Up* (67), in the sequence in which David Hemmings, a photographer, disports naked with models, and in 1968 Lindsay Anderson's compelling story of revolution in a British public school, *If . . .*, showed an erotic coupling between Malcolm McDowell and Christine Noonan, in which genitals were again exposed without causing a flutter.

Some directors were able to use the more liberal climate of opinion to explore themes which would previously have been *verboten*. Roman Polanski's *Repulsion* (65) was concerned with a woman (Catherine Deneuve) whose fear of sex leads her to withdraw into paranoid isolation and brutally murder her boyfriend and landlord when they attempt to establish contact with her. It was a lean, finely-etched film, full of powerful images which the British censor, John Trevelyan, left untouched. Interestingly, Hitchcock's masterpiece of the

who would continue with *The Hill* (65) and *The Group* (65) through to *Serpico* (74) and *Dog Day Afternoon* (75).

The Pawnbroker makes no attempt to exploit nudity. In a crucial scene a whore, desperate for money to stop her boyfriend drifting into crime, takes some jewelry to Nazerman (Steiger), a pawnbroker with a reputation for misanthropy. His offer is $20 less than the sum she needs so she offers him her body to raise the extra money, removing her dress to show her breasts. Her skinny

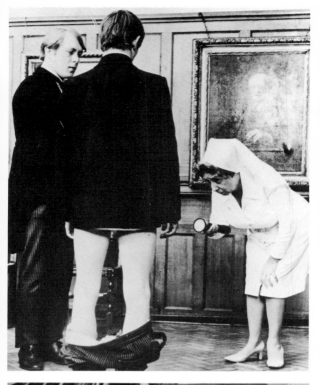

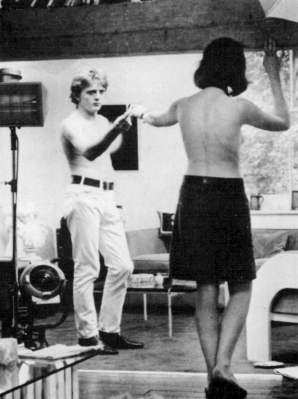

decade, *Psycho* (60), with its famous shower murder, brilliantly composed of a mosaic of shots – including naked breasts – stitched together with almost subliminal speed to deceive the eye into believing it is seeing something far more graphic and explicit than it is, was subjected to some cuts by Trevelyan because he thought it sadistic. Fourteen stabs were reduced to three.

Polanski's next film, *Cul-de-Sac* (66), oozed sexuality, including homosexuality, and then he turned to the horror genre and spoofed it amusingly (a Jewish vampire is undeterred by an upheld crucifix) in *Dance of the Vampires* (67, aka *The Fearless Vampire Killers*). He went to the States, where he made the genuinely chilling, modern-day demonic tale, *Rosemary's Baby* (68), in which the

above left
If . . ., director Lindsay Anderson (Paramount, 68)

above
Mia Farrow in *Rosemary's Baby*, director Roman Polanski (Paramount, 68)

Sex grows more explicit: (*centre*) David Hemmings and Vanessa Redgrave in *Blow-Up*, director Michelangelo Antonioni (MGM, 67); (*below left*) Anthony Perkins in *Psycho*, director Alfred Hitchcock (Paramount, 60), and (*below*) Catherine Deneuve in *Repulsion*, director Roman Polanski (Compton/Tekli, 65)

terrified Mia Farrow is raped with her husband's
(John Cassavetes) complicity by the Devil and bears
his child. There followed a controversially sexual
version of *Macbeth* (71) and an excellent elliptical
thriller, *Chinatown* (74).

The barriers against sex and violence were down
but the battles were not over. In 1971 there was a
tremendous furore about a film that contained both
and which virtually started a backlash against the
new permissiveness. Had not *A Clockwork Orange*
been made by Stanley Kubrick, one of the most
brilliant and respected of all the new directors, it
would undoubtedly have had a fearful mauling by
the censor.

He started the Sixties in rather untypical style
with a historical epic, *Spartacus* (60), which was
superior to most. The only predictable thing about
Kubrick – apart from the individuality of his vision
and the quality of his work – is his unpredictability.
From revolting slaves he turned to a potential
sexual minefield: *Lolita* (62), Vladimir Nabokov's
story of a middle-aged man besotted by a nymphet.
The subject matter made difficult film material but,
thanks to Kubrick's very discreet touch, there
was no outcry even though Sue Lyon (who played
Lolita) was only 14 and it was clear that James
Mason (as Humbert Humbert) has more than a
fatherly interest in her.

Next Kubrick made the blackest, bleakest comedy
of the decade (and one of the grimmest ever) with
Dr Strangelove or How I Learned to Stop Worrying

and Love the Bomb (63). Madness runs through the
film: the madness of the people who have un-
leashed the ultimate horror; the madness of keeping
and 'improving' such weapons of destruction; and
the madness of building systems that allow no call-
back. It is an unlikely subject for comedy but by
suggesting the terrifying absurdities by which the
nuclear holocaust could be precipitated Kubrick
makes his points more tellingly than did Sidney

left
Peter Sellers in *Dr Strangelove*, director Stanley Kubrick (Columbia, 63)

above
The Planet of the Apes, director Franklin J. Schaffner (20th Century-Fox, 68)

below left
Tony Curtis as *The Boston Strangler*, director Richard Fleischer (20th Century-Fox, 68)

below
Bette Davis in *The Anniversary*, director Roy Ward Baker (Hammer, 67)

opposite
2001: A Space Odyssey, with Keir Dullea (*bottom*), director Stanley Kubrick (MGM, 68)

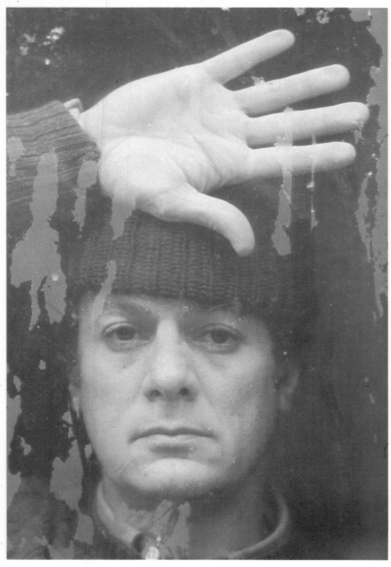

Hitchcock directs Tippi Hedren: (*above*) in *The Birds* (Universal, 63), and (*above right*) in *Marnie* (Universal, 64)

Lumet with his grippingly convincing and realistic essay on the same theme, *Fail Safe* (64). *Strangelove* was justifiably admired at the time and it is a sorry commentary that as the world entered the Eighties the film was as relevant as it had been in the Sixties. It also provided Peter Sellers with a tremendous acting opportunity. He played three roles, including the deranged Strangelove, and displayed a genius he had all too few chances to exhibit.

One of the themes of *Strangelove* was the way in which man's sophisticated machines ultimately dominated their creator. Kubrick developed this notion in one of the most visually stunning, thought-provoking films ever made, *2001 : A Space Odyssey* (68).

Again his individual vision, his tremendous imagination, and his painstaking ability to render that imagination into brilliant cinematic effects made this a quite outstanding movie. It starts in prehistory, The Dawn of Man, showing a hominid

Fantastic Voyage, director Richard Fleischer (20th Century-Fox, 66)

who makes the giant mental leap to tool-using by
grasping a bone and then, of course, to weapon-
wielding. The murder instrument is thrown aloft in
jubilation and becomes a space craft – the odyssey
through space is analagous with man's own
odyssey to civilization. Once into space the
spectacle becomes eye-boggling; so beautiful, so
realistic are the images that it seems as if it must
have been made on location! The story – or fable or
parable, call it what you will – is not easy to follow;
there are probably as many interpretations of
Kubrick's intention as there are people who have
seen the film. Much discussion centred around the
Cosmic Ride sequence; at the time many people
were convinced it was a recreation on film of an
LSD trip. The debate was irrelevant – *2001* stands
as a singular, extraordinary cinematic experience.

To describe it as a science-fiction film is seriously
to understate the case; it *is* that and so very much
more. It stands so far above other examples of the
genre in the decade – *Fantastic Voyage* (66), in
which miniaturized scientists are injected into a
patient's bloodstream, *Marooned* (69), John Sturges's
adventure thriller about astronauts stranded in
space, or *The Planet of the Apes* (68), which started
promisingly but quickly declined into a samey but
financially successful series – that comparison is
invidious. However, it did show the way for others
with vivid imaginations and, usually, very limited
budgets, who in the early Seventies made clever,
thoughtful movies in the sci-fi genre. One was
Douglas Trumbull's *Silent Running* (71), in which

Bruce Dern and three charming clones – Huey,
Dewey and Louie – run a space station devoted to
raising a forest which will one day re-stock
holocaust-stricken Earth. Another was George
Lucas's *THX 1138* (70).

Directors like Lucas showed that a great deal
could be achieved on a very small budget, a lesson
Hollywood had already been given in 1969. That
year it was shaken rigid by the success of a movie
which cost a paltry $375,000 and which, according
to Variety in its 1980 list of All-Time Film Rental
Champs, had taken over $19 million in rentals from
exhibitors (its gross at the box office is thought to
exceed $40 million).

Easy Rider was that rare thing, the movie of the
time, the one that strikes the right chord with the
audience. A rambling, free-wheeling odyssey of
two bikers (Dennis Hopper and Peter Fonda) who
set off on a drugged, drunken 'trip' (in every sense
of the word, remembering this was the time of
LSD trips) across America and the people (notably
Jack Nicholson) they meet. It became a cult.

It looked, for a period, as though it might be one
of the most influential pictures of the era, pointing
the direction for 'new' Hollywood, for smaller
budgets and tightly-made pictures. In the event, it
stands out now as an exception to the rule. The new
Hollywood film was not getting smaller. It was
getting bigger and bigger. By the middle of the
Seventies, superlatives (at least for size and monetary success) would run out. The day of the monster
block-buster, the mega-grosser was dawning.

'60s Oscars

YEAR	BEST FILM	BEST ACTOR	BEST ACTRESS
1960	*The Apartment/* Mirisch-UA	Burt Lancaster/ *Elmer Gantry*	Elizabeth Taylor/ *Butterfield 8*
1961	*West Side Story/* Mirisch-UA	Maximilian Schell/ *Judgement at Nuremberg*	Sophia Loren/ *Two Women*
1962	*Lawrence of Arabia/* Horizon-Columbia	Gregory Peck/ *To Kill a Mockingbird*	Anne Bancroft/ *The Miracle Worker*
1963	*Tom Jones/* Lopert-UA	Sidney Poitier/ *Lilies of the Field*	Patricia Neal/ *Hud*
1964	*My Fair Lady/* Warner Brothers	Rex Harrison/ *My Fair Lady*	Julie Andrews *Mary Poppins*
1965	*The Sound of Music/* 20th Century-Fox	Lee Marvin *Cat Ballou*	Julie Christie/ *Darling*
1966	*A Man for All Seasons/* Columbia	Paul Scofield/ *A Man for All Seasons*	Elizabeth Taylor/ *Who's Afraid of Virginia Woolf?*
1967	*In the Heat of the Night/* Mirisch-UA	Rod Steiger/ *In the Heat of the Night*	Katharine Hepburn/ *Guess Who's Coming to Dinner*
1968	*Oliver!/* Romulus-Columbia	Cliff Robertson/ *Charly*	Katharine Hepburn/ *The Lion in Winter*
1969	*Midnight Cowboy/* UA	John Wayne/ *True Grit*	Maggie Smith/ *The Prime of Miss Jean Brodie*

60s Oscars

BEST DIRECTOR	BEST SUPPORTING ACTOR	BEST SUPPORTING ACTRESS	YEAR
Billy Wilder/ *The Apartment*	Peter Ustinov/ *Spartacus*	Shirley Jones/ *Elmer Gantry*	1960
Robert Wise, Jerome Robbins/ *West Side Story*	George Chakiris/ *West Side Story*	Rita Moreno/ *West Side Story*	1961
David Lean/ *Lawrence of Arabia*	Ed Bagley/ *Sweet Bird of Youth*	Patty Duke/ *The Miracle Worker*	1962
Tony Richardson/ *Tom Jones*	Melvyn Douglas/ *Hud*	Margaret Rutherford/ *The VIPs*	1963
George Cukor/ *My Fair Lady*	Peter Ustinov/ *Topkapi*	Lila Kedrova/ *Zorba the Greek*	1964
Robert Wise/ *The Sound of Music*	Martin Balsam/ *A Thousand Clowns*	Shelley Winters/ *A Patch of Blue*	1965
Fred Zinnemann/ *A Man for All Seasons*	Walter Matthau/ *The Fortune Cookie*	Sandy Dennis/ *Who's Afraid of Virginia Woolf?*	1966
Mike Nichols/ *The Graduate*	George Kennedy/ *Cool Hand Luke*	Estelle Parsons/ *Bonnie and Clyde*	1967
Carol Reed/ *Oliver!*	Jack Albertson/ *The Subject Was Roses*	Ruth Gordon/ *Rosemary's Baby*	1968
John Schlesinger/ *Midnight Cowboy*	Gig Young/ *They Shoot Horses Don't They?*	Goldie Hawn/ *Cactus Flower*	1969

opposite left
(Left to right) Jeremy Brett, Audrey Hepburn and Rex Harrison in *My Fair Lady*, director George Cukor (CBS/Warners, 64)

opposite right
Jack Lemmon and Shirley Maclaine in *The Apartment*, director Billy Wilder (United Artists, 60)

left
(Left to right) Elizabeth Taylor, George Segal, Richard Burton and Sandy Dennis in *Who's Afraid of Virginia Woolf?*, director Mike Nichols (Warners, 66)

199

the Seventies

In 1973 an old man – 100 years old – was honoured in Hollywood, a Hollywood which had changed beyond recognition since he produced his first film in 1913. Adolph Zukor had been a mogul, head of Paramount Pictures. Now the great studios were broken up, their backlots sold off as real estate, their wardrobes and props auctioned to souvenir-hunting buffs. Once-mighty companies were being taken over by oil corporations and the moguls ousted by accountants who knew nothing about picture-making, except that it was showing too much red on the balance sheet. He had, in short, lived to see Hollywood go broke.

He addressed the young men around him and offered them an old, old adage: 'There's nothing wrong with this business,' he said, 'that a few good movies can't cure.' It seems that someone heeded his words for you only have to look down Variety's list of All-Time Film Rental Champs (the films that took most money in rentals paid by exhibitors to the distributor in the States and Canada) at the end of the decade to see the trend against movie-going had been reversed.

Star Wars (77) was No. 1; it had taken a scarcely credible $175,849,013 in rentals. Then came *Jaws* (75, $133,429,000), *Grease* (78, $93,292,000), *The Exorcist* (73, $88,100,000), *The Godfather* (72, $86,275,000), *Superman* (78, $81 million), *The Sound of Music* (65, $79 million), *The Sting* (73, $78,889,000), *Close Encounters of the Third Kind* (77, $77 million), and *Gone with the Wind* (39, $76,700,000).

These were big, big films: big in budget; big in conception and ultimately big in returns. Five of them demanded huge investments because they relied so heavily on monstrously expensive special effects to achieve their impact and there was a new type of inflation entering the film business – the incredible price stars were asking for their services.

The curious aspect of this success story was that many of the directors who made the biggest impact on the decade had started it – and made their names – turning out dazzling movies on incredibly small budgets. Steven Spielberg (*Jaws* and *Close Encounters*) had arrested attention with a brilliant little TV movie, *Duel* (71), a chilling road joust

George C. Scott in *Patton*, director Franklin J. Schaffner (20th Century-Fox, 70)

Tora! Tora! Tora!, directors Richard Fleischer, Toshio Masuda and Kinji Fukasaku (20th Century-Fox, 70)

between a car driver (Dennis Weaver) and a juggernaut lorry that was so outstanding it escaped the box and was successfully shown in cinemas. George Lucas (*Star Wars*) had scraped together finance for a modest but clever sci-fi pic, *THX 1138* (71), and then gone on to *American Graffiti* (73), which cost a mere $750,000 and grossed about $50 million. And Peter Bogdanovich – *The Last Picture Show* (71), *What's Up Doc* (72), and *Paper Moon* (73) – made his first feature, *Targets* (68), for pocket money – $125,000.

The Seventies was an extraordinary decade in all respects for Hollywood. It was a decade of trends, of directors, and of stars. At various times each of these seemed to hold the key to success, but ultimately no trend, no one director, no star could guarantee that the audiences would pay their money at the box office.

The trends came and went. Perhaps the first discernible one was for disaster movies. These were films that depicted disaster – the term took on another meaning when some did disastrous business.

Sarah Miles and Robert Mitchum in *Ryan's Daughter*, director David Lean (MGM, 70)

Disaster movies: (*left*) Jack Lemmon and Olivia de Havilland in *Airport '77*, director Jerry Jameson (Universal), and (*below*) Richard Chamberlain caged in *The Towering Inferno*, director John Guillermin (20th Century-Fox/Warners, 74)

Perhaps the first of the sub-genre was *Airport* (70), a well-made drama translated from the Arthur Hailey novel chronicling the mishaps that strike a modern airfield. With its strong cast – Burt Lancaster and Dean Martin in the lead – it provided a few thrills, some tension, and played on the widespread fear of air travel. It also took a lot of money. *Airport '75* (74), the sequel, did well enough to initiate a series, including *Airport '77* and *Concorde – Airport '80* which yawned along, the plots getting more preposterous and the acting more cardboard.

In 1972 Ronald Neame took another novel, this time by Paul Gallico, about a cruise liner that turns turtle, trapping assorted survivors who struggle to work their way out. It was a good idea and worked well on film. Another strong cast – Gene Hackman, Ernest Borgnine, Shelley Winters, and Red Buttons among others – aided the good production values, and, although the actors were inevitably submerged (in every sense) beneath the special effects, *The Poseidon Adventure* made exciting viewing. It also established producer Irwin Allen as the doyen of disaster.

His next was a biggie in every sense. The world's tallest skyscraper is consumed by fire on its opening night. Here we are presented with the twin fears of fire and vertigo AND Paul Newman AND Steve McQueen (the first and only time they acted together), William Holden, Faye Dunaway, Fred Astaire, Richard Chamberlain, Robert Vaughn, Robert Wagner, etc, etc. *The Towering Inferno* (74) didn't actually *need* these stars – after all, one human torch is much like another – but that's Hollywood.

In the meantime others had climbed on the bandwagon and in 1974 *Earthquake* swallowed Los Angeles and Charlton Heston, Ava Gardner and

right
Ali MacGraw and Ryan
O'Neal in *Love Story*,
director Arthur Hiller
(Paramount, 70)

below
Glenda Jackson in *The
Music Lovers*, director Ken
Russell (United Artists, 70)

which young teens could see – mainly because in
the late Sixties and early Seventies the high sex
content of even thriller and adventure films gave
them certificates which excluded young people
under 18. The disaster movies eschewed sex (there
wasn't much time for it anyway, when people were
swimming, jumping or running for their lives).
Being fairly simple in plot (not to say simple-
minded) and packed with thrills, the kids started
going back to the flicks.

It was just a matter of time before Hollywood
woke up to the fact that there was a market out
there which was being neglected. There had been
some rock films in the Sixties but nothing as big as
Woodstock (70), which was a glossy, documentary
record of the biggest open-air rock festival to date.
No plot, just a big-screen (occasionally multi-
screen, thanks to split images) celebration of some

of the best rock artists of the time – Joe Cocker, Crosby, Stills, Nash and Young, Jimi Hendrix, Sly and The Family Stone, Ten Years After, The Who, etc. etc. It was a big movie and it made big, big money.

But nothing as compared to George Lucas's *American Graffiti* (73). This was sold on nostalgia – 'Where were you in '62?' the posters asked – and harked back to an adolescence that was not confronted with Vietnam. In fact, *American Graffiti* is not true to its period. Although supposedly set in the Sixties, most of the music that accompanies it, and nearly all the period detail, the atmosphere, and the attitudes owe more to the Fifties. No matter, it is a warm evocation of past times.

The plot is slight – Curt (Richard Dreyfuss) and Steve (Ronny Howard) are due to go away to college. On the last night before their departure they and their friends – Terry, the gimpish clown (Charlie Martin Smith), and John, the cool James

Ken Hutchison and Susan George in *Straw Dogs*, director Sam Peckinpah (Talent Associates/ Amerbroco, 71)

The theme of violence: (*above*) Charles Bronson in *Death Wish*, director Michael Winner (Paramount/Dino de Laurentiis, 74), and (*right*) Malcolm McDowell in *A Clockwork Orange*, director Stanley Kubrick (Warners, 71)

Dean look-alike (Paul Le Mat) – cruise around town. The movie follows them through a long, drifting night, packed with small incidents. On its own it might have been a well-considered cult movie. But Lucas realized that the best way to create the atmosphere of the time was to accompany it with the hits of the day, so he spent about 10% of his modest budget paying for the right to use 40 rock classics.

American Graffiti worked brilliantly as a package. It didn't matter if you were hardly born in '62. You somehow knew that this picture was not only for you; it was of and about you. It made a fortune and George Lucas now had the clout to command millions.

Graffiti proved that there was a big market for rock. In 1973 the most phenomenal rock musical of all time was transferred, with only marginal success, from the stage to the screen. *Jesus Christ, Superstar* showed the way for other such exercises. Two other stage successes, *Hair* (79) and *The Rocky Horror Picture Show* (75), also made the transition. In the meantime had come the 'film of the album'. Ken Russell led the way with his typically eccentric and extravagant vision of The Who's rock opera – *Tommy* – in 1975. A similar trick performed on The Beatles' long-player *Sgt Pepper's Lonely Hearts Club Band* (78) was an unmitigated disaster. But other, less overblown and pretentious movies did deservedly, if modestly, well. *The Buddy Holly*

below
Twiggy and Christopher Gable in *The Boyfriend*, director Ken Russell (MGM, 71)

right
Ted Neeley as *Jesus Christ, Superstar*, director Norman Jewison (Universal, 73)

below centre
Harrison Ford (*left*) and Paul Le Mat in *American Grafitti*, director George Lucas (Universal, 73)

Rock movies: (*left*) Tim Curry (centre) and Richard O'Brien (right) in *Rocky Horror Picture Show*, director Jim Sharman (20th Century-Fox, 75) and (*below*) Roger Daltrey in *Tommy*, director Ken Russell (Hemdale, 75)

Quadrophenia, director
Franc Roddam (The Who
Films, 79)

Story (78), *The Kids Are Alright* (79) and *Quadro-phenia* (79, the last two inspired by the work of The Who) were more faithful to their subjects and showed some respect for the audience they sought.

However, all these were dwarfed by two block-busters starring one young man. It's difficult to analyse the appeal of John Travolta – he was no Adonis, he could dance a bit, sing a bit, and act hardly at all. And yet he was in two movies on the trot which had teens and sub-teens scrabbling to get into the cinemas. In 1977–78 he was the biggest thing since the Beatles, since James Dean. By 1980, you couldn't give him away. Perhaps it wasn't his innate appeal that made him so popular. Certainly, as soon as he attempted to break away from the young, dancing/singing hero he was cooked.

Saturday Night Fever (77) had him as a young man whose life is empty except for the one night of the week he can don his figure-hugging gear and strut his stuff on the floor of the disco. It was a film no critic admired. But, of course, the critics are not teens. A teenage girl sees that sexy ass moving; a teenage boy sees a guy he'd like to emulate. And the critics have got cloth ears.

The critics liked *Grease* (78) still less. And they liked Olivia Newton John least of all. What matter?

This inane story of young love in the Fifties, of the kewpie doll who becomes a siren in order to cap-ture the affections of a James Dean look-alike *is* thin and fatuous and silly. But the film is also lively, energetic and, yet again, full of hummable, sing-able songs. And it was *exactly* what the teeny-boppers were wanting.

Grease did even better than *Fever*; it became the most successful musical ever made. Next Travolta played a young non-singing, non-dancing stud who reawakens the passion of an older woman (Lily Tomlin) in *Moment by Moment* (78) and the audience just melted away. By the turn of the decade, in spite of *Urban Cowboy*, John Travolta was poised to become an historic figure – the man who shot to the heights and then plunged to the depths quicker than any other star.

The young had another and very unlikely hero in the Seventies, who specialized in a type of film which equalled the Spaghetti Western in its un-expected success. The Far East had had a large, prolific, profitable but entirely parochial film in-dustry for years; its most dependable product was films about the Chinese martial arts, which came to be known in the West as kung-fu. The basis of a kung-fu film was a pure-hearted hero who fights

John Travolta: in *Saturday Night Fever* (*above*), director John Badham (Paramount, 77), and in *Grease* (*right*), with Olivia Newton John, director Randal Kleiser (Paramount, 78)

Liza Minnelli (upstage) in *Cabaret*, director Bob Fosse (ABC/Allied Artists, 72)

Barbra Streisand and Kris Kristofferson in *A Star Is Born*, director Frank Pierson (Warners/Barwood/ First Artists, 76)

oppression and seeks revenge by taking on any number of opponents and smashing them to the accompaniment of grunts, groans, and very loud slapping and crunching noises. At its best it is balletic, athletic and dizzying; at its worst bloody, brutal and nasty.

It seemed unlikely that kung-fu movies would ever find an audience in the West outside the cinemas in various Chinatowns which sprang up wherever expatriate Chinese settled. However, Bruce Lee changed all that. He was an expert in the martial arts, he was very good-looking, and he had worked in Hollywood (mostly in TV). Bruce Lee first came to Western attention in *Marlowe* (69), when he explodes onto the screen, sets about hacking apart James Garner's office with his fists, and

James Bond: by Sean Connery (*right*) with Jill St John in *Diamonds Are Forever,* director Guy Hamilton (United Artists, 71), and by Roger Moore (*below*) in *Live and Let Die,* director Guy Hamilton (United Artists, 73)

then exits to his death via the window. It is the liveliest moment in one of the duller remakes of Raymond Chandler novels.

However, Hollywood was not ready for him and so he took off for Hong Kong, where he made *The Big Boss* (72, aka *Fist of Fury*), *Fist of Fury* (72, aka *The Chinese Connection* – there is considerable confusion about the titles; they seem to have different names in different territories), *Way of the Dragon* (73, aka *Return of the Dragon*) and *Enter the Dragon* (73, which despite its title was made after the other). They were all much of a muchness but elevated above the slew of other kung-fu movies which flooded the market in their wake by reason of Lee's presence. He seemed set to be a huge star, although it's difficult to see where he would have gone after the fad for kung-fu inevitably waned. However, any speculation was removed by Lee's sudden and rather mysterious death.

Bruce Lee (left) in *Enter the Dragon,* director Robert Clouse (Warners/Concord, 73)

215

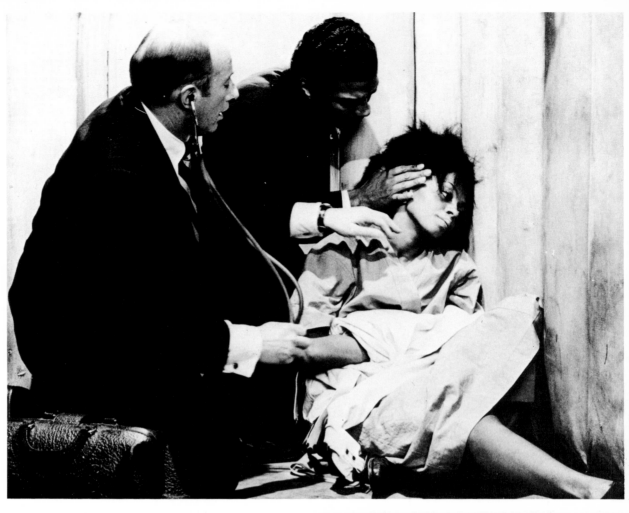

Hollywood was slow to recognize Lee's appeal partly because of his race. In effect, he was the victim of the sort of discrimination that had kept American blacks out of films for decades. Apart from Sidney Poitier, there were no black stars at the start of the decade and those blacks appearing in big movies were little more than tokens – O.J. Simpson in *The Towering Inferno* (75), Richard Roundtree in *Earthquake* (74) and so on.

Poitier, aware of his unique position and the responsibility he owed to his fellow blacks, conscientiously tried to further their cause as star, director and producer. He plugged away with *Buck and the Preacher* (72), *A Warm December* (73) and *Uptown Saturday Night* (74), the latter a comedy with Bill Cosby, Harry Belafonte, Flip Wilson and Richard Pryor, which was successful but no match for its successor, *Let's Do It Again* (76, Poitier directed both), which reteamed him with Cosby.

However, Poitier was viewed with considerable suspicion by many who thought he played 'a white man's nigger'. The mood of blacks in America was changing fast. They were now demanding films that reflected their lives and their problems. Decent attempts – like *Sounder* and *Lady Sings the Blues* (both 72) – were all very well: they were black stories with black actors and actresses (in the latter Diana Ross played Billie Holliday) but they were written and directed by whites.

Billie Holliday was a black woman in a white world; soon American blacks were flocking to see films set in the urban ghettoes in which they lived, films in which whites seldom impinged except as villains or cops. Gordon Parks supplied them with a hero who makes out in the urban jungle, a street-wise, cool, often violent private eye called *Shaft*

Cicely Tyson (centre) in *Sounder*, director Martin Ritt (20th Century-Fox, 72)

Richard Roundtree (right) in *Shaft*, director Gordon Parks (MGM, 71)

The identity of the Australian aborigine: David Gulpilil in *The Last Wave* (*right*), director Peter Weir (Ayer Productions, 77) and (*bottom*) Tommy Lewis (left) and David Gulpilil in *The Chant of Jimmie Blacksmith*, director Fred Schepisi (Film House/Australian Film Commission, 78)

(71). Richard Roundtree in the name part was not really much different from most other private dicks of the time, but he gave black audiences a hero they could cheer. The movie was a big hit and Parks sequelled it with *Shaft's Big Score* (72). However, a sign that Hollywood was riding a trend is that the third in the series, *Shaft in Africa* (73), was directed by a white man, John Guillermin.

There wasn't much social comment in these films; they were slick black thrillers which left aside a message in favour of entertainment. But their heroes moved in an environment of fear,

violence, sexuality and decay which was a reflection of the desperate conditions experienced by the audience.

Regrettably, the movement towards an American black cinema quite quickly descended into exploitation, the films becoming routine and stereotyped – there were black heroines of the Modesty Blaise variety, *Cleopatra Jones* and *Coffy* (both 73) and even a black vampire, *Blacula* (72). Amid them, honest attempts to further the cause, like Gordon Parks Sr's *Leadbelly* (75), the life of Huddie Ledbetter, were lost.

Tamara Dobson as *Cleopatra Jones*, director Jack Starrett (Warners, 73)

219

In the end, the black movie became just another
Seventies trend. It had its day just as, for example,
the Devil had his day. The lead given by Polanski's
Rosemary's Baby (68) in the Sixties was taken up by
William Friedkin in 1973 with *The Exorcist*. This,
like the disaster movies, seemed to touch an
atavistic fear; the audience, it appeared, liked to be
shocked and scared and even disgusted. *The
Exorcist* is a common enough plot – a young girl
(Linda Blair) is possessed by the Devil and transformed into a monster; attempts are made to
exorcize her, lives are lost in the battle against the
foul demon. What perhaps made this film stand out
from the rest was the graphic detail with which her
possession is portrayed.

It was an old-fashioned horror film made in a
very modern way, full of suspense and shocks, and
it won Oscars for Best Screenplay and Best Sound.
Its quite astonishing success ensured that it
spawned not only its own sequel, *Exorcist II: The
Heretic* (77), but a very successful imitator – *The
Omen* (76). This time it's a boy who is invaded by
Satan, and it produced its own sequel, *Omen II:
Damien* (78). The Devil as superstar? So it seemed
as Michael Winner got in on the act with *The
Sentinel* (77); then came a purportedly true (later dis-
proved) story of a family who move into a house
infested with diabolical terrors, *The Amityville
Horror* (79). They all made a lot of money.

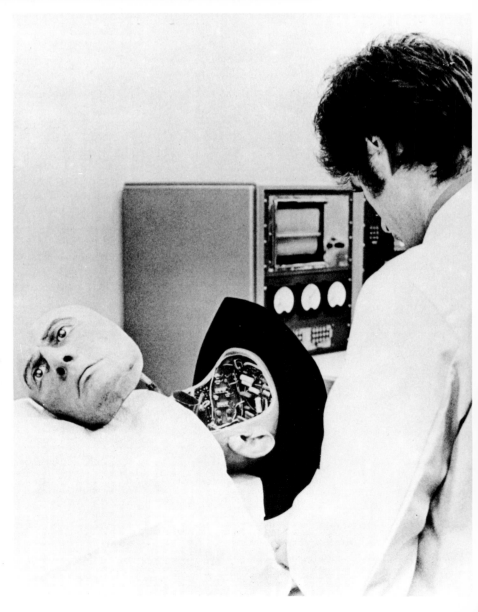

None of these trends, however, proved to be as
financially rewarding as science fiction. The new
sci-fi movies took a number of forms. In 1973 there
was a relatively modest film with an intriguing
idea: what happens when a humanoid gunslinger
robot blows a circuit in a leisure centre designed to
look like a Western township where people go to
indulge their fantasies? Such was the plot for
Westworld (starring Yul Brynner), which cleverly

Sissy Spacek in *Carrie*, director Brian DePalma (United Artists/Red Bank Films, 76)

contrived to mix two genres – the Western and the sci-fi flick. It was a success, seeded a follow-up, *Futureworld* (76), and initiated a run of pictures which took a look into our future on Earth.

Some were desolate: *Soylent Green* (73) glimpses New York in 2022 and the inhabitants' dependence on artificial food; *Logan's Run* (76) postulates that every person must be killed at the age of 30 and is really a futuristic chase movie about those, including Michael York and Jenny Agutter, who try

221

left
Soylent Green, director
Richard Fleischer (MGM, 73)

below
Bruce Dern in *Silent Running*,
director Douglas Trumbull
(Universal, 71)

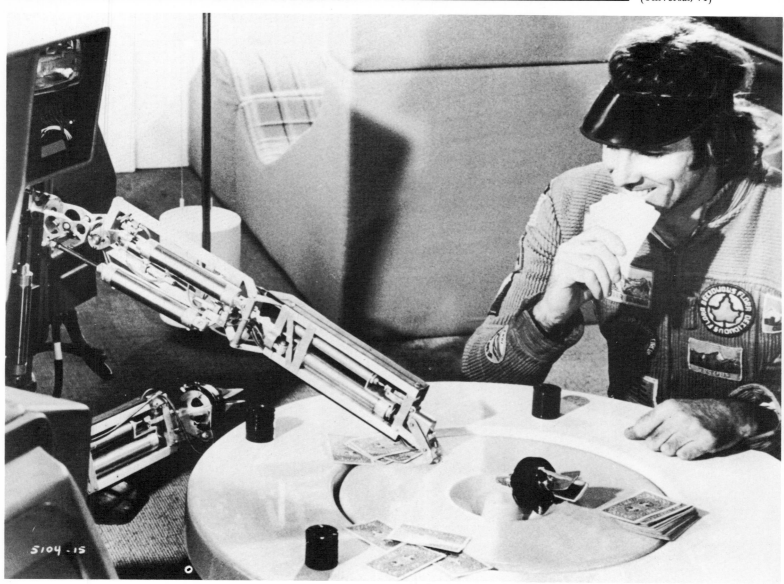

Rollerball, director Norman Jewison (United Artists, 75)

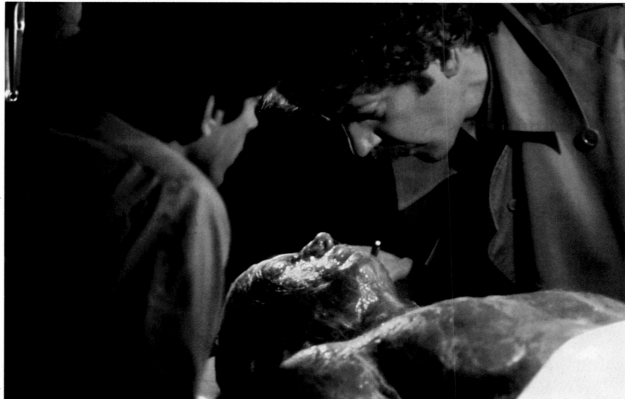

Donald Sutherland (right) in *Invasion of the Body Snatchers*, director Philip Kaufman (United Artists, 78)

to escape that fate; *Zardoz* (74), starring Sean Connery in a more pretentious effort by John Boorman, is set in 2293, with Earth devastated and humans split into two classes, the Brutals and the Exterminators; *Rollerball* (75) looks to the next century too, when the discontent of the masses is channelled into an exceedingly vicious sport; and a similar theme is explored and exploited in *Death Race 2000* (75), where the sport is cross-country motor racing with the purpose to rack up as many casualties as possible.

Meanwhile, some old favourites in the broadly science-fiction category were not forgotten. *King Kong* was remade in 1976 at colossal expense. For all the technical wizardry of the new Kong, he lacked the appeal (one might almost say the humanity) of the 1933 original. The rebirth was futile in entertainment and financial terms. There was no need for a new Kong while the old one still had the power to enthrall and captivate. Another remake, this time of Don Siegel's superior Fifties movie *The Invasion of the Body Snatchers* (56 and 78), was just as unnecessary but probably rather more rewarding financially. However, one old hero *did*

benefit from new screen technology. *Superman* (78) really gained from it; so good were the effects that we almost *did* believe a man could fly. It also boasted an amiable, amusing hero in Christopher Reeve, who looked good both as timid Clark Kent and invincible Superman himself. On the debit side, however, was a rather weak plot and some entirely unmenacing villains, notably Gene Hackman who was wasted. Nonetheless, *Superman* was one of the most entertaining and spectacular pictures of the decade and probably deserved its tremendous success.

It was when the movies went into space that they became astronomic: there had never been anything to rival the success of *Star Wars* (77). In other respects, there was nothing new about it. The story borrowed heavily from other genres, not least the Western. Luke Skywalker (Mark Hamill) gets mixed up in someone else's war; he meets a mysterious, monkish man, Ben Obi-Wan Kenobi (Alec Guinness), who invests him with a laser sword and the watchword 'The Force be with you' and sets him on his

way to help a beautiful princess (Carrie Fisher) fight against evil Darth Vader and the power of the Empire, aided by a pair of robots – R2D2 and C3PO.

It was a simple-minded plot, kid's stuff. And that was the point. George Lucas was making a film for children: 'I saw that kids today don't have any fantasy life the way we had – they don't have Westerns, they don't have pirate movies, they don't have that stupid serial fantasy we used to believe in.'

He took the basic elements of the fairy tale and updated them. He used every technical resource to hand (and occasionally invented some). Visually the film is often stunning, otherwise it is a *Flash Gordon* serial in modern garb. How many years is it since an audience was so caught up by the sheer magic of the movies that they 'oohed' and 'aahed' and gasped in horror and then in wonder? When people say, 'They don't make movies like they used to', it should be pointed out that George Lucas did just that. It cost a lot of money but it made so very much more.

Peter Mayhew as the Wookie, Mark Hamill, Alec Guinness and Harrison Ford in *Star Wars*, director George Lucas (20th Century-Fox, 77)

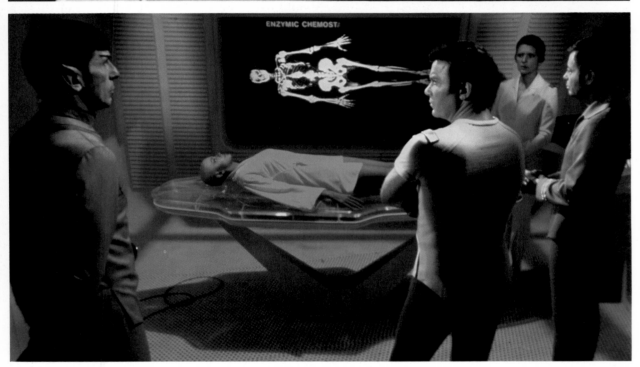

Star Trek: *The Movie* with (foreground, left to right) Leonard Nimoy, William Shatner and DeForest Kelley, director Robert Wise (Paramount, 79)

Nothing came within laser-blasting distance of *Star Wars*. There were other simple-minded attempts at the genre. *Star Trek* (79) finally made the transition from TV to film after years of lobbying from its large band of fanatical supporters. *Buck Rogers* (79) was born again from serial to superscreen (and TV), and then there was *Battlestar Galactica* (78), which was a TV serial *and* a movie but not very convincing as either. Disney even got onto the spacewagon with *The Black Hole* (79), but none of them touched *Star Wars* commercially or even in intent – they were childish rather than childlike. *Alien* (79) positioned itself for adults and mixed the genres – sci-fi meets *The Exorcist* – dealing out shocks as the Thing erupts horribly from John Hurt's stomach.

The nearest anyone got was Steven Spielberg

with *Close Encounters of the Third Kind* (77). This was not a space movie; it was an Earth movie in which the extraterrestrials visit and touch the lives of very ordinary Americans. Where *Close Encounters* differs from the rest of the sci-fi blockbusters is in its attention to people, rather than technology. The massive, glittering, glowing ship is there, but not until the very end. Spielberg wanted his movie to be full of suspense; his declared aim was 'to write a mystery story as opposed to a special-effects movie'.

It was a big movie but set within a smaller frame of reference. Spielberg's skies aren't great playgrounds; they are menacing because they are seen in relationship to human scale. Nevertheless, it was an enormously expensive film to make. $19 million were spent on it and there were some cold feet at

Alien, director Ridley Scott
(20th Century-Fox, 79)

Columbia. The gamble paid off – it's indubitably the most profitable movie the studio's ever made.

These films and others had made the names, and fortunes, of a handful of young directors who were being hailed as *wunderkinder* and upon whose talent the salvation of Hollywood seemed to rest. They had come into films at exceptionally young ages – Spielberg was only 26 when he made *Jaws* – and very few of them had served traditional apprenticeships.

Three, however, had paid some of their dues, working with the single-minded and maverick producer/director Roger Corman. He was the king of the drive-in movies: the very cheap, very sensational pics which were staple fare for teenage Saturday nights.

During the Fifties he had churned out such nonsense as *It Conquered the World* (56), *Attack of the Crab Monsters* (57) and *Wasp Women* (59), occasionally making excursions into gutsy, bloody gangster pics like *Machine Gun Kelly* (58). In the Sixties he ventured into more classic horror, roping in the acting talents of old hands like Boris Karloff and Peter Lorre and creating a new horror star in Vincent Price. His most successful work of the period was campy, grand guignol versions of Edgar

Allen Poe stories – *The Fall of the House of Usher* (60), *The Pit and the Pendulum* (61), *The Premature Burial* (62) and others, including a splendidly jokey version of *The Raven* (63), which had as its young leading man (the stars were Price, Lorre and Karloff) a Corman protegé, Jack Nicholson. In the late Sixties he turned his attention to other matters – mostly a heady, not particularly savoury, mixture of drugs, speed, sex and violence with *The Wild Angels* (66), a biker movie that set the scene for *Easy Rider* (69), and a controversial movie about LSD, *The Trip* (67), which simulated an acid experience and was roundly condemned and much banned.

Quickies were Corman's stock in trade. He made his Fifties movies in a fortnight and his bigger, colour efforts from Poe in less than a month! He often managed to bring in a film under budget and before schedule. Which was how he happened to have two spare days of work from Boris Karloff owing to him. He also had a young ex-journalist on the payroll of AIP studios who was desperate to become a director. So Corman handed Peter Bogdanovich the following problem – see what you can do with the remaining days on Karloff's contract, 18 minutes of unused shooting from a previous film, *The Terror* (63), and a budget not exceeding $125,000.

Bogdanovich came up with *Targets* (68), a dazzling little suspense movie in which an ageing horror star (Karloff, of course) is the target for a deranged young sniper who plans to assassinate him as he is premiering his new film (*The Terror* out-takes) at a drive-in! It didn't earn much money but it made Bogdanovich's reputation. The young director went on to make *The Last Picture Show* (71), set in the Fifties, in which the closing of a cinema in small-town Texas is paralleled with the end of adolescence. This garnered a great deal of praise, perhaps too much.

Bogdanovich, whose journalistic work had most often been in re-establishing the reputations of Hollywood directors from the golden age, continued to look back. His next, *What's Up Doc?* (72), had a contemporary setting but was a homage to the screwball comedies of the Thirties. Starring Ryan O'Neal and Barbra Streisand, it was fast and fairly funny but it was evidence that Bogdanovich lacked Howard Hawks's sure touch with comedy. He harked back again, this time with far more success, in *Paper Moon* (73). It was a warm, affectionate, often funny story of a Bible-selling

conman and a smart, precocious child (Ryan and Tatum O'Neal) as they travel across the mid-West, living off their wits. It was saved from mawkishness by the really quite extraordinary playing of 10-year-old Tatum O'Neal, who picked up the Supporting Actress Oscar that year.

With these behind him, Bogdanovich was top of the heap. But suddenly it all started going wrong. He commenced a well-publicized romance with Cybill Shepherd (who'd appeared in *The Last Picture Show*) and his love seemed to blind him to her limitations as an actress. First he put her into a version of Henry James's *Daisy Miller* (74), but subtlety eluded her. And then he tried to do for the Thirties musical what he had failed to do for the screwball comedy. *At Long Last Love* (75) had Shepherd and Burt Reynolds. It would, perhaps,

have helped if they'd shown any proficiency at singing and dancing!

Bogdanovich followed this with yet another retrospective glance, this time to the early days of Hollywood (the industry was much given to celebrating its own history at the time, the compilation *That's Entertainment* in 1974 was a big and rather unexpected hit). *Nickelodeon* (77) looked like it might restore his reputation. Ryan and Tatum O'Neal had served him well before, Burt Reynolds was fast becoming a bankable star, but again something was missing. By the end of the decade a career that had rocketted was now looking rocky in the extreme.

Too much, too soon. This seemed to be the problem with another Corman graduate, Martin Scorsese. Corman produced his first cinema feature as

Ryan (right) and Tatum O'Neal in *Paper Moon*, director Peter Bogdanovich (Paramount, 73)

More from Bogdanovich:
(*above*) Ryan O'Neal and
Barbra Streisand in *What's
Up Doc?* (Warners, 72), and
(*right*) *The Last Picture Show*
with (left to right) Ben
Johnson and Timothy and
Sam Bottoms (Columbia, 71)

director, *Boxcar Bertha* (72), about a girl who rides the railroads in the Depression, which got a lot of admiring attention. Next he journeyed back to his own troubled, unhappy childhood in New York's Little Italy to direct a fine study of harsh lives in *Mean Streets* (73). *Alice Doesn't Live Here Anymore* (74) took a wider view; Ellen Burstyn is the woman who, on the death of her husband, sets off on the road with her son. It starts as a feminist story of a woman who cuts herself free of dependency on men

Martin Scorsese directs:
(*left*) Ellen Burstyn and
Alfred Lutter in *Alice
Doesn't Live Here Anymore*
(Warners, 74), and (*below*)
Robert De Niro in *Taxi
Driver* (Columbia, 76)

Marlon Brando as *The Godfather*, director Francis Ford Coppola (Paramount, 72)

but ends up with her forming a new relationship (with Kris Kristofferson) that is not so very different from that she'd had.

Scorsese returned to the streets of New York for the deeply disturbing, rather tortured *Taxi Driver* (76), a study in breakdown as a Vietnam veteran (Robert De Niro) seems to find echoes of the horrors he has experienced on the sidewalk of the city. It was a film which showed the squalor of urban low-life very realistically and De Niro was magnificent as the disintegrating avenging angel.

Scorsese seemed to be at his best with grim, claustrophobic stories full of fear and a certain amount of disgust. However, for his next subject he turned to a musical. *New York, New York* (77) had many elements of *A Star Is Born* – the band singer (Liza Minnelli) outstrips the success of her man (De Niro) – and too many uncomfortable echoes in Minnelli's performance of her mother, Judy Garland, who had played 'Mrs Norman Maine' in the second remake. Somewhere along the way *New York, New York* got out of hand. It cost $12 million and the rough cut lasted more than four hours. This was reduced to two-and-a-half hours and then trimmed by a further 16 minutes. It seemed that the young lions were biting off more than they could chew.

This never looked more true than when Francis

Ford Coppola set out to make *the* film about the Vietnam war – *Apocalypse Now*. But until he started work on it, in 1975, Coppola's career seemed to have been far steadier than those of the new generation he had helped. Francis Coppola (he dropped 'Ford' during the shooting of *Apocalypse*) is older than the other members of the Hollywood 'new wave' and has acted as something of a godfather (no pun intended) to several of them, particularly George Lucas. He had a more solid grounding in the industry, working in many capacities for Corman from the early Sixties. His first big feature as director was *You're a Big Boy Now* (67) and after that he was handed a huge assignment – directing Fred Astaire, Petula Clark and Tommy Steele in the musical *Finian's Rainbow* (68). He did a decent job but was disenchanted with the Hollywood system, decamped to San Francisco, and set up his own company, American Zoetrope. His energy seems to have been phenomenal. Not only did he write and direct the picaresque *The Rain People* (69), he also wrote scripts, notably *Patton* (70) and *The Great Gatsby* (74). And he produced the work of others, particularly George Lucas's first two movies, *THX 1138* (72) and *American Graffiti* (73).

It was something of a surprise, however, when he was asked to direct the film from Mario Puzo's blockbusting book, *The Godfather* (72). He didn't

233

More from Francis Ford Coppola: (*left*) John Cazale in *The Godfather Part Two* (Paramount, 74), and (*above*) Gene Hackman in *The Conversation* (Paramount, 74)

have an easy ride. For a start, the story is so huge that the organization of the material into a workable script must have been daunting (as it was, he had enough left to bring out *The Godfather Part Two* in 1974). Then the studio was under considerable pressure from influential Italian-American lobbies, who were howling that the story was a vile slur on their reputation. And thirdly, the studio was unhappy about two of his cast – Brando as Don Corleone and Al Pacino as Michael.

In the event, it was these performances (among many other fine ones) which helped to raise the movie to a very elevated plane. (Let it be remembered that not only did *The Godfather* win the Best Film Oscar, not only did Brando win – and reject – the Best Actor Oscar, not only did Coppola and Puzo win the Script Oscar, but three of the actors – James Caan, Robert Duvall and Al Pacino – were nominated for Best Supporting Oscar which, in the event, went to Joel Grey for *Cabaret*).

The Godfather was an exception in the Seventies – a movie that was staggeringly successful financially but also of the very highest artistic merit and

integrity. A serious film as well as an exciting and entertaining one, it has been described as 'arguably the most important American film of the Seventies' and, taken together with its fine sequel, it is undoubtedly one in which commerciality and story-telling, action and the serious exploration of ethics, of family relationships, and of the immigrant struggle in the States come consummately together.

In between the two parts, Coppola took a smaller subject but one which touched the nerves of the audience. Although he had conceived *The Conversation* (74) before the revelations of Watergate and the Nixon tapes, he made it at a time when the US was particularly sensitive to the subject of bugging. *The Conversation* is an elliptical, often puzzling film about a 'surveillance and security technician', Harry Caul (Gene Hackman at his introspective, subtle best), who is nothing without his job.

It's a teasing film which poses more questions than it answers. Caul is frozen; he comes to realize the immorality of his work and yet seems powerless to do anything more than follow events. Had he acted, the film might have found more favour

with audiences who, in the wake of Watergate, needed to be reassured. (Which is why Woodward and Bernstein, the Washington Post reporters who dug and dug until they had uncovered the truth of Nixon's White House, became contemporary heroes and one reason why *All The President's Men* (76) was such a financial success at a time when 'serious' films were finding it hard to win at the box office.)

Nonetheless, *The Conversation* was a considerable achievement but was Coppola prepared for his next project, *Apocalypse Now*? He started it in 1975 and the making was an epic in itself. It took four years and the money put into it may have been $25 or $40 million. From all reports the struggles to get it made – not to say the hardship of the years on location in the Philippines – nearly broke him financially and physically.

Whether it is a masterpiece or the definitive film statement on the Vietnam war is still debatable. It was regarded as a flawed work – the latter sequences in which Brando appeared were subject to considerable criticism – but the majority view was that it was a film of great stature, and that if it failed to achieve everything Coppola had hoped for, then it was probably because he had set himself impossible targets.

It is rather surprising that *Apocalypse Now* was only the fourth major film to appear around the theme of Vietnam. Perhaps it was too recent in the memory, too painful to bear investigation. Hollywood had never shown itself so reticent about war

ance won her the Oscar, which must have brought an ironic smile to her face as only a few years before she was virtually ostracized by Hollywood for her vociferous opposition to the US's involvement in Vietnam.

Michael Cimino's film about buddies from a Pennsylvanian steelworks who go off to the war, *The Deer Hunter* (78), was initially hailed as one of the finest, most moving and truthful essays on the subject. It won the Best Film Oscar and a Best Supporting Actor Oscar for Christopher Walken but before long there was a backlash. Criticism hinged around the scenes of Russian roulette played by Viet Cong guards on their prisoners. It never happened, asserted the war correspondents. Cimino made contradictory statements. He had, it seems, blurred the distinction between reportage and interpretation; a film that purports to tell truth cannot lightly claim artistic licence. This is an inherent danger when film-makers tackle controversial films which engage the passions. In a sense it should not matter whether the events did happen. Whatever the merits, *The Deer Hunter* was an infinitely more faithful, sincere and honest film than *The Green Berets*.

The Vietnam war: (*opposite*) *Apocalypse Now*, with Martin Sheen (*below*), director Francis Coppola (United Artists, 79); (*above*) Jane Fonda and Bruce Dern in *Coming Home*, director Hal Ashby (United Artists, 78); and *The Deer Hunter* (*below*) with John Savage (right), director Michael Cimino (Universal, 78)

in the past. In the Sixties John Wayne had made a tub-thumping, stereotyped, right-wing movie, *The Green Berets* (68), which made no attempt to portray the conflict accurately.

Coming Home (78) was more concerned with the aftermath than the war zone; Jon Voight played a paraplegic veteran who has an affair with the wife (Jane Fonda) of another veteran – a martinet Marine officer (Bruce Dern), rigid, unbending, the antithesis of the cripple. The film's implications were rather lost in the attention devoted to the sexuality of the paralyzed man. However, Fonda's perform-

Film-makers were on safer ground when they took a topical issue and from it projected what *might* happen, as Jane Fonda did with *The China Syndrome* (79). This was an excellent example of serious film-making that provoked thought (and even some alarm) while being grippingly entertaining. The subject was one close to Fonda's heart

(she produced), and its treatment indicated she had learned that the best way to make a point in the cinema is to set it within a strong drama. It was pure coincidence that the release of *The China Syndrome* was almost simultaneous with a near-disaster at a nuclear plant in Harrisburg, Pennsylvania, but even without that the film would probably have done more to alert the general public to the potential risks of nuclear energy than a dozen documentaries. *The China Syndrome*, a particularly well-made and excellently acted film (not least by Fonda and the marvellous Jack Lemmon, who seemed to get better as he got older), showed that Jane Fonda had lost much of her stridency but none of her sincerity.

She emerged as an undisputed female superstar of the Seventies, but only after she had been through a period as one of the most unpopular women in the US. Her career has taken a number of twists and bumps. For a start it was not easy for her to prove that she was not merely Henry Fonda's daughter but an actress in her own right. Then she had a difficult time in Hollywood, where she reacted strongly against attempts to mould her into a Monroe-style sex-symbol. She fled to France, met and married Roger Vadim, who promptly turned her into a Bardot-style sex symbol!

She worked between France and Hollywood in the mid Sixties. In the States she made the excellent *Cat Ballou* (65), starred opposite Robert Redford in *The Chase* (66), and after a couple more, hit a very high peak indeed, again opposite Redford, in *Barefoot in the Park* (67). Her French work was less satisfactory, although Vadim's bizarre, kinky, futuristic *Barbarella* (68) caused much attention, little of it complimentary.

By now she was gaining a deep political awareness and starting to make some very controversial statements on a number of subjects but mostly the US's dubious presence in Vietnam. She was marvellous in an excellent movie about the Depression, *They Shoot Horses, Don't They?* (69), but was beginning to fall from favour in the Nixon years.

In *Klute* (71) she was just one good thing in Alan J. Pakula's off-beat, gripping thriller. Donald Sutherland as the determined, righteous ex-cop, John Klute, was so good it was difficult to realize he was acting; his still, rawboned features registered such subtlety. Nonetheless, as the strung-out hooker, Bree Daniels, who is trying to give up the game and who is threatened by a sadistic pervert, Fonda is brilliant, veering between cocky independence and frail insecurity. She won the Oscar that year and forebore from using the opportunity to proselytize her causes, merely commenting in her acceptance speech, 'There is a great deal to say, but I'm not going to say it.'

She was not so restrained thereafter and her militancy won her many enemies. She and Sutherland co-starred again, in *Steelyard Blues* in 1972, but between 1971 and 1977 the work was thin. Things picked up with a mild comedy opposite George Segal, *Fun with Dick and Jane* (77), and then she was terrific opposite Vanessa Redgrave in *Julia* (77) from one of Lillian Hellman's autobiographical

Jane Fonda: in (*opposite top*) *The China Syndrome*, director James Bridges (Columbia, 79) and (*opposite bottom*) with Vanessa Redgrave in *Julia*, director Fred Zinnemann (20th Century-Fox, 77)

Australian films about women: (*top*) Helen Morse in *Caddie*, director Donald Crombie (Anthony Buckley Productions, 76), and (*right*) Judy Davis and Sam Neill in *My Brilliant Career*, director Gillian Armstrong (NSW Films/Margaret Fink, 79)

right
Robert Redford in *Little Fauss and Big Halsy*, director Sidney J. Furie (Alfran/Furie for Paramount, 70)

below
Redford and Paul Newman (right) in *The Sting*, director George Roy Hill (Universal, 73)

opposite top
Robert Redford and Barbra Streisand in *The Way We Were*, director Sydney Pollack (Columbia, 73)

opposite bottom
Mia Farrow and Redford in *The Great Gatsby*, director Jack Clayton (Paramount, 74)

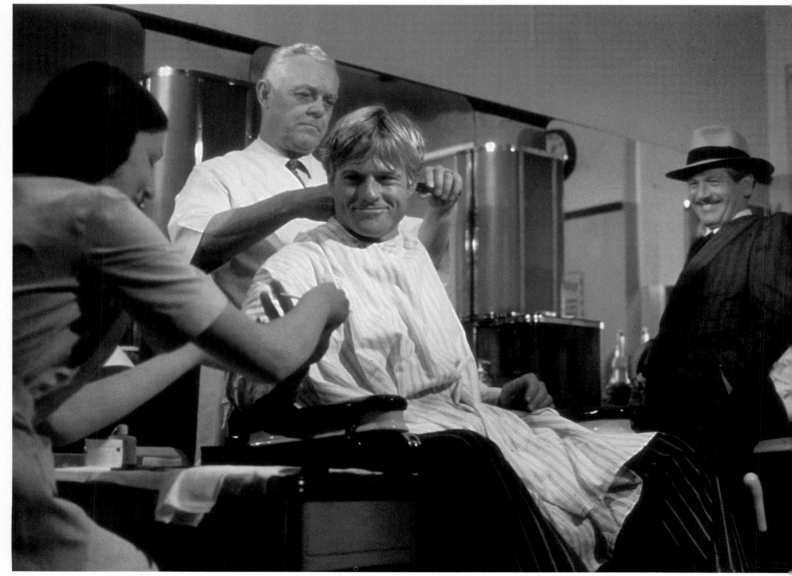

books and one of the few films of a male-dominated era which gave women meaty parts. She's at her best when tackling a subject that she feels strongly about as *Julia, Coming Home* (78) and *The China Syndrome* (79) showed.

In 1979 she made her third movie with Robert Redford, *The Electric Horseman*, which didn't live up to its promise. In many ways Redford is Fonda's male equivalent. Both have well-articulated social consciences, both have tried to prove that they are more than pretty faces, and both have had an uneasy relationship with Hollywood. Both entered the Eighties as superstars.

Redford's career has always gone in fits and starts, mainly because he seems to get bored after a while and decides to retreat from the cameras. His work in the early Sixties was patchy and he found the roles he was offered so unsatisfactory that he dropped out. He was tempted back for *Barefoot in the Park* (67) and scored such a hit he was offered a number of projects, including *The Graduate*, but seemed to be committing professional suicide by turning them down.

Then came *Butch Cassidy* (69) and some films he might have turned down but didn't – *Tell Them Willy Boy Is Here* (69), *The Downhill Racer* (69), *Little Fauss and Big Halsy* (70), *The Hot Rock* (72), *Jeremiah Johnson* (72) and *The Candidate* (72). Most of them were well-intentioned but somehow lost their way and, occasionally, his deficiencies as an actor were exposed. Somehow his beautiful face is not as expressive as Newman's or as impish as McQueen's; he has a neat sense of comedy but when it comes to the more serious stuff he seems to make heavy going of it as if he's always thinking and not allowing himself to relax into the part.

left
Faye Dunaway, Cliff
Robertson and Robert
Redford in *Three Days of the
Condor*, director Sydney
Pollack (Paramount, 75)

Don Siegel directs Eastwood:
(*below*) in *Dirty Harry*
(Warners, 72) and (*right*)
with Elizabeth Hartman in
The Beguiled (Universal, 71)

He remained popular after this bunch but had reached a plateau. *The Way We Were* (73) opposite Streisand was not particularly brilliant but it *was* extremely popular and *The Sting* (73) was an absolute monster. *The Great Gatsby* (74), we were assured, was going to be as big but Redford was adjudged lacking in the title part and it fell comparatively flat. *The Great Waldo Pepper* (75) was fun; he seemed to enjoy being in a purely entertainment vehicle and playing the devil-may-care barnstorming pilot. But it was not a particular success and probably didn't do as well as his next, *Three Days of the Condor* (75), a rather murky thriller with Watergate undertones.

In the meantime he had bought the story of the Watergate disclosures and set up the production of *All the President's Men* (76), a project into which he poured a considerable personal commitment. His sincerity was evident and he possibly gave his finest performance to date as Bob Woodward, playing brilliantly off the equally good portrayal of Carl Bernstein by Dustin Hoffman. It could have been a worthy, dull film, but Pakula's direction and their acting made it both faithful and gripping.

After that he seemed to withdraw again. He did little for a lot ($2 million) in the over-loaded, over-long *A Bridge Too Far* (77) and went back to his mountaintop retreat until re-emerging in 1979 for *The Electric Horseman* and then another part which engaged his sympathies, that of a reforming prison governor who gets screwed by the system, *Brubaker* (80). At the threshold of the new decade, it remained to be seen if he would continue acting.

Redford took a very long time coming to the

Clint Eastwood: (*left*) in *Thunderbolt and Lightfoot*, director Michael Cimino (United Artists, 74); (*below left*) with Jessica Walter in *Play Misty for Me*, director Eastwood (Universal, 71); (*below*) in *High Plains Drifter*, director Eastwood (Universal, 72); and (*right*) in *Every Which Way But Loose*, director James Fargo (Warners, 78)

conclusion that there was only one small, dark, Jewish actor who could play Carl Bernstein in *All the President's Men*. Or at least that is what Dustin Hoffman claims. It's certainly difficult now to think of anybody who might have fitted the part better. Similarly it's impossible to imagine anyone else as Benjamin Braddock, the stumbling hero of *The Graduate* (67). Since his overnight leap to stardom, Hoffman seems to have had a charmed voyage, but the facts don't necessarily bear this out.

He can be a very good actor, but, as he acknowledges, anybody can shine in a grotesque part like Ratso in *Midnight Cowboy* (69); Jon Voight had a much more difficult job and brought it off brilliantly. Actually, there have been periods when it looked as though Hoffman's success may have been a flash in the pan. *John and Mary* (69) was a comparative failure. He was excellent as the guy who was on all the wrong sides in all the wrong places at all the wrong times in the history of the American

West but still managed to survive in *Little Big Man* (70) and then got himself into a stinker with an impossible title – *Who Is Harry Kellerman and Why Is He Saying All Those Terrible Things About Me?* (71). Peckinpah's *Straw Dogs* (72) was slammed for its unpleasantness and his entry into the Seventies looked tentative at best. An Italian film *Alfredo Alfredo* (73) didn't help.

Papillon (73) opposite Steve McQueen should have done, and *Lenny* (74), the biopic of Lenny Bruce, should have shown his range as an actor but neither quite hit the mark. *President's Men* saved the situation, *Marathon Man* (76) was a popular thriller, but *Straight Time* (78) didn't do very good business and *Agatha* (79), about crime writer Agatha Christie's disappearance for a few days in the Twenties, was an unmitigated disaster. By the end of the decade things were looking rocky for Hoffman. And nobody expected *Kramer vs Kramer* (79) to sweep the board at the Oscars and tug the heartstrings of millions, who wept at this rather thin story of a kid shuffled around in a divorce.

Hoffman, like Fonda and Redford, survived, despite the strong pressure on them from a whole new generation of actors, and a couple of fellows who had been around for a while but really hit the jackpot in the Seventies.

Jack Nicholson was a graduate *cum laude* from the Corman school of horror-schlock movies. He entered the academy in the Fifties and learned his trade the hard way. He also wrote scripts and turned producer; most are not worth remembering but a couple attained small cult status in the psychedelic Sixties. He wrote *The Trip* (67), which brought him together with Peter Fonda and Dennis Hopper, and wrote and co-produced one of the

Dustin Hoffman: (*left*) in *Little Big Man* with Robert Mulligan, director Arthur Penn (National General, 70); in (*below*) *All the President's Men*, with Robert Redford, director Alan J. Pakula (Warners, 76); and in (*opposite, top left*) *Kramer vs Kramer* with Justin Henry, director Robert Benton (Columbia, 79)

Warren Beatty: (*opposite, top right*) with Goldie Hawn (left) and Lee Grant in *Shampoo*, director Hal Ashby (Columbia, 75), and (*opposite bottom*) with Julie Christie in *Heaven Can Wait*, directors Buck Henry and Warren Beatty (Paramount, 78)

Charles Bronson: in (*above*)
Chato's Land, director
Michael Winner (United
Artists, 72), and (*above
centre*) *The Valachi Papers*,
director Terence Young
(Cinema International, 72)

right
James Coburn in *Pat Garrett
and Billy the Kid*, director
Sam Peckinpah (MGM, 73)

most extraordinary rock movies ever, *Head* (68), which featured The Monkees, who were then very big news. It should have been a big hit but it so baffled the business and the critics that it hardly surfaced.

Then the trio who made *The Trip* re-formed for *Easy Rider* (69). The film could have changed the face of Hollywood, instead it made a star out of Nicholson. Oddly, he had already been offered a part that might have broken him through, playing opposite Streisand in *On a Clear Day You Can See Forever* (70) but when that appeared his impact was negligible.

Instead he was tremendous in *Five Easy Pieces*

Jack Nicholson in *Five Easy Pieces*, director Bob Rafelson (Columbia, 70)

Bjorn Andresen and Dirk Bogarde in *Death in Venice*, director Luchino Visconti (Warners, 71)

(70) as Bobby Dupree, a drifter who is equally uncomfortable in the privileged background he springs from and in the rough oilfields he adopts. This shows the Nicholson persona at its best, one that seems to be an extension of his own personality. He just goes his own way, a born loner, a misfit who doesn't give a damn and who recognizes his own hopelessness with self-deprecating humour. But, for all his smiling nonchalance, he can 'go critical' if pushed. He seems to know that life is futile and mainly accept it, but every now and again a loathing – for the world and himself – seems to overwhelm him and he has no answer except to lash out.

Nicholson, however, is more than an actor who plays to type. He is one of the most interesting to watch. His pointed, sharp face has two (at least) smiles – one radiant and charming, the other like the sneer of the shark. And the first can switch unexpectedly to the second. You just don't know if it will unless you watch his eyes; they are the most expressive on screen. He uses his body too – flat, still and motionless one moment, bursting into humorous mime or whirlwind action the next. Nicholson thinks about his acting but he doesn't show it; on screen he just *is*. There probably wasn't a better actor with a greater range making movies in the Seventies.

Drive He Said (70) followed *Five Easy Pieces* and then Mike Nichols put him into *Carnal Knowledge* (71). Of all the hard-core, soft-core and sexually-oriented films of the decade – and they abounded from *Deep Throat* (72) and *The Devil in Miss Jones* (73) at the hard end through the 'significant', because Brando was in it, *Last Tango in Paris* (72) to the glossy *Emmanuelle* at the other – *Carnal Knowledge* was probably the most challenging movie about sex. As might be expected from this director – *The Graduate* (67) and *Catch 22* (70) – the

film was not merely cashing in on the new permissive climate; it was a study of the sexual awakening, confusion, obsession, and disillusion of two friends (Nicholson and Art Garfunkel) from their college days in the Fifties through to middle age. Nicholson gained considerable acclaim as the man who finally becomes so jaded that he needs

above
Marlon Brando and Maria Schneider in *Last Tango in Paris*, director Bernardo Bertolucci (United Artists, 72)

left
Sylvia Kristel (left) in *Emmanuelle, The Joys of a Woman*, director Francis Giacobetti (Paramount, 75)

252

Child-actress Brooke Shields in *Pretty Baby*, director Louis Malle (Paramount, 78)

Jack Nicholson and Julia Anne Robinson in *The King of Marvin Gardens*, director Bob Rafelson (Columbia, 73)

the services of a fellating prostitute to derive any satisfaction.

He was also excellent as a disc jockey in *The King of Marvin Gardens* (73) and much better still in *The Last Detail* (73) as a gruff sailor who, with another, has to escort a not very bright lad to jail, takes pity on him, and breaks all the rules by giving him a wild night on the town before delivering him to his sentence. It seemed that no one could play the contemporary man confronted by modern pressures better than Nicholson. But, just to keep everyone guessing, he switched and played, with evident relish, a Thirties private dick, J.J. Gittes, who is embroiled in a case of municipal

Jack Nicholson: in (*right*) *Chinatown*, director Roman Polanski (Paramount, 74), and (*below*) in *The Passenger* (aka *Profession: Reporter*), with Claud Mulbehill, director Michelangelo Antonioni (MGM, 75)

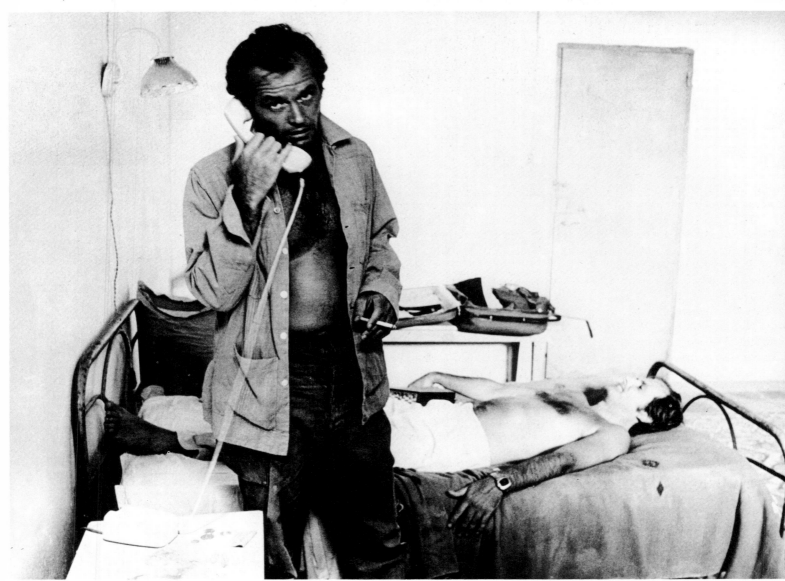

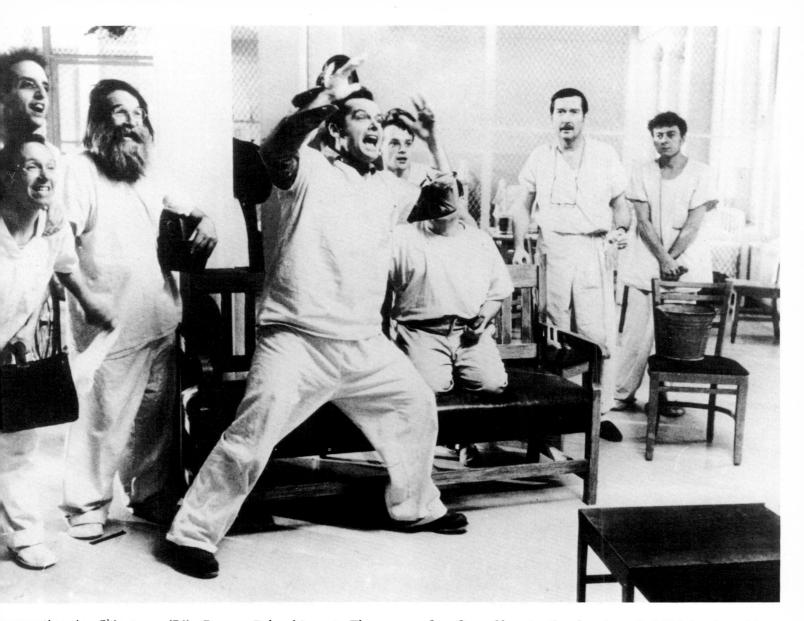

corruption in *Chinatown* (74). Roman Polanski directed *and* played a convincingly evil runt who slits Gittes's nostril, and brought to the first job an oblique vision that raised the film above the normal gumshoe fare. Nicholson invested the part with a great deal of throwaway humour.

Next there was a rather barren patch – Antonioni's confused *The Passenger* (75), a small part in Russell's *Tommy* (75), and a not too successful Mike Nichols comedy, *The Fortune* (75) – before he gave his ultimate performance as the individualist who battles against oppression in *One Flew Over the Cuckoo's Nest* (76). On the surface this is a comedy and a very, very funny one at that. Nicholson the oddball is confined to a mental hospital where he clashes with Nurse Ratched (a superb, Oscar-winning performance from Louise Fletcher), a woman whose rigidity and unbending interpretation of the rules amounts to a negation of humanity.

The comedy ends in tragedy for Nicholson, who is surgically reduced to a vegetable, but the human spirit prevails when a huge Indian (Will Sampson), who has conducted his own form of rebellion by pretending to be mute, is so devastated by the treatment accorded to Nicholson that he breaks

out. There were few finer films in the decade; Milos Forman directed it with enormous humanity and elicited memorable performances from all the cast and one from Nicholson that brought him an Oscar. And not before time.

That peak was followed by an inevitable dip – *The Last Tycoon* (76), *Missouri Breaks* (77) and *Goin' South* (78, which he directed) – but there were high expectations of Stanley Kubrick's exploration of the horror/supernatural genre, *The Shining* (80). These were not quite matched artistically; critics found that Kubrick's individual vision was not in evidence. However, Nicholson's essay into psychosis was interesting, if rather overdone.

There's no comparison, in acting terms, between Nicholson and Burt Reynolds. Reynolds doesn't act; he doesn't even claim to act. Reynolds was a star in the Seventies in much the same way (although of a lesser magnitude) that Gable had been. In fact, they share that all-man image, while being secure enough to make fun of their own masculinity. Reynolds worked hard to make himself into a star, even posing naked for a women's magazine. By the start of the Eighties he was acknowledged as one of the biggest names in Hollywood and yet he had made only one film of

(Left to right) Ned Beatty, Jon Voight, Ronny Cox and Burt Reynolds (right) in *Deliverance*, director John Boorman (Warners, 72)

Jill Clayburgh and Burt Reynolds in *Starting Over*, director Alan J. Pakula (Century Associates, 79)

any merit (other than pure entertainment) and very few that were really big box-office. Reynolds was a star because he looked and acted like one.

His career up to the Seventies can be summarized in two words – TV and rubbish. However, in 1972 he was in John Boorman's unusual adventure movie, *Deliverance*. Superficially concerned with four men on a weekend's boating/hunting trip, it carries deeper resonances. In the end they have to seek into their innermost resources to survive against a real and cruel enemy as they hunt and are hunted by men on whose territory they have encroached. Reynolds played the butchest of the trippers, the one who seems to have all the answers.

The role suited Reynolds well. The main dif-

ference between the character and the real man was that the former was humourless; the real Burt Reynolds has a strong streak of laughter running through him and, over the decade, he was to develop an individual screen persona of the 'good old boy'.

He followed *Deliverance* with *Fuzz* (72), an over-jokey version of the Ed McBain characters from his 87th Precinct series of crime novels. Then, after *The Shamus* (72), he made his first venture into the 'good old boy', moonshine-toting, car-chasing redneck character in *White Lightning* (73). He developed it in *W.W. and the Dixie Dance Kings* (75, this time he was peddling a C&W band instead of gutrot), *Gator* (76, the sequel to *White Lightning* and his directorial debut), and then the apotheosis of the type, *Smokey and the Bandit* (77), which seemed devoted to smashing up a variety of vehicles, making the police look stupid, and generally causing disruption. However, it was done with such enjoyment that the fun was infectious and few could resist his larger-than-life performance.

At Long Last Love (75), in which he seems to have tried for the mantle of Cary Grant, is best forgotten, as are *Lucky Lady* (76) and *Nickelodeon* (76). He was better as a sportsman in *The Longest Yard* (74) and *Semi-Tough* (77) and as a stuntman in *Hooper* (78), roles closer to the ruggedness of his physique.

Smokey and the Bandit was not only one of the most successful comedies of the decade, it was, according to the Variety ratings, one of the most successful of all time. Only two beat it in purely monetary terms – *The Sting* (73) and *National Lampoon Animal House* (78), the latter being a knockabout farce of American campus life. Undergraduate humour struck it rich there, but perhaps it was a

Veteran stars: (*above*) John
Wayne in *The Cowboys*,
director Mark Rydell
(Columbia, 72), and (*left*)
Laurence Olivier, with
Michael Caine, in *Sleuth*,
director Joseph L.
Mankiewicz (Palomar, 72)

Olivier in *The Marathon Man*, director John Schlesinger (Paramount, 76)

Peter Ustinov in *Death on the Nile*, director John Guillermin (EMI, 78)

one-off. It was certainly a world away from the postgraduate humour of Woody Allen, who by the mid-Seventies had given up the slapstick and was going for cerebral jokes.

Woody Allen is a bundle of neuroses; rather he keeps telling us he is and we are forced to believe him. From them spring his comedy, the comedy of the little guy who doesn't cope too well. He started in films as an actor and/or writer – *What's New Pussycat?* (65) and *Casino Royale* (67) – but always had a yen to direct. His first effort was *Take the Money and Run* (69), also playing an inept thief,

followed by *Bananas* (71), where he was a schmuck
mixed up in a South American revolution. Both
were curate's eggs – good and funny in parts. He
didn't direct *Play It Again Sam* (72), although it
was his own screenplay from his Broadway play
and he starred as a neurotic with woman problems.
This established his little worried-man persona,
unequal to the struggles of the modern world,
nervous and hesitant about sex, the pimply, four-
eyed gimp who can never quite believe a woman
will fancy him but can't stop trying for the most
unattainably beautiful women he sees.

Thereafter he was back to direction (still acting).
*Everything You Always Wanted to Know About Sex
But Were Afraid to Ask* (72) mostly conforms to the
rule of longer the title, thinner the material, being
a series of sketches around a theme and very patchy.
Sleeper (73) was a decided improvement; although
it still consisted of sketches, they were now strung
together to give a narrative thrust, and his adventures as a twentieth-century man (still a schlemiel)
who is resuscitated in the distant future were
packed with sight gags and some very funny one-
liners about the state of contemporary America.
Love and Death (76), a parody of extremely long
Russian novels, was intended to show his ability
to make clever, witty jokes but it looked like he was
showing off his knowledge and taking himself too
seriously. He got even more serious with *Interiors*
(78), a homage to Bergman which was a failure
commercially and considered pretentious by critics.

In between, however, he had come right back
into form with *Annie Hall* (77), one of the few films
of the decade to deal sensitively and sympathetic-
ally with women and to give a woman – Diane
Keaton – a really cracking, truthful part. It helped,
of course, that Annie bore more than a passing
resemblance to Diane, who had been Allen's lover,
on and off, for several years. If it was autobiographical, it was not indulgent; it was, in fact,
very warm, very witty and very amusing. It caught
the public imagination and cleaned up the Oscars

Allen in *Everything You Always Wanted to Know About Sex But Were Afraid to Ask,* director Allen (United Artists, 72)

Allen and Keaton in *Manhattan,* director Woody Allen (United Artists, 79)

– one, deservedly, for Keaton, two to Allen (Director and Writer, shared with his frequent collaborator, Marshall Brickman) and Best Film.

Allen struck back after *Interiors* with another movie that garnered rich praise and pulled in the crowds. His hymn to New York, *Manhattan* (79),

proved that he was at his best when his humour projected the inadequacies of his own character.

Mel Brooks also enjoyed a good comic run in the decade. His best, funniest film, *The Producers* (68), was one of the biggest sleepers in movies. It wasn't until it appeared on TV that it was generally hailed as one of the most outrageous and amusing films of modern years.

In fact, Brooks won an Oscar for the screenplay in 1968, which must be one of the few occasions when the Academy was actually ahead of the public. However, it ought to be said that there are those who consider it tasteless, lacking in style, and entirely unamusing. Perhaps the idea of a fat, venal producer (brilliant Zero Mostel) seducing nice, rich old ladies for their money and then selling off 2500% of the shares in a hideously awful musical on the assumption that it will flop and make him a fortune does not appeal. But who can resist Gene Wilder as a cringing accountant, Kenneth Mars as a thick-headed Nazi playwright, and Dick Shawn as a hippie whose brain has been blasted by drugs? And failing all that, is it possible not to laugh until you have to stuff a handkerchief in your mouth at the grossest Berkeley-style dance routine ever staged to the strains of 'Springtime For Hitler'?

Admittedly, Brooks's next, *The Twelve Chairs* (70), left a great deal to be desired and there were some doubts as to whether he could find the spark

again, but in 1974 he almost equalled the manic hilarity of *The Producers* with *Blazing Saddles*, which was packed with jokes about Westerns, Hollywood, movies, and virtually everything else. Having seen off the Western, Brooks now turned his wicked eye to other film genres. The horror pic was well duffed up in *Young Frankenstein* (75), which was far more disciplined than *Blazing Saddles* and also made with a loving regard for the original. But the joke was becoming over-stretched, Gene Wilder and Marty Feldman – stalwarts of Brooks films – tried their hands at sending up old movies with *The Adventures of Sherlock Holmes's Smarter Brother* and *The Last Remake of Beau Geste* to little success. Brooks himself turned to Hollywood's pre-talkie days with *Silent Movie* (76), which was exceptionally noisy although only one person had any dialogue (famous mime, Marcel Marceau!), and then had a go at Hitchcock with *High Anxiety* (78), by which time the in-jokes were leaving audiences cold.

They did not, unaccountably, seem to bore of the Pink Panther series. This had started in 1963 with *The Pink Panther*, in which Peter Sellers created the role of incompetent Inspector Clouseau, who mangles language with his idiosyncratic pronunciations – 'boermp' for 'bump', 'murth' for 'moth', etc. It was a huge success and Clouseau returned in *A Shot in the Dark* (64), which was, if anything, funnier than the original with Sellers at the height of his comic powers. The character was briefly and inadequately taken over by Alan Arkin in *Inspector Clouseau* (68) and then disappeared until 1975 when he was brought back for *The Return of the Pink Panther*, which was a surprisingly big hit. Next in line was *The PP Strikes Again* (77) and *The Revenge of the PP* (78). Although still popular, these demanded little of Sellers, whose recent work was well

Comedy from Mel Brooks: (*opposite top*) the 'Springtime for Hitler' number from *The Producers* (Embassy, 68); (*opposite bottom*) Marty Feldman in *Young Frankenstein* (20th Century-Fox, 75); (*above*) Feldman and Dom De Luise in *Silent Movie* (20th Century-Fox, 76); and (*right*) *Blazing Saddles* (Columbia/EMI/Warners, 74)

below par; the series might have continued indefinitely but for the actor's death in 1980.

It would have been sad if his last years were remembered by roles which allowed him to show so little of his massive comic talent. Fortunately, *Being There* (79), a gently satiric parable, gave him a welcome opportunity to display his gifts and stands as part testament to his brilliance, perhaps genius.

The Panther series was formula comedy but there were enough examples of more adventurous attempts at humour to make the decade rather brighter in this area than in some other genres. Michael Ritchie's sadly neglected *Smile* (75) was a sly satire on small-town America, set around a beauty contest · and exposing the smug self-satisfaction of the community. It is far more stinging and acerbic than that director's next, and vastly more successful, movie *The Bad News Bears* (76),

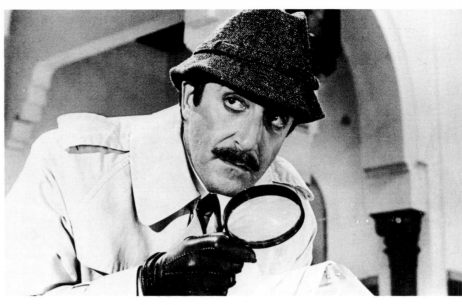

Peter Sellers: (*above*) as Clouseau in *The Return of the Pink Panther*, director Blake Edwards (United Artists, 75), and (*left*) in *Being There*, director Hal Ashby (United Artists, 79)

264

in which ever dependable Walter Matthau coaches a no-hope kids baseball team. (This didn't start out as formula comedy but its success spawned two sequels.)

As dependable as Matthau was playwright Neil Simon, who contributed 11 films during the decade of varying quality. The best were *The Out of Towners* (70, Jack Lemmon and Sandy Dennis), *The Prisoner of Second Avenue* (75), in which Lemmon is brilliant as the jobless man in a mid-life crisis, *The Sunshine Boys* (75) with Matthau and George Burns as ex-vaudevillians who worked the

boards for years and can't stand the sight of each other, and *The Goodbye Girl* (77), which brought Richard Dreyfuss an Oscar.

Dreyfuss had very quietly and unassumingly built himself an enviable career during the decade. Seldom flashy on the screen, he had nevertheless contributed considerably to the films he was in. And he was in some of the biggest ever; the trouble was, he was so damned good you sometimes overlooked him – his performance sort of snuck into your mind later and generally brought a smile of satisfaction. He was undoubtedly the best thing in

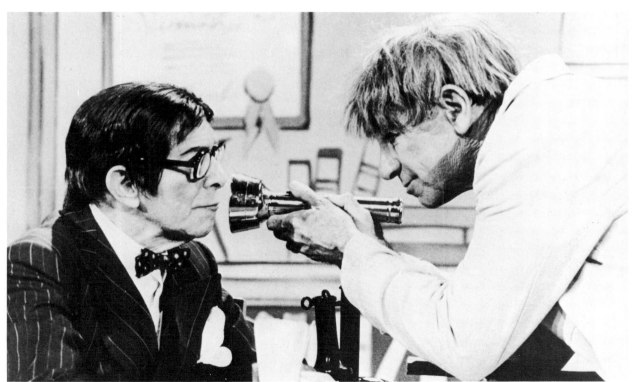

Richard Dreyfuss in *The Apprenticeship of Duddy Kravitz*, director Ted Kotcheff (Fox/Rank, 74)

American Graffiti (73), apart from the music, just right as Curt, the half-confident, half-fearful loner. He was full of chutzpah in *The Apprenticeship of Duddy Kravitz* (74). He was concerned as the ichthyologist in *Jaws* (75), a fairly thankless role, overshadowed by the harassed policeman (Roy Scheider) and hamminess of Robert Shaw. He was absolutely central to *Close Encounters of the Third Kind* (77) as the family man obsessed by the extra-terrestrial visitants. And he got a deserved Best Actor Oscar for *The Goodbye Girl*, in which his obvious talent for comedy was given full rein.

Comedy in the Seventies did not go in the direction that two early films seemed to indicate. Both took a black and bleakly funny look at medicine. One was *The Hospital* (71), in which George C. Scott is a surgeon whose personal life is in ruins and whose career seems to be disintegrating along with the hospital in which he works. This movie looked set to confirm Scott as one of the great actors of his

generation, especially as he had recently won, and refused to accept, the Best Actor Oscar for *Patton* (70). However, he was a prickly individual whose irascibility frequently alienated fellow workers and whose ego was not always matched by his performance or box-office popularity. The rest of the decade was marked by a series of flops, frequently because the pictures didn't warrant his talents.

The other gory, laugh-or-go-mad look at medicine was *M*A*S*H* (70), which many thought would start a trend for macabre comedy. Robert Altman's story of the Korean War was achingly funny at the time (it's less so now) and did a great deal to propel the careers of Elliott Gould and Donald Sutherland. It also marked Altman as one of the most idiosyncratic and individual directors in the States, a man who has possibly taken more praise and more abuse for his work than any other director.

He took a lot of stick for *Buffalo Bill and the*

left
George Hamilton and Susan Saint James in *Love at First Bite*, director Stan Dragoti (AIP, 79)

below
Donald Sutherland (third from right) in *M*A*S*H**, director Robert Altman (20th Century-Fox, 70)

Indians (76) with good reason, and a great deal for his updated version of *The Long Goodbye* (72) because he was not faithful to Raymond Chandler's novel (although he was faithful to the spirit of it). He has also been overpraised for *Nashville* (75). It's a considerable achievement, a multi-layered patchwork of a film centring around a number of themes, mostly concerned with politics and country music, with fine performances from its 24 principal actors. A landmark film, certainly. But also it is overlong and just a shade too clever.

At least two others have been rather neglected. *Thieves Like Us* (73) is about child-like adults who get caught in the trap of believing what they read of themselves. Bowie is a not terribly intelligent young man who turns to crime and is swept along inexorably as the press builds him up into a figure of glamour. The film gets a superb performance not just from the man (Keith Carradine), but also from his sad moll (Shelley Duvall). *California Split* (74), Altman's study of compulsive gamblers, also deserves more consideration than it got at the time. There were complaints that the dialogue was confusingly fuzzy, which is to miss the point; the film has a drive that mirrors the manic intensity with which Elliott Gould and George Segal speed themselves towards the vicarious perils of any game on which they can hazard their money. It is probably the best, certainly the funniest, film ever made on the subject.

Segal and Gould were two actors who were consistently reliable throughout the decade but seemed to hover just below the level of superstardom. Together with Donald Sutherland, they seldom turned in a bad performance but did not, perhaps, attract the notice that was accorded to an actor like Al Pacino: for fine performances in Sidney Lumet's *Serpico* (74), *Dog Day Afternoon* (75)

above
Donald Sutherland and Julie
Christie in *Don't Look Now*,
director Nicolas Roeg
(British Lion, 73)

left
Al Pacino (centre) in *Serpico*
director Sidney Lumet
(Paramount, 73)

and both parts of *The Godfather* (72 and 74). It
became increasingly difficult to work out where
anyone stood on the Hollywood stardom pecking-
order. Gene Hackman was undoubtedly a star after
The French Connection (71) but he just didn't look

like one and although he did excellent work in
excellent (if often undervalued) films like *Scarecrow* (73, with Pacino), *The Conversation* (74) and
Night Moves (76) he couldn't pull the crowds into
the cinemas on his name alone.

270

Donald Sutherland: in
(*right*) *Klute*, director Alan
J. Pakula (Warners, 71), and
in (*below*) *Steelyard Blues*
with Jane Fonda, director
Alan Myerson (Columbia/
EMI/Warners, 72)

left
Al Pacino in *Dog Day Afternoon*, director Sidney Lumet (Columbia/Warners, 75)

below
Gene Hackman in *The French Connection*, director William Friedkin (20th Century-Fox, 71)

opposite top
Freebie and the Bean, director Richard Rush (Warners, 74)

opposite bottom
James Caan throws the dice in *The Gambler*, director Karel Reisz (Paramount, 75)

Nor could Robert De Niro, although he was one of the most admired of the new-wave actors, especially for his work in *The Godfather Part Two*, *Taxi Driver* (76), in which he was quite brilliant, and *The Deer Hunter* (78). And for all this, he couldn't save *New York, New York* (77) from going down the pan. For a brief moment Sylvester Stallone seemed to hold the magic key, especially after the totally unexpected success of *Rocky* (76, which he also wrote), but he had trouble sustaining the impetus and only time would tell whether he could persuade the public to see him in other parts.

Never before in Hollywood's history have men (repeat, men; women had a lean time during the decade) become stars so quickly, made so much money, and then been discarded so ruthlessly. In the old studio system, for all its faults, an actor like James Caan would have been nurtured, given progressively better and bigger parts until it was judged he was ready for the full treatment. In the Seventies James Caan was said to be a star on very little evidence. He got a lot of attention in *The Godfather* but there was nobody ready to help him build on that. He did *Slither* (73), which meant nothing, *Cinderella Liberty* (73) which, for all its merits, meant little, and *Freebie and the Bean* (74), which was just another cops-car-chases-spectacular-smashes movie, albeit rather more successful than some. He was good in *The Gambler* (74), which did little better than the superior *California Split*; then came *Funny Lady* (75), which looked as though it would be big but wasn't, and *Rollerball* (75), which also failed to match its ballyhoo. Two real flops followed, and then he was in *A Bridge Too Far* (77) but who wasn't – the cast seemed bigger than the audience. By which time James Caan was demanding $2 million for appearing in *Apocalypse Now* (79). Coppola evidently did not think he was worth it.

Two million dollars! Who is to criticize him? Or Hackman, who asked, and got, the same for a brief appearance in *Superman*? After all, inflation was one of the dominant issues of the Seventies and nowhere were the effects more spectacular than in Hollywood. The reason was that the rewards were, in theory, enormous. But for one *Star Wars* how many films were there that never even covered their costs? We'll never know because Hollywood does not publicize its failures. By 1980, a *cheap* American film cost $3 million, and Hollywood was wondering where the movies were going with minimum budgets at that level. Bigger and better? Or bust?

70s Oscars

YEAR	BEST FILM	BEST ACTOR	BEST ACTRESS
1970	*Patton*/ 20th Century-Fox	George C. Scott/ *Patton* (award declined)	Glenda Jackson/ *Women in Love*
1971	*The French Connection*/ 20th Century-Fox	Gene Hackman/ *The French Connection*	Jane Fonda/ *Klute*
1972	*The Godfather*/ Paramount	Marlon Brando/ *The Godfather* (award declined)	Liza Minnelli/ *Cabaret*
1973	*The Sting*/ Zanuck-Brown-Universal	Jack Lemmon/ *Save the Tiger*	Glenda Jackson/ *A Touch of Class*
1974	*The Godfather Part II*/ Paramount	Art Carney/ *Harry and Tonto*	Ellen Burstyn/ *Alice Doesn't Live Here Anymore*
1975	*One Flew Over the Cuckoo's Nest*/ Fantasy-UA	Jack Nicholson/ *One Flew Over the Cuckoo's Nest*	Louise Fletcher/ *One Flew Over the Cuckoo's Nest*
1976	*Rocky*/ Chartoff-Winkler-UA	Peter Finch/ *Network*	Faye Dunaway *Network*
1977	*Annie Hall*/ Rollins-Joffe-UA	Richard Dreyfuss/ *The Goodbye Girl*	Diane Keaton/ *Annie Hall*
1978	*The Deer Hunter*/ EMI-Cimino-Universal	Jon Voight/ *Coming Home*	Jane Fonda/ *Coming Home*
1979	*Kramer v Kramer* Jaffe-Columbia	Dustin Hoffman/ *Kramer v Kramer*	Sally Field/ *Norma Rae*

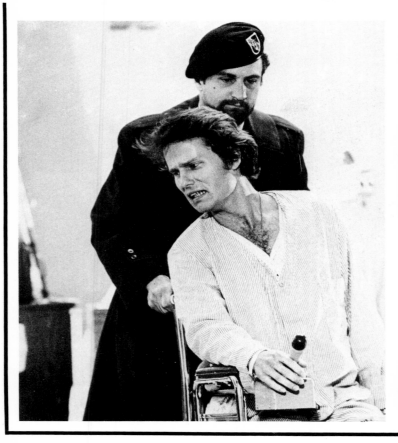 

70s Oscars

BEST DIRECTOR	BEST SUPPORTING ACTOR	BEST SUPPORTING ACTRESS	YEAR
Franklin J. Schaffner/ *Patton*	John Mills/ *Ryan's Daughter*	Helen Hayes/ *Airport*	1970
William Friedkin/ *The French Connection*	Ben Johnson/ *The Last Picture Show*	Cloris Leachman/ *The Last Picture Show*	1971
Bob Fosse/ *Cabaret*	Joel Grey/ *Cabaret*	Eileen Heckart/ *Butterflies Are Free*	1972
George Roy Hill/ *The Sting*	John Houseman/ *The Paper Chase*	Tatum O'Neal/ *Paper Moon*	1973
Francis Ford Coppola/ *The Godfather Part II*	Robert De Niro/ *The Godfather Part II*	Ingrid Bergman/ *Murder on the Orient Express*	1974
Milos Forman/ *One Flew Over the Cuckoo's Nest*	George Burns/ *The Sunshine Boys*	Lee Grant/ *Shampoo*	1975
John G. Avildsen/ *Rocky*	Jason Robards/ *All the President's Men*	Beatrice Straight/ *Network*	1976
Woody Allen/ *Annie Hall*	Jason Robards/ *Julia*	Vanessa Redgrave/ *Julia*	1977
Michael Cimino/ *The Deer Hunter*	Christopher Walken/ *The Deer Hunter*	Maggie Smith/ *California Suite*	1978
Robert Brenton/ *Kramer v Kramer*	Melvyn Douglas/ *Being There*	Meryl Streep/ *Kramer v Kramer*	1979

opposite left
Three major awards for *The Deer Hunter*, with Robert De Niro and John Savage (in chair), director Michael Cimino (Universal, 78)

opposite right
Awards for Diane Keaton and Woody Allen in *Annie Hall*, director Allen (United Artists, 77)

left
Best Actor Richard Dreyfuss and Marsha Mason in *The Goodbye Girl*, director Herbert Ross (Warners, 77)

first rushes for the Eighties...

The Eighties started inauspiciously for Hollywood. Michael Cimino, who had had such a hit with *The Deer Hunter* (78), finally got *Heaven's Gate* (80), a huge, unwieldy, and apparently almost incomprehensible Western into a cinema only to have it pulled out again after *one* performance. He was ordered by United Artists to cut it down to a reasonable length (it was four hours long) and try to find a plot. No one had any great hopes he would succeed and, at $36 million, *Heaven's Gate* was potentially the biggest flop in cinema history.

There were other, lesser failures and for a while it looked as though no one was immune. Kubrick's *The Shining* (80) fell far short of expectation and

even Woody Allen took a critical and commercial hammering for *Stardust Memories* (80). These failures, compounded by an actors' strike which is said to have cost the studios about $40 million per *week*, left Hollywood in very bad shape.

In Britain things were hardly better. The Rank Organisation pulled out of film production; Denham studios finally went the way of so many others and was pulled down for property development; and, although many of the most successful films of the period – *Star Wars* (77) and *Superman* (78) to name two – were made in Britain using British knowhow and technicians (said to be the best in the world, especially for special effects), the money

Brooke Shields and Christopher Atkins in *The Blue Lagoon*, director Randal Kleiser (Columbia/EMI/ Warners, 80)

Shelley Duvall in *The Shining*, director Stanley Kubrick (Columbia/EMI/Warners, 80)

behind them was American and the profits flowed back to the States. It was almost impossible for a British film-maker to get British money to make a British movie, although the few who did produced interesting, comparatively low-budget films – *Babylon* and *Breaking Glass* (both 80) stand out. However, their appeal abroad was limited and thus expected profits were small.

In fact, there was no reason why Britain should not have a successful film industry despite its size. And there was no reason why Hollywood couldn't bring in a successful film for well under $30 million.

Germany, with approximately the same population as Britain and with a much smaller language market, and Australia, with a tiny population, had industries which flourished.

Germany had a group of young film-makers whose intentions were similar to those of the French new wave 20 years before. 'The new cinema, they asserted, 'needs new forms of freedom: from the conventions and clichés of the established industry, from interventions from commercial partners, and finally freedom from . . . other vested interests.' In 1980 Rainer Werner

above left
Nancy Allen in *Dressed to Kill*, director Brian DePalma (Filmways, 80)

above
Jamie Lee Curtis in *The Fog*, director John Carpenter (Avco Embassy, 80)

left
Prom Night, director Paul Lynch (Avco Embassy, 80)

above
John Hurt in *The Elephant Man*, director David Lynch (Paramount, 80)

right
Nastassia Kinski in *Tess*, director Roman Polanski (Columbia, 80)

Fassbinder received considerable international acclaim for *The Marriage of Maria Braun* and seemed to have launched a new sex symbol (although she detested the tag) in Hanna Schygulla, who recalled Dietrich in *The Blue Angel* (30). The film was a commercial breakthrough for a man whose reputation on the 'art' circuit was already considerable. Together with Werner Herzog, Hans Jurgen Syberberg, Wim Wenders and others, he revived a flagging industry and injected new life into film-making.

The success of the Australian film industry was even more surprising. Regarded for years as a joke, it suddenly developed its own style and tremendous creative confidence in the Seventies thanks to enlightened financial support from government and individual states. In 1980 *Breaker Morant* (80), set in the Boer War, starring Edward Woodward and directed by Bruce Beresford, appeared to spearhead success in the new decade, following that of Peter Weir's *Picnic at Hanging Rock* (75) and *The Last Wave* (78), Ken Hannam's *Sunday Too Far* (75), Donald Crombie's *Caddie* (75), and Fred Schepisi's *The Devil's Playground* (76) and *The Chant of Jimmie Blacksmith* (78) in the previous five years.

The experience of the German and Australian industries seemed to prove that cinema need not die in the Eighties. And even Hollywood occasionally got it right, the first detectable trend seeming to be for 'terror' movies, a reworking of the old horror genre with gloss. It was epitomized by *Dressed to Kill* (80), which although strongly attacked for the violence, especially to women, it portrayed, hit big on the circuit and did much to resuscitate Michael Caine's flagging career.

One trend from the Seventies seemed to continue undiminished. Following the success of comic-strip heroes, producers continued casting back for other super-beings to delight young audiences. *Superman II* was in production and film-makers turned to the weekly serials of the Thirties in which Buster Crabbe as Flash Gordon pitted himself against the evil Ming the Merciless of the planet Mongo. The new, glossy, extravagant *Flash Gordon* (80), played by Sam Jones, battled mightily against Max von Sydow's Ming and had the children cheering.

However, in 1980 Hollywood itself recognized it was at a crossroads. Huge profits were possible if the right films were produced. But whether the movie capital could rise to the challenge or whether it would finally succumb to the twin attacks of TV and video (on which recent movies could be seen at very low cost and in home comfort) was one of the most interesting and crucial questions that had faced Hollywood in the 50 or so years since the talkies began.

Acknowledgments

Sources

Anger, Kenneth: *Hollywood Babylon*, Dell, New York, 1976.

Annan, David: *Cinefantastic: Beyond the Dream Machine*, Lorrimer, London, 1974.

Anobile, Richard J. (editor): *A Flask of Fields*, Avon Books, New York, 1973; *Frankenstein*, Avon Books, New York, and Picador Books, London, 1974; *The Maltese Falcon*, Avon Books, New York, and Picador Books, London, 1974.

Barbour, Alan G.: *Humphrey Bogart*, Pyramid Books, New York, 1973, and Star Books, London, 1974.

Baxter, John: *Hollywood in the Thirties*, Zwemmer, London, and A.S. Barnes, New York, 1968; *Ken Russell: An Appalling Talent*, Michael Joseph, London, 1974; *Stunt: The Story of the Great Movie Stuntmen*, Macdonald, London, 1973, and Doubleday, New York, 1974.

Behlmer, Rudy (editor): *Memo from David O. Selznick*, Avon Books, New York, and Macmillan, London, 1973.

Bergman, Ingrid and Alan Burgess: *Ingrid Bergman: My Story*, Michael Joseph, London, and Delacorte Press, New York, 1980.

Blum, Daniel: *A Pictorial History of the Talkies*, G.P. Putnam, New York, 1973, and Spring Books, London, 1974.

Bogdanovich, Peter: *John Ford*, University of California Press, Berkeley, 1968.

Braudy, Leo and Morris Dickstein (editors): *Great Film Directors: A Critical Anthology*, Oxford University Press, London, and New York, 1978.

Brownlow, Kevin: *The Parade's Gone By*, Abacus Books, Tunbridge Wells, 1973, and University of California Press, Berkeley, 1976.

Brownlow, Kevin and John Kobal: *The Pioneers*, William Collins, London, 1979, and Alfred A. Knopf, New York, 1980.

Campbell, Joanna: *The Films of Steve McQueen*, Barden, Castell, and Williams, London, 1973.

Castle, Charles: *Noel: Biography of Noel Coward*, Abacus Books, Tunbridge Wells, 1974.

Chandler, Charlotte: *Hello, I Must Be Going: Groucho Marx and His Friends*, Penguin Books, New York, 1979, and Sphere, London, 1980.

Chaplin, Charles: *My Autobiography*, Penguin, London, 1973, and Simon and Schuster, New York, 1978.

Earley, Steven C.: *An Introduction to American Movies*, New American Library, New York, 1978, and Mentor Books, London, 1979.

Edwards, Anne: *Vivien Leigh: A Biography*, Simon and Schuster, New York, 1977, and Coronet Books, London, 1978.

Essoe, Gabe and Ray Lee: *Gable*, Price, Stern, and Sloan Publishers, Los Angeles, 1967.

Eyles, Allen: *The House of Horror: Story of Hammer Films*, Lorrimer, London, 1973.

Flynn, Errol: *My Wicked, Wicked Ways*, Pan Books, London, 1972, and Berkely Publishing, New York, 1974.

Fox Sheinwold, Patricia: *Too Young To Die: Stars the World Tragically Lost*, Cathay Books, London, 1980.

French, Philip: *The Movie Moguls*, Pelican, London and New York, 1971.

Frewin, Leslie: *Dietrich*, Frewin, London, 1967, and Avon Books, New York, 1972.

Gifford, Denis: *A Pictorial History of Horror Movies*, Hamlyn, London, and Chartwell, New York, 1973.

Glaessner, Verina: *Kung Fu: Cinema of Vengeance*, Lorrimer, London, 1974.

Green, Stanley and Burt Goldblatt: *Starring Fred Astaire*, Dodd, Mead and Company, New York, 1973, and W.H. Allen, London, 1974.

Griffith, Richard and Arthur Mayer: *The Movies*, Simon and Schuster, New York, 1970, and Spring Books, London, 1971.

Halliwell, Leslie: *The Filmgoer's Book of Quotes*, Granada Publishing, London and New York, 1978; *Halliwell's Film Guide*, Granada Publishing, London and New York, 1979; *Halliwell's Filmgoer's Companion* (seventh edition), Granada Publishing, London and New York, 1980.

Hossent, Harry: *Gangster Movies*, Octopus Books, London, 1974.

Houston, Penelope: *The Contemporary Cinema: 1945–63*, Penguin, London and New York, 1963.

Jeavons, Clyde: *A Pictorial History of War Films*, Hamlyn, London, and Citadel Press, New York, 1974.

Jordan, René: *Clark Gable*, Pyramid Books, New York, 1973, and Star Books, London, 1974; *Marlon Brando*, Pyramid Books, New York, 1973.

Kael, Pauline: *The Citizen Kane Book*, Little, Boston, 1971, and Secker and Warburg, London, 1972.

Knight, Arthur: *The Liveliest Art: A Panoramic History of the Movies* (revised edition), Mentor Books, London, 1978, and New American Library, New York, 1979.

Kobal, John: *Gotta Sing, Gotta Dance: A Pictorial History of Film Musicals*, Hamlyn, London, and Chartwell, New York, 1972; *Marilyn Monroe*, Hamlyn, London, and Crescent, New York, 1974.

Lesley, Cole, Graham Payn and Sheridan Morley: *The Life of Noel Coward*, Jonathan Cape, London, 1976, and Penguin, New York, 1978; *Noel Coward and His Friends*, Weidenfeld and Nicolson, London, and William Morrow, New York, 1979.

Marill, Alvin H.: *Katharine Hepburn*, Pyramid Books, New York, 1973, and Star Books, New York, 1974.

Mast, Gerald: *The Comic Mind: Comedy and the Movies* (second edition), Bobbs-Merrill, New York, 1973, and New English Library, London, 1974.

Monaco, James: *American Film Now: The People, the Power, the Money, the Movies*, Oxford University Press, Oxford, 1979.

Mountbatten of Burma: *Mountbatten: Eighty Years in Pictures*, Macmillan, London, and Viking Press, New York, 1979.

Niven, David: *Bring On the Empty Horses*, Dell Publishing, New York, 1976 and Coronet Books, London, 1977; *The Moon's A Balloon*, Hamish Hamilton, London, 1971 and Dell Publishing, New York, 1973.

Parkinson, Michael and Clyde Jeavons: *A Pictorial History of Westerns*, Hamlyn, London, and Chartwell, New York, 1972.

Parrish, James Robert and Leonard De Carl: *The Forties Gals*, Arlington House, Westport, Connecticut, 1980.

Pascall, Jeremy (editor): *Hollywood and the Great Stars*, Phoebus, London, 1976; (author) *The Illustrated History of Rock Music*, Hamlyn, London, and Galahad, New York, 1978; *The King Kong Story*, Phoebus, London, 1976.

Pascall, Jeremy and Clyde Jeavons: *A Pictorial History of Sex in the Movies*, Hamlyn, London, and Chartwell, New York, 1975.

Perry, George: *The Great British Picture Show*, Hill and Wang, New York, 1974 and Paladin, London, 1975.

Robertson, Patrick: *Guinness Book of Film Facts and Feats*, Guinness Superlatives, London, 1980.

Sennett, Ted: *Warner Brothers Presents*, Arlington House, New Rochelle, New York, 1971.

Shaw, Arnold: *Sinatra*, Holt, Rinehart and Winston, New York, and W.H. Allen, London, 1968.

Shipman, David: *The Great Movie Stars: The Golden Years* (second edition), Hamlyn, London, and Crown, New York, 1970; *The Great Movie Stars: The International Years*, Angus and Robertson, London, 1972 and St Martin's Press, New York, 1973.

Stallings, Penny and Howard Mandelbaum: *Flesh and Fantasy*, St Martin's Press, New York, 1978 and Macdonald and Jane's, London, 1979.

Symons, Julian: *Crime and Detection: An Illustrated History*, Panther, London, 1968.

Tatham, Dick: *Elvis*, Phoebus, London, 1977.

Thomas, Tony and Aubrey Solomon: *The Films of Twentieth Century-Fox*, Citadel Press, New York, 1980.

Tozzi, Tomano: *Spencer Tracy*, Pyramid Books, New York, 1973.

Trevelyan, John: *What the Censor Saw*, Michael Joseph, London, 1973.

Truffaut, François: *The Films in My Life*, Simon and Schuster, New York, 1978 and Allen Lane, London, 1980; *Hitchcock*, Touchstone Books, New York, 1969, and Paladin, London, 1978.

Ustinov, Peter: *Dear Me*, Penguin Books, London and New York, 1979.

Vermilyme, Jerry: *Bette Davis*, Pyramid Books, New York, 1973, and Star Books, London, 1974; *Cary Grant*, Pyramid Books, New York, 1973.

Walker, Alexander: *Stanley Kubrick Directs* (enlarged edition),

Sphere, London, and Harcourt Brace Jovanovich, New York, 1972.
Williams, Neville: *Chronology of the Modern World 1763–1965*, Penguin, London and New York, 1975.
Wise, Arthur and Derek Ware: *Stunting in the Cinema*, Constable, London and St Martin's Press, New York, 1973.
Wolf, William and Lillian K.: *Landmark Films: The Cinema and Our Century*, Paddington Press, New York, 1979.
Zierold, Norman: *The Moguls*, Avon Books, New York, 1972.
Marx Brothers: *Monkey Business/Duck Soup* (Film Scripts Classics Series), Simon and Schuster, New York, 1973, and Lorrimer, London.

Photographs

The Publishers would like to thank Michelle Snapes and her staff at The National Film Archive, the Information and Documentation Department of The British Film Institute, and all the staff at The Kobal Collection for their invaluable assistance and invariable patience during the compilation of this book.

Colour

Cinema Bookshop, London 115 top, 175 top right; The Kobal Collection, London endpapers, title page, 10, 11 bottom, 14 top, 15 top left, 15 top right, 82 top left, 82 top right, 82 bottom, 83 top, 83 bottom, 91, 94 top, 94 bottom, 95 bottom, 114 top, 114 bottom, 115 bottom, 122 centre, 123 top, 131 top, 131 bottom, 134 top, 135 top, 135 bottom, 139 top, 142 top, 142 bottom, 143, 162 top, 162 bottom, 166 top, 166 bottom, 166–7 top, 166–7 bottom, 167 bottom, 170 top, 170 bottom right, 174 top, 174 bottom left, 174 bottom right, 175 top left, 175 bottom, 178 bottom left, 178–9 top, 182 centre left, 182 bottom left, 182–3, 183 top, 183 bottom, 186 left, 187 top, 187 bottom, 190, 194 top right, 195 top, 200, 201, 202, 203, 207, 209, 211 right, 213 top, 213 bottom, 214 bottom, 215 top, 215 centre, 215 bottom, 220, 221, 223, 225, 226, 227, 228–9, 230, 232, 235, 236 top, 236 bottom, 237, 238, 240 top, 240 bottom, 241, 242, 247, 248, 249 top, 250 bottom, 250–1, 251, 252, 253, 256, 258 top, 259 bottom, 263, 265, 266, 271 top, 271 bottom, 272, 276, 281; National Film Archive, London 14 bottom, 138 top, 163 top, 163 bottom, 170 centre left, 170 bottom left, 171, 178–9 bottom, 179 top right, 179 bottom right, 182 top, 191, 194 top left, 194 bottom left, 194 bottom right, 195 bottom, 204, 206, 210–11, 214 top, 216, 222, 223, 233, 249 bottom, 250 top left, 254, 256, 258 bottom, 259 top, 260, 272 bottom.

Black and white

Hamlyn Picture Library 12–13, 18 centre, 67 top, 79 top, 99 bottom, 106 top, 112 bottom, 116 bottom, 127 centre left, 152 top, 157 bottom right, 173 bottom left, 181 top right, 184 left, 191 bottom right, 193 top right, 196 top right, 207, 208, 226, 228, 247; The Kobal Collection, London 8 bottom left, 12 bottom, 13 top, 13 bottom right, 15 bottom, 20 top, 22 top left, 22 bottom left, 24 top, 26 bottom right, 27 top, 28 bottom, 31 top, 33 top, 37 bottom, 41, 42 bottom, 43, 50 top left, 51 bottom, 55, 60, 61, 62 top, 62 bottom, 63 top, 63 centre, 63 bottom left, 63 bottom right, 64 bottom, 65 top left, 65 top right, 65 bottom, 67 bottom left, 67 bottom right, 68, 69 top, 69 bottom, 70 top, 70 bottom, 75 top right, 76 top, 76 bottom, 77 bottom, 80 bottom, 81 top, 81 bottom, 84 top, 84 bottom, 85 bottom, 86, 88 top, 88 bottom, 89, 90 top, 93 top, 96, 97, 98 top, 98 bottom, 99 top right, 100 top, 102 top left, 102 bottom, 104 top, 106 bottom, 107 top right, 111 top, 112–13, 119 bottom right, 120 top, 120 centre, 120 bottom, 121 bottom left, 122 top right, 123 centre, 123 bottom left, 123 bottom right, 124, 125 bottom, 126 bottom right, 127 top, 127 centre right, 130 top, 133 top, 137 top, 137 bottom left, 138 bottom left, 140 top right, 149 top, 150 right, 151 left, 156 top, 157 centre, 158 bottom, 159 top left, 165 top, 172 top, 173 top, 173 bottom right, 177 top, 178, 180 top, 184–5, 185, 188 bottom left, 190 bottom, 210–11, 218 bottom, 224, 239 bottom, 245, 252, 262 top, 264 bottom, 267 top, 270 top, 274 right, 275, 278 top left, 278 top right, 278 bottom, 279 top, 279 bottom, 280 top, 280 bottom; National Film Archive, London 8 top left, 8 bottom right, 9 left, 9 right, 10–11, 11 top right, 12 top, 16 top, 16 bottom left, 16 bottom right, 17 top left, 17 top right, 17 bottom, 18 top, 18 bottom, 19, 20 bottom, 21 top, 21 bottom, 22 top right, 22 bottom right, 23 top, 23 bottom, 24 bottom, 25 top, 25 centre, 25 bottom, 26 top, 26 bottom left, 27 bottom, 28 top, 29, 30 top, 30 bottom, 31 bottom, 32 top, 32 bottom, 33 bottom, 34, 35 top, 35 bottom, 36 top, 36 bottom, 37 top, 38 top left, 38 top right, 38 bottom, 39, 42 top, 44 top left, 44 top right, 45 top, 45 bottom, 46, 47 top, 47 centre, 47 bottom, 48 top, 48 bottom, 49 top left, 49 top right, 49 centre, 49 bottom, 50 top right, 50 bottom, 51 top, 51 bottom, 52 top, 52 bottom, 53, 54 top, 54 bottom, 56 top, 56 bottom, 57, 58, 59, 64 top, 66 top, 66 centre, 66 bottom, 69 centre left, 69 centre right, 70 centre, 71 top, 72 top left, 72 top right, 72 bottom, 73 top, 73 bottom, 74 top left, 74–5, 75 bottom, 77 top, 78, 79 bottom, 80 top, 85 top left, 85 top right, 87, 90 bottom, 92 top, 92 centre, 92 bottom, 93 bottom, 95 right, 99 top left, 100 centre, 100 bottom, 101 top, 101 bottom, 102 top right, 103, 104 bottom, 105 top, 105 bottom, 107 top left, 107 bottom, 108, 109 left, 109 right, 111 bottom, 113 bottom, 116 top left, 116–17, 117 top right, 117 bottom, 118, 119 top left, 119 top right, 119 bottom left, 121 top right, 121 top left, 121 bottom right, 122 top left, 122 bottom left, 122 bottom right, 125 top, 125 bottom right, 126 top, 126 bottom left, 127 bottom, 128 top, 128 centre, 128 bottom, 129 top left, 129 top right, 129 centre left, 129 centre right, 129 bottom, 130 bottom left, 130 bottom right, 132 top left, 132 top right, 132 bottom, 133 bottom left, 133 bottom right, 134 bottom left, 134 bottom right, 136 left, 136 right, 137 bottom right, 138 bottom right, 139 bottom left, 139 bottom right, 140 top left, 140 bottom left, 140 bottom right, 141 top, 141 bottom, 142, 143 left, 143 right, 144, 145 top, 145 bottom, 146 top, 146 bottom, 147 bottom, 148 top, 148 centre, 148 bottom, 149 centre left, 149 centre right, 149 bottom left, 149 bottom right, 150 left, 151 right, 152 bottom, 153 top, 153 bottom, 154 top, 154 bottom left, 154 bottom right, 155 top, 155 bottom left, 155 bottom right, 156 bottom left, 156–7, 157 top, 158 top, 159 top, 159 bottom, 160 top, 160 bottom, 161, 164, 165 centre, 165 bottom, 167, 168 top, 168 bottom, 169 top, 169 bottom, 171, 172 bottom, 173 centre left, 176 top, 176 centre, 176 bottom, 177 centre, 177 bottom, 180 bottom, 181 top left, 181 bottom, 184–5 top, 185 centre, 185 bottom, 186 left, 186 right, 186–7, 188 top, 188 bottom right, 189 top left, 189 top right, 189 bottom left, 189 bottom right, 190 top, 191 top, 191 centre, 191 bottom left, 192 top, 192 bottom, 193 top left, 193 bottom right, 196 top left, 196 bottom, 197, 198 left, 198 right, 199, 201, 202, 204, 205, 206, 209, 210 left, 211 right, 212, 216, 217 top, 217 bottom, 218 top, 219, 220, 222, 231 top, 231 bottom, 232, 234, 237, 238, 239 top, 241, 242, 244 top, 244 bottom left, 244 bottom right, 246, 248, 249, 251, 253, 254, 255, 257 top, 257 bottom, 260, 261 top, 261 bottom, 262 bottom, 263, 264 top, 265, 267 bottom, 268, 269, 270 bottom, 273 top, 273 bottom, 274 left, 277; Walt Disney Productions, Burbank, California 40, 95 left.

Film title Index

General Index

Figures in italics refer to illustration captions.